IF
YOU
WILL ASK

Discovery House Publishers

Books, music, and videos that feed the soul with the Word of God

Box 3566 Grand Rapids, MI 49501

IF YOU WILL ASK

REFLECTIONS ON THE **POWER OF PRAYER**

OSWALD CHAMBERS

If You Will Ask
© 1937 Oswald Chambers Publications Association.

This edition © 1989 Oswald Chambers
Publications Association Limited. All rights reserved.

Discovery House Publishers is affiliated with RBC Ministries,
Grand Rapids, Michigan 49512.

Discovery House books are distributed to the trade exclusively by
Barbour Publishing Inc., Uhrichsville, Ohio 44683.

Unless otherwise indicated, Scripture quotations are from the
New King James Version, © 1979, 1980, 1982 Thomas Nelson, Inc.

Interior design by Sherri L. Hoffman

Library of Congress Cataloging-in-Publication Data
Chambers, Oswald, 1874–1917.
If you will ask: reflections on the power of prayer/Oswald
    Chambers.
       cm.
    ISBN 0-929239-06-7
Prayer—Christianity. 1. Title.
BV215C513 1966
2483'2—dc20   96-33345

Printed in the United States of America

03 04 05 06 07 08 09 10 11 12 / CHG/ 32 31 30 29 28 27 26 25 24

CONTENTS

FOREWORD

Oswald Chambers' closest friends knew him as a person for whom prayer was a natural and joyful aspect of everyday life. In 1912, while serving as interim pastor for a church in Dunstable, England, Oswald would arrive on Saturday morning for his weekend of ministry. He began by taking several young men from the church for a hike. "Those walks!" wrote one of the participants. "Happy talk, jokes, tales, then—'Off with your hats, it is good to pray everywhere,' and there would follow brief prayer."

A student at the Bible Training College in London, where Oswald was Principal, recalled walking with Chambers one evening through a little country village. "He just very naturally stopped and prayed, asking for God's blessing on the village," she said, "and it seemed so like what Our Lord would have done when He was on earth."

In late October 1915, Oswald Chambers arrived in Egypt to serve as a Y.M.C.A. chaplain during World War I. A few days later he announced that there would be a week-night religious service in their camp just outside Cairo. Skeptics told him no one would come because the soldiers just wanted to write letters, smoke, play cards and enjoy refreshments from the canteen. Religion was for Sunday morning. But on November 4, 400 men packed the large hut to hear Chambers speak on the topic, "What Is the Good of Prayer?" That message is the first chapter in this book.

"It is only when a man flounders beyond any grip of himself and cannot understand things that he really prays," he told the troops, many of whom had cried out to God for the first time during the war. "When a man is at his wits' end, it is not a cowardly thing to pray, it is the only way to get in touch with Reality."

Chambers has been called a mystic, but his words and actions reveal him as spiritual realist who believed that prayer was not a means of getting things from God, but a way of getting to know God Himself. In *If You Will Ask* he challenges us to enter a new dimension of communion with our Heavenly Father, and to discover that "the good of praying is that it gets us to know God and enables God to perform His order through us."

David McCasland, author
Oswald Chambers: Abandoned to God

INTRODUCTION

Source

*I*f *You Will Ask* is from lectures given at the Bible Training College[2] London (1911–1915); at League of Prayer[3] gatherings in Britain; to British Commonwealth troops in Egypt[4] during World War I.

Where known, date and place appear on the first page of each sermon.

Publication History

- As articles: Many of these chapters appeared first as articles in *Tongues of Fire/Spiritual Life* magazines or in the *Bible Training College (BTC) Monthly Journal.*[5]
- As a book: The material was first published as *If Ye Shall Ask* in 1937. Drawing on her store of notes from Britain and Egypt, Mrs. Chambers compiled this collection expressing the heart of Oswald's teaching on prayer and his practice of it. She selected the short prayers at the beginnings of chapters 2 through 12 from Oswald Chambers' personal prayer journal and from meetings at the Bible Training College.

[From the Introduction composed by David C. McCasland for *If Ye Shall Ask*, included in *The Complete Works of Oswald Chambers*, copyright © 2000 by Oswald Chambers Publications Association, Limited. *The Complete Works of Oswald Chambers* is available from Discovery House Publishers, Grand Rapids, Michigan.]

One

WHAT'S THE GOOD OF PRAYER?

Therefore I exhort first of all that supplications, prayers, intercessions, and giving of thanks be made for all men, for kings and all who are in authority, that we may lead a quiet and peaceable life in all godliness and reverence. For this is good and acceptable in the sight of God our Savior, who desires all men to be saved and to come to the knowledge of the truth. For there is one God and one Mediator between God and men, the Man Christ Jesus, who gave Himself a ransom for all, to be testified in due time, for which I was appointed a preacher and an apostle—I am speaking the truth in Christ and not lying— a teacher of the Gentiles in faith and truth. I desire therefore that the men pray everywhere, lifting up holy hands, without wrath and doubting (1 TIMOTHY 2:1–8).

Only when a man flounders beyond any grip of himself and cannot understand things does he really pray. Prayer is not part of the natural life. By "natural" I mean the ordinary, sensible, healthy, worldly-minded life. Some say that a man will suffer in his life if he does not pray. I question it. Prayer is an interruption of personal ambition, and no person who is busy has time to pray. What will suffer is the life of God in him, which is nourished not by food but by prayer.

If we look on prayer as a means of developing ourselves, there is nothing in it at all, and we do not find that idea in the Bible. Prayer is other than meditation; it develops the life of God in us. When a man is born from above, the life of the Son of God begins in him, and he can either starve that life or nourish it.

Prayer nourishes the life of God. Our Lord nourished the life of God in Him by prayer. He was continually in contact with His Father. We generally look upon prayer as a means of getting things for ourselves, but the biblical idea of prayer is that God's holiness, purpose, and wise order may be brought about. Our ordinary views of prayer are not found in the New Testament.

When a man is in real distress he prays without reasoning. He does not think things out, he simply blurts it out. "Then they cried out to the LORD in their trouble, and He saved them out of their distresses" (Psalm 107:13). When we get into a tight place our logic goes to the winds and we work from the implicit part of ourselves.

What's the Good of Prayer?

"Your Father knows the things you have need of before you ask Him" (Matthew 6:8). Then why ask? Very evidently our ideas about prayer and Jesus Christ's are not the same. Prayer to Him is not a way to get things from God, but so that we may get to know God. Prayer is not to be used as the privilege of a spoiled child seeking ideal conditions to indulge his spiritual propensities. The purpose of prayer is to reveal the presence of God, equally present at all times and in every condition.

A man may say, "Well, if the Almighty has decreed things, why need I pray? If He has made up His mind, what is the use of my thinking I can alter His mind by prayer?" We must remember that there is a difference between God's order and God's permissive will. God's order reveals His character; His permissive will applies to what He permits. For instance, it is God's order that there should be no sin, no suffering, no sickness, no limitation, and no death; His permissive will is all these things. God has so arranged matters that we are born into His permissive will, and we have to get at His order by an effort of our own, that is, by prayer. To be children of God, according to the New Testament, does not mean that we are creatures of God only, but that we grow into a likeness to God by our own moral character.

I question whether the people who continually ask for prayer meetings know the first element of prayer. It is often an abortion of religious hysterics, a disease of the nerves taking a spiritual twist. Jesus says we are to pray in His name, that is, in His nature, and His nature is shed abroad in our hearts by the Holy Spirit when we are born from above (see Luke 11:13; Romans 5:5). Again, Jesus did not promise to be at every prayer meeting, but only at those "where two or three are gathered together in My name," meaning, in His nature (Matthew 18:20). Jesus Christ does not pay any attention to the gift of "religious gab." His words,

"And when you pray, do not use vain repetitions as the heathen do. For they think that they will be heard for their many words" (Matthew 6:7) refer not to the mere repetition and form of the words, but to the fact that it is never our earnestness that brings us into touch with God. Rather, it is our Lord Jesus Christ's vitalizing death (see Hebrews 10:19).

In His teaching about prayer our Lord never once referred to unanswered prayer. He said God always answers prayer. If our prayers are in the name of Jesus or in accord with His nature, the answers will not be in accord with our nature but with His. We are apt to forget this and to say without thinking that God does not always answer prayer. He does every time, and when we are in close communion with Him we realize that we have not been misled.

"Ask, and it shall be given you." We grouse before God and are apologetic or apathetic, but we ask very few things; yet what a splendid audacity a child-like child has! And our Lord says, "Unless you . . . become as little children . . ." (Matthew 18:3). Jesus says, "Ask . . . God will give" (John 11:22). Give Jesus Christ a chance. Give Him elbow room, but no one ever does it until he is at his wits' end. During a war many pray for the first time. It is not cowardly to pray when we are at our wits' end. It is the only way to get in touch with reality. As long as we are self-sufficient and complacent, we don't need to ask God for anything. We don't want Him. It is only when we know we are powerless that we are prepared to listen to Jesus Christ and to do what He says.

Then again our Lord says, "If you abide in Me, and My words abide in you, you will ask what you desire" (John 15:7), or rather, you shall ask "what your will is in." There is very little our wills are in. Consequently it is easy to work up false emotions. We intercede in a mechanical way. Our minds are not in it. Jesus said to two of His disciples, "You do not know what you ask" (Mark 10:38).

15

Be yourself exactly before God and present your problems—the things you have come to your wits' end about. Ask what you will, and Jesus Christ says your prayers will be answered. We can always tell whether our will is in what we ask by the way we live when we are not praying.

The New Testament view of a Christian is that he is one in whom the Son of God has been revealed, and prayer deals with the nourishment of that life. It is nourished by refusing to worry over anything, for worry means there is something over which we cannot have our own way, and in reality is personal irritation with God. Jesus Christ says, "Don't worry about your life. Don't fear them which kill the body. Be afraid only of not doing what the Spirit of God indicates to you."

"In everything give thanks" (1 Thessalonians 5:18). Never let anything push you to your wits' end, because you will get worried, and worry makes you self-interested and disturbs the nourishment of the life of God. Give thanks to God that He is there, no matter what is happening. Many a man has found God in the belly of hell in the trenches during the days of war. They came to their wits' end and discovered God. The secret of Christian quietness is not indifference, but the knowledge that God is my Father, He loves me, I shall never think of anything He will forget, and worry becomes an impossibility.

It is not so true that "prayer changes things" as that prayer changes us, and then we change things. Consequently we must not ask God to do what He has created us to do. Jesus Christ is not a social reformer. He came to alter us first, and if there is any social reform to be done on earth, we must do it. God has so constituted things that prayer on the basis of redemption alters the way we look at things. Prayer is not altering things externally, but working wonders within our disposition. When we pray, things remain the same but we begin to be different. The same thing occurs when we fall in love. The circumstances and conditions are the same—we have a sovereign preference in our heart for another person that transfigures everything. If we have been born from above and Christ is formed in us, instantly we begin to see things differently: "If anyone is in Christ, he is a new creation" (2 Corinthians 5:17).

> *Heaven above is brighter blue;*
> *Earth around is sweeter green!*
> *Something lives in every hue*
> *Christless eyes have never seen.*
> *Birds with gladder songs o'erflow,*
> *Flowers with deeper beauties shine,*
> *Since I know, as now I know,*
> *I am His, and He is mine.*

The good of praying is that it gets us to know God and enables God to perform His order through us no matter what His permissive will may be. We are never what we are in spite of our circumstances, but because of them. As Reader Harris[6] once said, "Circumstances are like featherbeds—very comfortable to be on top of, but immensely smothering if they get on top of you." Jesus Christ, by the Spirit of God, always keeps us on top of our circumstances.

What's the Good of Prayer?

We need it—Luke 11:1.

Human wits have an end—Psalm 107:13, 19, 27–28.

Human wills have an end—Romans 8:26.

Human wisdom has an end—James 1:5.

Prayer alters *me*.

We must do it—Luke 18:1.
    If we would know God—Matthew 6:8.
    If we would help men—John 14:12–13.
    If we would do God's will—1 John 5:14–16.
        Prayer alters *others*.

We can do it—James 5:16.
    By asking—John 15:7.
    By seeking—John 15:7.
    By knocking—Matthew 7:7.
        Prayer alters *circumstances* through me.

How beautiful is this undisturbed morning hour with God!

O Lord, this day keep my soul focused upon You as Creator of the world, and upon our Lord Jesus Christ as Creator of His life in me. O for the power of Your Spirit to adore You completely!

"What shall I render to the Lord *for all His benefits toward me? I will take the cup of salvation." Can I think of anything so gracious and complete in surrender and devotion and gratitude as to take from You? O Lord, I desire a livelier sense of You and of Your blessings continually with me.*

O Lord, this day may Your beauty and grace and soothing peace be in me and upon me. May no wind or weather or anxiety ever touch Your beauty and Your peace in my life or in this place.

Two

THE SIMPLICITY
OF PRAYER

Watch and pray, lest you enter into temptation. The spirit indeed is willing, but the flesh is weak (MATTHEW 26:41).

These words were spoken in the supreme moment of our Lord's agony. We are immensely flippant if we forget that. No words our Lord ever spoke weigh more. We are dealing with the sacred simplicity of prayer. If prayer is not easy, we are wrong. If prayer is an effort, we are out of it. There is only one kind of person who can really pray, and that is the child-like saint—the simple, stupid, supernatural child of God. I do mean "stupid."

We try to explain why God answers prayer on the ground of reason. This is nonsense. God answers prayer on the ground of redemption and on no other ground. Let us never forget that our prayers are heard, not because we are in earnest, not because we suffer, but because Jesus suffered. Because our Lord Jesus Christ went through the depths of agony to the last ebb in the Garden of Gethsemane, because He went through Calvary, we have "boldness to enter the Holiest" (Hebrews 10:19).

Let us take ourselves across Kidron to the Garden of Gethsemane. We can never fathom the agony in Gethsemane, but at least we need not misunderstand. This is not the agony of a man. This is the distress of God in Man, or rather the distress of God as Man. It is not human in any phase, and it is fathomless to a human mind. But we have several lines to go on so as not to misunderstand. Always beware of the tendency to think of our Lord as an extraordinary human being. He was not. He was God incarnate.

The Undiscerned Word of Our Lord.

Watch and pray . . .

"Stay here and watch with me" (Matthew 26:38). Is our idea of prayer based on the keen watching that Jesus Christ asked of His disciples? He did not say "pray for anything" or "ask God for anything." His attitude toward them was wrapped up in the words "watch with me." Our Lord did not say sentimental or pious things about prayer. He said practical and intensely real things, and this is one of them.

Probably our biggest difficulty is that our Lord is not really Master. We use the word "Master," but we use it in a more or less pious way. We do not intend to make Him Master practically. We are much more familiar with the idea that Jesus is our Savior, our sanctifier, anything that puts Him in the relationship of a supernatural comrade. We advocate anything that Jesus does, but we do not advocate Him.

The Appropriate Place of Our Lord's Arranging. "Sit here while I go and pray over there" (Matthew 26:36). In one sense it is quite right to take our Lord as an example of how to pray, but in the fundamental sense He is not. The relationship we have to God is not the same as Jesus Christ's relationship to His Father—especially on this occasion. His is not a relationship, it is a redemption. So until we are sure about our Lord's redemption we are to "sit here and wait." People ask, "Why do you waste your time in a Bible Training College? Fancy spending all your time studying the Bible. Think of the people who need to be looked after. Think of the thousand and one things there are to do." Well, they have to be done, but that is not the point. The point is, are we prepared for our Lord to say to us, "Sit here while I go and pray over there"? Are we prepared to give due weight to the fact that we are not our own masters? Are we devotees to a cause or disciples of the Lord Jesus Christ? He said to the disciples, "Sit here." If they had been like some of us they would have said, "No, it is absurd. We must go and do something."

The more we get into the atmosphere of the New Testament the more we discover the unfathomable and unhastening leisure of our Lord's life, no matter what His agony. The difficulty is that when we do what God wants us to do, our friends say, "It is all very well, but suppose we all did that?" Our Lord did not tell all the disciples to sit there while He prayed. He told only three of them. The point is that we must take as from God the haphazard arrangements of our lives. If we accept the Lord Jesus Christ and the domination of His lordship, we also accept that nothing happens by chance because we know that God orders and engineers circumstances. The fuss has gone, the amateur providence has gone, the amateur disposer has gone, and we know that "all things work together for good to those who love God" (Romans 8:28). If Jesus says, "Sit here while I go and pray over there," the only appropriate thing we can do is to sit.

The Appointed Place of Our Lord's Associates. "And He took with Him Peter and two sons of Zebedee." Our Lord opened His sorrow to these three. Peter may stand for the first temptation that beset our Lord—the sensible, material side of things, for help and assistance. James may stand for the second temptation that beset our Lord—the intensely ritualistic. And John may stand for the last temptation—the temptation to compromise everything to win. These three were appointed by our Lord for one purpose—to see His agony. "Stay here and watch with me." He did not put them there to go to sleep, He put them there to wait and watch. The twelve disciples were all He had. He knew that one had gone to

The Simplicity of Prayer

betray Him, that Peter would shortly deny Him with oaths and curses, and that all of them would forsake Him and flee. But He took these three with Him to see the unveiling of His heart—and they slept for their own sorrow.

The Autobiographic Place of Our Lord's Agony. He "began to be sorrowful and deeply distressed" (Matthew 26:37). Our Lord said to these disciples what He never said to the others. In John 12:27, He said in soliloquy something similar. "Now my soul is troubled, and what shall I say?" Here He really said to these three, "My soul is exceedingly sorrowful, even to death" (Matthew 26:38). Have we for one second watched Jesus pray? Have we ever understood why the Holy Spirit and our Lord Himself were so exceptionally careful about recording the agony of Gethsemane? This is not the agony of a man or a martyr. This is the agony of God as Man. It is God, as Man, going through the last lap of the supreme, supernatural redemption of the human race.

We ought to give much more time than we do—a great deal more than we do—to brooding on the fundamental truths on which the Spirit of God works the simplicity of our Christian experience. The fundamental truths are redemption and the personal presence of the Holy Spirit, and these two are focused in one mighty personality, the Lord Jesus Christ. Thank God for the emphasis laid on the efficacy of the Holy Spirit to make experientially real the redemption of Jesus Christ in individual lives.

Remember, what makes prayer easy is not our wits or our understanding, but the tremendous agony of God in redemption. A thing is worth just what it costs. Prayer is not what it costs us, but what it cost God to enable us to pray. It cost God so much that a little child can pray. It cost God Almighty so much that anyone can pray. But it is time those of us who name His name knew the secret of the cost, and the secret is here: "My soul is exceedingly sorrowful, even to death." These words open the door to the auto-biography of our Lord's agony. We find the real key to Gethsemane in Matthew 4, which records the temptations of our Lord. Here they come again in a deeper and more appealing manner than ever before. We are not looking here (as we do when we deal with the temptations) at the type of temptation we have to go through. We are dealing here with the grappling of God as Man in the last reaches of historical redemption.

"But these truths are so big." Why shouldn't they be? Have we to be fed with spooned meat[7] all the time? Is it not time we paid more attention to what it cost God to make it possible for us to live a holy life? We talk about the difficulty of living a holy life, but there is the absolute simple ease of Almighty God in living a holy life because it cost Him so much to make it possible. Beware of placing the emphasis on what prayer costs us. It cost God every-thing to make it possible for us to pray. Jesus did not say to these men, "Agonize!" He said, "Watch with me." Our Lord tried to lift the veil from before these disciples that they might see what He was going through. Think who He was—the Son of God. "My soul"—the reasoning mind of the Lord Jesus Christ—"is exceedingly sor-rowful, even to death. Stay here and watch with Me."

The Lure of Wrong Roads to the Kingdom

. . . lest you enter into temptation . . .

Whenever Jesus talked about His kingdom the disciples misinter-preted what He said to mean a material kingdom to be established on this earth. But Jesus said, "My kingdom is not of this world. If my kingdom were of this world, My servants would fight, so that I

The Simplicity of Prayer

should not be delivered to the Jews" (John 18:36). And again He said, "The kingdom of God does not come with observation; . . . for indeed, the kingdom of God is within you" (Luke 17:20).

The only way to be saved from the lure of the wrong roads is by doing what our Master tells us, that is, "Watch and pray, lest you enter into temptation." If we do not watch and pray we shall be led into temptation before we know where we are. "Nevertheless, when the Son of man comes, will He really find faith on the earth?" said Jesus (Luke 18:8). He will find faith in individual men and women, but the general organized form of the Christian church has slipped almost wholesale onto wrong roads to the Kingdom.

The Material Road of Deliverance (Matthew 4:1–4). "If You are the Son of God, command that these stones become bread." This temptation is profoundly human. If we could only find some means of curing everybody of disease, of feeding them and putting them on a good social basis, what a marvelous thing it would be. That is the way we are being told that the Kingdom of God is to be established on this earth. "We do not need any more of this talk about the atonement and the shedding of blood; what is needed today is to spend ourselves for others." But that is the lure of the wrong road to the Kingdom, and we cannot keep out of it if we forget to watch and pray. "Watch with me," said Jesus. "Mine is the only road to the kingdom."

We have to continue with Him in His temptations. "Command that these stones become bread." In other words, Satan was saying, "Satisfy Your own needs and the needs of men and You will get the kingship of men." Was Satan right? Read John 6:15: "Therefore when Jesus perceived that they were about to come and take Him by force to make Him king, He departed again to the mountain by Himself alone." Why? He had just fed five thousand of them! Yes, but Jesus "departed . . . alone." He would not be king at that price.

The Mysterious Road of Devotion (Matthew 4:5–7). Here we are dealing with our Lord's presentation of His own temptation. In the most sacred matters we must rely only on the Holy Spirit, no one else.

This temptation presents a wild reach of possibility. "You are the Son of God. Do something supernatural that will stagger men, and the world will be at your feet." Was Satan right? Absolutely. Is there not a lure along that road today more than ever? There are miraculous dealings that lure to destruction, such as the seeking for signs and wonders. Almost without exception the people lured down this wrong road are those who have been told to fast and concentrate for something for themselves, whereby the Lord may show how marvelous He is. It does look right to human reason when it is just touched on the first outer fringe by the Holy Spirit, but it contradicts emphatically what our Lord teaches, namely, that importunity in intercession is never for ourselves but for others.

"The kingdom of God does not come with observation" (Luke 17:20). It is at work now. The manifestation of the Kingdom of God externally is another thing. The disciples still had their own ideas of the Kingdom. They were blind to what Jesus Christ's Kingdom meant, and they were so totally depressed that they slept for their own sorrow. "Watch with me." How could they? They had no idea what He was after.

The Mental Road of Dominion (Matthew 4:8–10). This is the temptation to compromise. Some say that evil is in the world, so we compromise with it, work with it judiciously. "All these things I will give You if You will fall down and worship me," Satan said. This temptation is the most subtle of all. People tell us, "Don't be so straight-laced. We have passed the day when we believe in a personal devil." May God forgive us. I am afraid we are past that stage. Will the church that bows down and compromises succeed? Of course it will. It is the very thing that the natural man wants, but it is the lure of a wrong road to the Kingdom. Beware of putting anything sweet and winsome in front of the One who suffered in Gethsemane.

The Light of Undisciplined Vision

The spirit indeed is willing, but the flesh is weak
(Matthew 26:41).

It is so easy when we see things in vision to start out and do them. We are caught up into the seventh heaven, far above all the grubby things of earth. It is magnificent for a time, but we have got to come down. After the Mount of Transfiguration comes the place where we have to live, namely, the demon-possessed valley. The test of reality is our life in the valley, not that we fly up among the golden peaks of the early morning.

The Triumphant Minute. "Blessed are you, Simon Bar-Jonah" (Matthew 16:17; see John 21:15–19). Peter had his triumphant minute, but he had to go through the mill after that. He went through a tremendous heartbreak before he was fit to hear Jesus say, "Feed my sheep." Peter would have done anything for his Lord— the spirit was willing, but the flesh was weak. We make allowances for the flesh, but we have no business to. We have to make manifest in the flesh the visions of the spirit. Thank God we are going to heaven when we die, but thank God we are not going before we die. We get glimpses of heaven, then we are brought down instantly into actual circumstances. Do not go too long in the light of undisciplined vision. Thank God for the triumphant minute, but we have to walk on earth according to what we saw in vision.

The Transfiguration Moment. "And He was transfigured before them" (Matthew 17:2). After seeing Jesus for that moment on the Mount, we see Him standing after the resurrection on the seashore in the early morning with "a fire of coals there, and fish laid on it, and bread" (John 21:9). Thank God for seeing Jesus transfigured, and for the almightiness of the visions He does give, but remember that the vision is to be made real in actual circumstances. The glory is to be manifested in earthen vessels. It has to be exhibited through fingertips, through eyes and hands and feet, wherever Jesus exhibited it. We are so like Peter on the Mount when we say, "O Lord, let me stay here."

The Transcendent Moment. "Even if I have to die with You, I will not deny You" (Matthew 26:35). Peter meant it every bit. It was a transcendent moment to him. He would have done anything for Jesus Christ, and yet he denied with oaths and curses that he ever knew Him. Peter was no hypocrite, but he did not watch and pray. Peter based his declaration on the keen generosity of his own heart, but he did not understand that he needed to be on another basis altogether—the basis of redemption.

Thank God for the heroic moments of life! It is comparatively easy to live in the heroic moments. We can all have halos at times. If we stand in the right place, with stained-glass windows behind us, and have the right kind of dress on, it is not at all difficult to look remarkably fine. But there is nothing in it. Not only is there nothing in it, but excessive dangers arise out of it. Beware of the transcendent moment that is a pose. A humorous sense of criticism is wholesome. Some people get to a transcendent moment and someone tells them they look remarkably fine, and forever after they try to live in that transcendent moment. We have to get down to the level where the reality works out, and the whole counsel comes back to this, "Watch and pray"—the secret of the sacred simplicity of prayer. Prayer imparts the power to walk and not faint, and the lasting remembrance of our lives is of the Lord, not of us.

O Lord, I come to You that I might find grace to praise and worship You aright.

Lord, lift up the light of Your countenance upon us. Send power and majestic grace.

O Lord, how good it is for me to know You! How vital it is for me to draw near to You! How can I falter when You are my Life!

Lord, our God, the Father of our Lord Jesus Christ, of whom Jesus is the very image, I look to You and make my prayer. Bless me this hour with the feeling of Your presence and the glow of Your nearness, for I do trust You and hope only in You.

IF YOU WILL ASK

Three

THE STRUGGLE FOR PRAYER

For we do not wrestle against flesh and blood, but against principalities, against powers, against the rulers of the darkness of this age, against spiritual hosts of wickedness in the heavenly places. Therefore take up the whole armor of God, that you may be able to withstand in the evil day, and having done all, to stand.

Stand therefore, having girded your waist with truth, having put on the breastplate of righteousness, and having shod your feet with the preparation of the gospel of peace; above all, taking the shield of faith with which you will be able to quench all the fiery darts of the wicked one. And take the helmet of salvation, and the sword of the Spirit, which is the word of God; praying always with all prayer and supplication in the Spirit, being watchful to this end with all perseverance and supplication for all the saints—and for me, that utterance may be given to me, that I may open my mouth boldly to make known the mystery of the gospel (EPHESIANS 6:12–19).

Paul takes the illustration of battle and applies it to what goes on in a saint's life. The whole meaning of taking the armor of God is for prayer. Prayer is the position the devil is struggling for. The struggle is around the position of prayer and the simplicity of prayer. Prayer is easy to us because of what it cost God to enable us to pray. It is the redemption of God, the agony of our Lord, that has made our salvation so easy and prayer so simple. When we emphasize the cost of prayer to us, we are wrong. The cost to us is nothing. It is a supreme and superb privilege marked by supernatural ease because of what it cost God.

We tend nowadays to worship prayer. We stress nights of prayer and the difficulty and cost of prayer. It is not prayer that is strenuous, but the overcoming of our own laziness. If we make the basis of prayer our effort and agony, we mistake the basis of prayer. The basis of prayer is not what it costs us, but what it cost God to enable us to pray.

The Christian Continually in Practice

It is all very well to have vision, but we must also have practice so that when we find ourselves in a tight place we are equipped to meet the emergency. One of the greatest difficulties in war is to find a man who can keep his head when everyone else is losing theirs. It is only done by steady practice. "Therefore take up the whole armor of God"—not to fight, but to stand. We are not told to attack or to storm the efforts of darkness. We are told to stand, unpanicky and unbudged, more than conquerors. A conqueror is one who fights and wins. A "more than conqueror" is one who easily and powerfully overcomes. The struggle is not against flesh and blood, it is against principalities and powers. We cannot touch them by intellect or organization, by courage or foresight or forethought. We cannot touch them at all unless we are based on the redemption.

"Therefore take up the whole armor of God." It is not given; we have to take it. It is there for us to put on, understanding what we are doing. We have the idea that prayer is for special times, but we have to put on the armor of God for the continual practice of prayer, so that any struggling onslaught of the powers of darkness cannot touch the position of prayer. When we pray easily it is because Satan is completely defeated in his onslaughts. When we pray with difficulty it is because Satan is gaining a victory. We have not been continuously practicing. We have not been facing things courageously. We have not been taking our orders from our Lord. Our Lord did not say, "Go" or "Do." He said, "Watch and pray."

If we struggle in prayer it is because the enemy is gaining ground. If prayer is simple, it is because we have the victory. There is no such thing as a holiday for the beating of our hearts. If there is, the grave comes next. And there is no such thing as a moral or spiritual holiday. If we attempt to take a holiday, the next time we want to pray it is a struggle because the enemy has gained a victory all around. Darkness has come down and spiritual wickedness in high places has enfolded us. If we have to fight, it is because we have disobeyed. We ought to be more than conquerors.

"And having done all, to stand"—a mental state of confidence, not panic. What is it that puts us into a panic? The devil is a bully, but he cannot stand for a second before God. When we stand in the armor of God he pays no attention to us, but if we tackle the devil in our own strength we are done for. If we stand in God's armor with the strength and courage of God, Satan cannot gain one inch of way. That is the only way to hold the position of prayer and to be untouched by Satan's wiles.

Confidence in the natural world is self-reliance. In the spiritual world it is God-reliance. We run away when we have not been practicing, when we have not been doing anything in private. Then, when there is a new onslaught of the wiles of the devil we lose heart instantly. Instead of standing we scuttle, and others have to fill the gap until we are sufficiently ashamed to come back.

We cannot stand against the wiles of the devil by our wits. The devil only comes along the lines that God understands, not along the lines we understand. The only way we can be prepared for him is to do what God tells us, to stand complete in His armor, indwelt by His Spirit, in complete obedience to Him. We do not have to wait for some great onslaught of the enemy. He is here all the time and he is wily. The secret of the sacred struggle for prayer lies in the fact that we must stand in the armor of God, practicing what God would have us do. Then we can hold the position of prayer against all the attacks of the devil.

If we are struggling in prayer it is because the wiles of the enemy are getting the upper hand, and we must look for the cause in our lack of discipline. There are some things we have not been strenuously practicing. We used to pray in the morning. Do we now? We used to commune with God over the Bible. Do we now? We used to be in contact with God wherever we went. Are we now? Put on the whole armor of God and continuously practice. Then the wiles of the devil cannot get you unaware.

The Christian's Courageous Preparation

"Stand therefore, having girded your waist with truth"—all active, sensible work is symbolized by a girded waist—"having put on the breastplate of righteousness." In other words, have no inordinate fear, no questionable affinities, no tampering with winsomeness, which all break down the armor. *Righteousness* means "rightness" in our relationship to other people and their best interests.

"And having shod your feet with the preparation of the gospel of peace." What kind of shoes do we wear? How many can say of us, "As soon as I heard your step I felt better?" Or do they say, "When your step came into my life all went wrong; when the step of your friendship began I started to lose out with God"? Put on the armor of God, keep the heart right with God, and wherever you go, you will shed the preparation of the gospel of peace. Wherever the saint goes there is the shedding of the benediction of the blessing of God, or there is the coming of the conviction of the Spirit of God.

"Above all, taking the shield of faith." Faith is unbreakable confidence in the personality of God, not in His power. There are some things over which we may lose faith if we have confidence in God's power only. There is so much that looks like the mighty power of God that is not. We must have confidence in God over and above everything He may do, and stand in confidence that His character is unsullied. Faith stands all tests—"Though He slay me, yet will I trust in Him." When we take the shield of faith, none of these things can get through without breaking the shield. We are protected by the covering shield.

"And take . . . the sword of the spirit." The Spirit brings to mind what the Lord Jesus has said. In every onslaught of the enemy around us, that is the position he is struggling for. To wield the sword of the Spirit, which is the Word of God, we must obey, and it takes the courageous heart to obey. If we try to apply the teaching of our Lord apart from the imparted nature of our Lord to our souls, we will make a muddle. It is not that we take the Sermon on the Mount as precepts and try to live up to them, but that when the Spirit of God brings some word of God back to mind, we will obey it. It will take courage, but as we obey, we withstand the wiles of the devil, and we stand.

The Christian's Competence in Prayer

This is where God puts His soldiers, clad in His armor, and indwelt by His Spirit. Can we pray in prayer, or are we beguiled by the devil? Have we been lured into a judicious winsomeness? Are we not quite so intense as we used to be? Have black and white become a neutral gray? Are we no longer so intense about sin as we used to be? Then we are out of place. We are exactly in the relationship of traitors. We give away God's position so that Satan can easily overcome us by surprise.

"Watch and pray," said Jesus in the center of His own agony. If we don't, we shall slip into the lure of wrong roads without knowing it. The only way to keep right is to watch and pray. The basis of prayer is not human earnestness, not human need, not the human will; it is redemption, and its living center is a personal Holy Spirit. Prayer on any other basis is stupid. A child can pray. Through His own agony in redemption, God has made it as easy to pray as it sounds. A rationally minded being can ridicule nothing more easily than prayer. "Praying always"—the unutterable simplicity of it! No panic, no flurry, always at leisure from ourselves on the inside.

"Being watchful to this end with all perseverance and supplication for all the saints." It is all very well to have prayer meetings,

37

but are we continually practicing in the armor of God, keeping our hearts stout in the courage of God's Spirit and taking our orders from Him? Or are we making an ingenious compromise? There is only one service that has no snares, and that is prayer. Preaching has snares to the natural heart; so has public service. Prayer has no snare because it is based on the redemption of the Lord Jesus Christ made efficacious all the time by the Holy Spirit.

"And for me, that utterance may be given unto me." We naturally suppose it is no use praying for prominent people. God will look after them all right. The prominent people for God are marked for the wiles of the devil, and we may pray for them all the time. Every now and again God gives us an alarming exhibition of what happens if we don't.

Lord God Omnipotent, how my soul delights to know that You care for sparrows and number the hairs of our head! Lord, breathe on me till I am in the frame of mind and body to worship You.

O Lord, I would seek Your face now, but what good is my seeking if You do not reveal Yourself? Show me Your face, O Lord. Keep me ever seeing You.

O Lord, to praise You aright is a great desire of mine, created and fostered by Your Spirit and grace. This morning, O Lord, I praise You for all the past—so wayward on my part, so wonderful and gracious and long-suffering and forgiving and tender and inspiring on Yours.

Four

THE CURRICULUM OF INTERCESSION

I will stand my watch

  And set myself on the rampart,

  And watch to see what He will say to me,

  And what I will answer when I am corrected.

Then the Lord answered me and said:

"Write the vision

  And make it plain on tablets,

  That he may run who reads it.

(Habakkuk 2:1-2).

Inspired Waiting

I will stand my watch and set myself on the rampart.

How steadily all through the Old and New Testament God calls us to stand on the watch and wait for His indications, and how often God's answers to our prayers have been squandered because we do not watch and wait. Are you thoroughly perplexed over God's way? Are you unable to reconcile God's clear way as revealed in His book with the way He is leading you? Take the line of this prophet during his perplexity. Stand and watch to see what God will say—watch at the right place.

There is a difference in the prayers of the Old and the New Testaments. In Chapter 3 the prophet Habakkuk bases his prayer on the character of God and appeals to God's great mercies. In the New Testament, prayer is based on a relationship with God through Jesus Christ. "When you pray, say, Our Father" (Luke 11:2). There is another difference—the prayers in the Old Testament have to do with an earthly people in an earthly setting. The prayers in the New Testament have to do with a heavenly state of mind in a heavenly people while on this earth. We are continually reminded that we wrestle not against flesh and blood, but against principalities and powers and the rulers of this world's darkness.

The first thing to remember is to watch at the right place, the place where God has put us. Watch, that is, for God's answer to our prayers, and not only watch, but wait. When God calls upon us to

The Curriculum of Intercession

pray, when He gives the vision, when He gives an understanding of what He is going to do through us in our Sunday school class, in our church or home—watch. How many of us have had to learn by God's reproof, by God's chastisement, the blunder of conferring with flesh and blood.

Are you discouraged where you are? Then get on this tower with God and watch and wait. The meaning of waiting in both the Old and New Testament is "standing under," actively enduring. It is not standing with folded arms doing nothing. It is not saying, "In God's good time it will come to pass." By that we often mean, "In my abominably lazy time I let God work." Waiting means standing under, in active strength, enduring till the answer comes.

We must never make the blunder of trying to forecast the way God is going to answer our prayer. When God made a tremendous promise to Abraham, Abraham thought of the best way to help God fulfill His promise and did the wisest thing he knew according to flesh-and-blood commonsense reasoning. But God refused to speak to him for thirteen years, until every possibility of his relying on his own intelligent understanding was at an end. Then God came to him and said, "I am Almighty God"—El Shaddai—"walk before Me and be blameless" (Genesis 17:1).

Over and over again God has to teach us how to stand and endure, watching actively and wondering. It is always a wonder when God answers prayer. We hear people say, "We must not say it is wonderful that God answers prayer." But it is wonderful. It is so wonderful that a great many people believe it impossible. "Whatever you ask in my name, that I will do" (John 14:13). Isn't that wonderful? It is so wonderful that I do not suppose more than half of us really believe it. "Everyone who asks receives" (Matthew 7:8). Isn't that wonderful? It is so wonderful that many of us have never even asked God to give us the Holy Spirit because we don't believe He will. "If two of you shall agree on earth as touching anything that they shall ask, it shall be done for them of my Father which is in heaven" (Matthew 18:19). Isn't that wonderful? It is tremendously wonderful. "The effective, fervent prayer of a righteous man avails much" (James 5:16). Isn't that wonderful?

If you have had a vision of how wonderfully God can answer prayer, are you watching today for Him to answer along His line? Are you on your tower, watching steadfastly every sign of God's goings? Or are you coming under the bitter blight that came on Meroz? When the Spirit of the Lord came on Deborah, the prophetess of the Lord, she cried, "Curse Meroz, . . . curse its inhabitants bitterly, because they did not come to the help of the LORD . . . against the mighty' (Judges 5:23).

The first chapter of Habakkuk speaks of the tremendous devastations that are to come upon Israel (see vv. 1–11). In our own day, the majority of us are sound asleep to the devastation going on. And we too will come under the bitter curse of Meroz if we do not rouse ourselves and stand with God against the mighty—spiritualism, supernaturalism, Christian Science, Millennial-dawnism[8]—all terribly widespread, sweeping, devouring errors. Are we thoroughly awake and watching, or are we crying in a cowardly way, "Tell us the things that please us, that rouse us up and kindle us on our own lines. Don't tell us about the perplexities of a prophet or handmaid of God?" God grant that every child of His may get on the watchtower and stand and watch.

As soon as a difficulty comes on the horizon and clouds gather, where is the intense watching? We sulk and turn aside. We turn our backs on God and on His messengers and say, "You have not brought us into a land flowing with milk and honey" (Numbers 16:14). God

43

grant that in times of perplexity we may get back again to the watch-tower, back again to inspired waiting, back again to the wide-eyed wonder of a child at God's answers to our prayers.

Intelligent Witnessing

And watch to see what He will say to me.

I do not think we have enough of the wondering spirit that the Holy Spirit gives. It is the child-spirit. A child is always wide awake with wonder. But as we get older we forget that a child's wonder is nearer the truth than our older knowledge. When through Jesus Christ we are rightly related to God, we learn to watch and wait, and wait wonderingly. "I wonder how God will answer this prayer." "I wonder how God will answer the prayer the Holy Spirit is praying in me." "I wonder what glory God will bring to Himself out of the strange perplexities I am in." "I wonder what new turn His providence will take in manifesting Himself in my ways."

The child-like wondering mind of the Holy Spirit, if I may say so reverently, was exhibited in the Lord Jesus Christ as everlasting wonder and expectancy at His Father's working. "I do not speak on my own authority," and "the Father who dwells in Me does the works" (John 14:10). Our Lord said that when the Holy Spirit is come, "He will not speak on His own authority, but whatever He hears He will speak" (John 16:13). The Lord Jesus spoke and worked from the great big child-heart of God. God Almighty became incarnate as a little child, and Jesus Christ's message in us must become as that of little children. God always keeps the minds of His children open with wonder, with open-eyed expectancy for Him to come in where He likes. I wonder how many of us have been getting our ideas and convictions and notions twisted. Thank God for the confusion if it is going to drive us straight to the watchtower with God. There our doctrines and creeds are going to be God's, not doctrines and creeds out of God's Book twisted to suit our preconceived ideas, but the doctrines of God woven into the flesh and blood tissues of our lives by the indwelling Holy Spirit— watching, waiting, wondering, and witnessing.

Take all the Old Testament prophets. God never spoke with them without a corresponding wonder on their part. Over and over again the prophets were staggered with wonder at the strange things God did, and if they leaned to their own intelligence without sufficiently relying on the tremendous power of God, there was instant confusion. We have to "receive, recognize, and rely on the Holy Spirit," and never get beyond that stage. God grant we may have the wonder of the child-heart that the Holy Spirit gives, and that He may keep our minds young and vigorous and unstagnant, never asleep, but always awake with child-eyed wonder at the next wonderful thing God will do. "The LORD reigns; let the earth rejoice" (Ps. 97:1).

God grant we may get to the place where the only thing we take seriously is the place God has put us, watching, waiting steadfastly for God's goings. Never take anything said by any man or woman, or in any book, without waiting and watching before God. "Try the spirits," test them, see if they be of God. I want you to beware of a mistake I have made over and over again of trying to interpret God's plan for other lives according to the way He has led me. Never do this! Keep open-eyed in wonder. Can God do what He likes in your life? Can He help Himself to you? Can He take you up and put you down? Can He introduce His schemes through you, and never tell you the reason? Can He make you a spectacle to men and angels, as He did Job, without giving you any explanation? Can He make you a wonder to yourself and to others, while

The Curriculum of Intercession

He gives you the implicit childlike understanding that somehow or other things are working out all right?

Inviolable Walking

Write the vision, and make it plain on tablets, that he may
run that reads it. No longer watching and waiting, but actively
set toward the divine goal to which God is calling.

Have you ever noticed the "wondering-ness" (if I may coin a word) of the people who go on with God? They never seem to be over-anxious or overconcerned and they always seem to be getting younger. What is the characteristic of the people of this world who have not got the child-heart? They are always sighing; they have mental and spiritual rheumatism and neuralgia, moral twists and perversities, and nothing can rouse them. Why? They need the child-spirit, the Spirit that was given to the disciples after the resurrection and in its fullness at Pentecost; then nothing will turn them aside.

After Pentecost came the sword and great persecution. The disciples were all scattered abroad, but nothing could stop them from preaching the Word. There was a hilarious shout all through these men's lives because of the mighty baptism of the Holy Spirit and fire. There was running then! No power on earth or heaven above or hell beneath could stop the tremendous strength of the child-life of the Holy Spirit in them. Have you got the wonder in your heart or are you sighing, "Thank God I have managed to squeeze enough grace out of God to last through this day?" Blessed be the name of God, all the unsearchable riches of Christ are at your disposal!

Thank God for every life that is running in the strength of the tremendous vision. Keep your eyes on your file leader, Jesus only,

46

Jesus ever, "and make straight paths for your feet" (Hebrews 12:13). Watch for His goings. When He stands and hides Himself in a cloud—stand, watch, and wait. When the meaning is clear, then you will run. A vision puts enthusiasm into you, a thrilling understanding of God's Word, and you soar above in tremendous ecstasy. Then you come down and run without being weary, and then you come to the grandest days and walk without fainting.

"For the vision is yet for an appointed time; but at the end it will speak, and it will not lie. Though it tarries, wait for it; because it will surely come, it will not tarry" (Habakkuk 2:3). "I heard the voice of the Lord, saying, 'Whom shall I send, and who will go for Us?'" (Isaiah 6:8). That is a wonderful point—"Who will go for Us?" Some say, "Lord, there is Mrs. So-and-so. She is ready, send her." Is that the answer you give? "O Lord, I know there ought to be a movement in my church and there is Mr. So-and-so. He's just the one, send him." If you have been watching, waiting, and wondering, you will say: "Here am I; send me." If God came to you tonight, would you say, "Here am I?" Do you know where you are? Some people live in a fog. They don't know where they are, but if you know anything about waiting on God and walking before Him, you will say, "Here am I, do what You like with me."

O Lord, explore down to the deepest springs of my spirit where Your Spirit works, and read my deepest prayer I cannot pray in expression. Lord, touch my body; it is Your temple. Shine out in and through it, O Lord.

The Curriculum of Intercession

O Lord, lift up the light of Your countenance upon us this day, and make us to fit in with Your plans with great sweetness and light and liberty, and a lilt to You all day.

O God my Father, the clouds are but the dust of Your feet. Let me discover in every cloud of providence or nature or grace no man but Jesus till there is no fear.

Five

AFTER GOD'S SILENCE— WHAT?

Now Jesus loved Martha and her sister and Lazarus. So, when He had heard therefore that he was sick, He stayed two more days in the same place where He was (JOHN 11:5–6).

The Absence of Audible Response

J esus stayed two days where He was without sending a word. We are apt to say, "I know why God has not answered my prayer. It is because I asked for something wrong." That was not the reason Jesus did not answer Martha and Mary. They desired a right thing. It is quite true God does not answer some prayers because they are wrong, but that is so obvious that it does not need a revelation from God to understand it. God wants us to stop understanding in the way we have understood and get into the place He wants us to get into. That is, He wants us to know how to rely on Him.

God's silences are His answers. If we only take as answers those that are visible to our senses, we are in a very elementary condition of grace. Can it be said of us that Jesus so loved us that He stayed where He was because He knew we had a capacity to stand a bigger revelation? Has God trusted us with a silence, a silence that is absolutely big with meaning? That is His answer. The manifestation will come in a way beyond our comprehension.

Are we mourning before God because we have not had an audible response? Mary Magdalene was weeping at the sepulcher. What was she asking for? The dead body of Jesus. Of whom did she ask it? Of Jesus Himself, and she did not know Him! Did Jesus give her what she asked for? He gave her something infinitely grander than she had ever conceived—a risen living, impossible-to-die Lord.

How many of us have been blind in our prayers? Look back and think of the prayers you thought had not been answered but now find that God has answered with a bigger manifestation than you ever dreamed. God has trusted you in the most intimate way He could trust you, with an absolute silence, not of despair but of pleasure, because He saw you could stand a much bigger revelation than you had at the time.

Some prayers are followed by silence because they are wrong, others because they are bigger than we can understand. Jesus stayed where He was—a positive staying, because He loved Martha and Mary. Did they get Lazarus back? They got infinitely more; they got to know the greatest truth moral beings ever knew—that Jesus Christ is the Resurrection and the Life. It will be a wonderful moment when we stand before God and find that the prayers we clamored for in early days and imagined were never answered, have been answered in the most amazing way, and that God's silence has been the sign of the answer. If we always want to be able to point to something and say, "This is the way God answered my prayer," God cannot trust us yet with His silence.

Here is where the devil comes in and says, "Now you have been praying a wrong prayer." You can easily know whether you have—test it by the word of God. If it has been a prayer to know God better, a prayer for the baptism of the Holy Spirit, a prayer for the interpretation and understanding of God's Word, it is a prayer in accord with God's will. You say, "But He has not answered." He has, He is so near to you that His silence is the answer. His silence is big with terrific meaning that you cannot understand yet, but presently you will. Time is nothing to God. Prayers were offered years ago and God answered the soul with silence. Now He is giving the manifestation of the answer in a revelation that we are scarcely able to comprehend.

The Attitude of Awful Repose

Picture Martha and Mary waiting day after day for Jesus to come, yet not till Lazarus' body had been in the grave four days did Jesus Christ appear on the scene. Days of absolute silence, of awful repose on the part of God! Is there anything analogous to it in your life? Can God trust you like that, or are you still wanting a visible answer? "Whatever we ask we receive from Him" (1 John 3:22). If God has given you a silence, praise Him. Think of the things you prayed to God about and tried to hold and, because of His love, He dare not let you hold them and they went. For a time you said, "I asked God to give me bread and He gave me a stone." But He did not, and you found that He gave you the bread of life. You prayed that you might keep the thing that seemed to make your life as a Christian possible. You asked that it might always be preserved by God, and suddenly the whole thing went to pieces. That was God's answer. After the silence, if we are spiritual and can interpret His silence, we always get the trust in God that knows prayers are answered every time, not sometimes. The manifestation of the answer in place and time is a mere matter of God's sovereignty. Be earnest and eager on the line of praying. One wonderful thing about God's stillness in connection with prayers is that He makes us still, make us perfect confident. The contagion of Jesus Christ's stillness gets into us—"I know He has heard me"—and His silence is the proof He has heard.

The Answer's Amazing Revelation

Could the answer that Jesus Christ gave ever have entered into the heart of Martha and Mary: a raised brother, the manifestation of the glory of God, and the understanding of Jesus Christ in a way that has blessed the church for twenty centuries?

Remember that Jesus Christ's silences are always signs that He knows we can stand a bigger revelation than we think we can. If He gives us the exact answer, He cannot trust us yet. "If two of you agree on earth concerning anything that they ask, it will be done for them by My Father in heaven" (Matthew 18:19). That is stated for people who are not spiritual. Our Lord's revelations about prayer in Luke 11 and 18 are for those who are spiritual, who remain in confidence in prayer. Because Jesus Christ keeps silence does not mean that He is displeased, but exactly the opposite. He is bringing us into the great run of His purpose, and the answer will be an amazing revelation. No wonder our Lord said, "Greater works than these he will do also; . . . . And whatever you ask in my name, that I will do" (John 14:12–13).

That is what prayer means—not that God may bless us. As long as we have the idea only that God will bless us in answer to prayer, He will do it, but He will never give us the grace of a silence. If He is taking us into the understanding that prayer is for the glorifying of His Father, He will give us the first sign of His intimacy—silence. The devil calls it unanswered prayer. In the case of Martha and Mary, the Spirit of God called it a sign that He loved them, and because He loved them and knew they were fit to receive a bigger revelation than ever they dreamed of, He stayed where He was. God will give us the blessings we want if we won't go any further, but His silence is the sign that He is bringing us into this marvelous understanding of Himself.

O Lord, I ask for the power of Your Spirit to adore You more fully. Keep my spirit brightly infused by Your Holy Spirit, O Lord, that thus energized, my Lord Jesus Christ and His perfections may be manifested in my mortal flesh.

O Lord, breathe on me till I am one with You in the temper of my mind and heart and disposition. I turn to You. How completely again I realize my lost-ness without You.

O Lord, I have no inkling of Your ways in external details, but I have the expectancy of Your wonders soon to be made visible. Lord, I look to You. How completely at rest I am, yet how free from seeing Your way. You are God and I trust in You.

Six

NOW THIS EXPLAINS IT

As You, Father, are in Me, and I in You (JOHN 17:21).

The Submission of Life

Jesus answered, "You could have no power at all against Me unless it had been given you from above. Therefore the one who delivered Me to you has the greater sin" (John 19:11).

We are not built for ourselves, but for God. Not for service for God, but for God. That explains the submissions of life.

"Then He went down with them . . . and was subject to them" (Luke 2:51). An amazing submission! For thirty years Jesus lived at home with brothers and sisters who did not believe in Him, and when He began His ministry they said He was mad. "As He is, so are we in this world." We say, "When I was born again I thought it would be a time of great illumination and service, and instead of that I have had to stay at home with people who have criticized me and limited me on the right hand and on the left. I have been misunderstood and misrepresented."

"A disciple is not above his teacher" (Matthew 10:24). Do we think our lot ought to be better than Jesus Christ's? We can easily escape the submissions if we like, but if we do not submit, the Spirit of God will produce in us the most ghastly humiliation before long. Knowing that Jesus has prayed for us makes us submit.

God is not concerned about our aims. He does not say, "Do you want to go through this bereavement, this upset?" He allows these things for His own purpose. We may say what we like, but God does allow the devil, He does allow sin, He does allow bad men to triumph and tyrants to rule, and these things either make us fiends or they make us saints. It depends entirely on our relationship with God. If we say, "Your will be done," we get the tremendous consolation of knowing that our Father is working everything according to His own wisdom. If we understand what God is after, we shall be saved from being mean[9] and cynical.

The things we are going through are either making us sweeter, better, nobler men and women, or they are making us more captious, more insistent on our own way. We are either getting more like our Father in heaven, or we are getting more mean and intensely selfish. How are we behaving ourselves in our circumstances? Do we understand the purpose of our life as never before? God does not exist to answer our prayers, but by our prayers we come to discern the mind of God, and that is declared in John 17:22: "That they may be one just as We are one." Am I as close to Jesus as that? God will not leave me alone until I am. God has one prayer He must answer, and that is the prayer of Jesus Christ. It does not matter how imperfect or immature a disciple may be, if he will hang in, that prayer will be answered.

Solitary Places of Life

Then Jesus, being filled with the Holy Spirit, returned from the Jordan and was led by the Spirit into the wilderness, being tempted for forty days by the devil. And in those days He ate nothing, and afterward, when they had ended, He was hungry (Luke 4:1–2).

There was nothing to mark our Lord from ordinary men except that He was insulated within. He did not choose the solitary places; He was driven by the Spirit of God into the wilderness. It is not good to be alone; evil will make a person want to be alone. Jesus Christ does not make religious hermits; He makes men and women fit for the world as it is (see John 17:15). We say, "I do wish Jesus did not expect so much of me." He expects nothing less than absolute oneness with Himself as He was one with His Father. God does not expect us to work for Him, but to work with Him.

Every man carries his kingdom within, and no one knows what is taking place in another's kingdom. "No one understands me!" Of course they don't; each of us is a mystery. There is only One who understands us, and that is God. We must hand ourselves over to Him.

Are you being subjected in this internal kingdom to tremendous temptations? Jesus was tempted of the devil. Perhaps you are also, but no one guesses it. There is never any comrade for your soul when you are tempted. Temptation tests the things we hold dear. If we withhold things from God, those are the lines along which temptation will come. This explains it—Jesus has prayed, "that they may be one just as We are one." Think of being one with Jesus, one in aim and purpose! Some of us are far off from this, and yet God will not leave us alone until we are one with Him, because Jesus has prayed that we may be. There is a risk in discipleship because God never shields us from the world, the flesh, and the devil. Christianity is character, not "show business."

If you are going through a solitary way, read John 17. It will explain exactly why you are where you are. Now that you are a disciple you can never be as independent as you used to be. Jesus has prayed that you might be one with the Father as He is. Are you helping God answer His prayer, or have you another end for your life?

The Sublimity of Life

And the glory which You gave Me I have given them,
that they may be one just as We are one (John 17:22).

"And the glory which You gave Me I have given them." The glory of our Lord was the glory of a holy life, and that is what He gives to us. He gives us the gift of holiness. Are we exercising it?

"The hope of His calling" is revealed in John 17, and it is the great light on every problem. God grant me that we may remain true to that calling. "We will come to Him and make Our home with him" (John 14:23), the triune God abiding with the saint. What else does a man need to care about after that!

O Lord, when I awake I am still with You. Quicken my mortal body with Your mighty resurrection life. Rouse me with a gracious flooding of Your Divine life for this day.

Lord, so much activity, so many things, so numberless the people, and yet You remain! Bless today with largeness of heart and beauty of character for Your glory.

O Lord, unto You do I look up. Enlighten me. Cause me to be radiant with Your countenance. I praise You for Your grace and for seeing a little of Your marvelous doings. Enable me more and more to manifest the life hidden with Christ in God.

Lord, through the dimness, come with dawning and drawing light. Breathe on me till I am in a pure, radiant frame of body and mind for Your work and for Your glory this day.

Seven

PRAYING IN THE HOLY SPIRIT

Praying always with all prayer and supplication in the Spirit
(EPHESIANS 6:18).

Praying in the Holy Spirit means using the power given to us by God to maintain a simple relationship to Jesus Christ, and it is most difficult to realize this simple relationship in the matter of prayer.

Prayer Pervaded by Pentecost

We have to pray relying upon what has been revealed by the sent-down Holy Spirit, and the first revelation is that we do not know how to pray (see Romans 8:26). We have to learn to draw on our relationship to Jesus Christ. As we do, we realize that the Holy Spirit keeps us in simple relationship to our Lord while we pray. When we pray in the Holy Spirit we are released from our petitions. "Your Father knows the things you have need of before you ask Him" (Matthew 6:8).

Then why ask? The whole meaning of prayer is that we may know God. The "asking and receiving" prayer is elementary; it is the part of prayer we can understand. But it is not necessarily praying in the Holy Spirit. Those who are not born again must ask and receive; but when we have received and have become rightly related to God, we must maintain this simplicity of belief in Him while we pray. Our minds must be saturated by the Revelation of prayer until we learn in every detail to pray in the Holy Spirit. Prayer is not an exercise, it is life.

Peculiar Sense of Need

A great many people do not pray because they do not feel any sense of need. The sign that the Holy Spirit is in us is that we realize that we are empty, not that we are full. We have a sense of absolute need. We come across people who try us, circumstances that are difficult, conditions that are perplexing, and all these things awaken a dumb sense of need, which is a sign that the Holy Spirit is there. If we are ever free from the sense of need, it is not because the Holy Spirit has satisfied us, but because we have been satisfied with as much as we have. "A man's reach should exceed his grasp." A sense of need is one of the greatest benedictions because it keeps our life rightly related to Jesus Christ.

Permeating Sense of Restraint

When we learn to pray in the Holy Spirit, we find there are some things for which we cannot pray. We sense a need for restraint. Never push and say, "I know it is God's will and I am going to stick to it." Beware. Remember the children of Israel: "He gave them their request; but sent leanness into their soul" (Psalm 106:15). Let the Spirit of God teach you what He is driving at and learn not to grieve Him. If we are abiding in Jesus Christ we shall ask what He wants us to ask, whether we are conscious of doing so or not (see John 15:7).

Profound Sense of Christ's Work

When we pray relaying on the Holy Spirit, He will always bring us back to this one point: we are not heard because we are in earnest, or because we need to be heard, or because we will perish if we are not heard. We are heard only on the ground of the Atonement of our Lord (see Hebrews 10:19).

The efficacy of the atoning work of Christ is one thing that the Holy Spirit works into our understanding. As He interprets the meaning of that work to us, we learn never to bank on our own earnestness or on our sense of need. We never have the idea that God does not answer; we become restfully certain that He always does.

The Holy Spirit will continually interpret to us that the only ground of our approach to God is "by the blood of Jesus." As we learn the spiritual culture of praying in the Holy Spirit, we find that God uses the common sense circumstances He puts us in, and the common sense people His providence places us among, to enable us to realize that the one fundamental thing in prayer is the atoning work of Jesus Christ.

Apprehension of God's Resources

When we pray in the Holy Spirit we begin to have a more intimate conception of God. The Holy Spirit brings all through us the sense of His resources. For instance, the Holy Spirit may call us to a definite purpose for our life and we know that it means a decision, a reckless fling over onto God, a burning of our bridges behind us, and there is not a soul to advise us when we take that step except the Holy Spirit.

Our clingings come in this way: We put one foot on God's side and one on the side of human reasoning. Then God widens the space until we either drop between or jump to one side. We have to take a leap—a reckless leap—and if we have learned to rely on the Holy Spirit, it will be a reckless leap to God's side. So many of us limit our praying because we are not reckless in our confidence in God. In the eyes of those who do not know God, it is madness to trust Him, but when we pray in the Holy Spirit we begin to realize the resources of God, that He is our perfect heavenly Father, and we are His children.

Always keep an inner recollection that God is our Father through the Lord Jesus Christ.

Atmosphere for Work

Praying in the Holy Spirit gives us a true insight into why Paul said we wrestle not against flesh and blood, but against principalities and powers, against spiritual wickedness in high places.

If the Holy Spirit is having His way in us, He will charge the atmosphere round about us. There are things that have to be cleared away by the Holy Spirit. Never fight; stand and wrestle. Wrestling is not fighting, it is confronting the antagonist on our own ground and maintaining a steady, all-embracing "stand" and "withstand." How many of us succumb to flesh-and-blood circumstances—"I did not sleep well" or "I have indigestion" or "I did not do quite the right thing there." Never allow any of these things to be your reason for not prevailing in prayer. Hundreds of people with impaired bodies know what it is to pray in the Holy Spirit.

In work for God never look at flesh-and-blood causes. Meet every arrangement for the day in the power of the Holy Spirit. It makes no difference what your work is or what your circumstances are if you are praying in the Holy Spirit. He will produce an atmosphere round about you, and all these things will result in the glory of God.

Apostolic Habit

"Pray without ceasing" (1 Thessalonians 5:17). Keep the child-like habit of continually exclaiming in your heart to God, recognize and rely on the Holy Spirit all the time. Inarticulate prayer, the impulsive prayer that looks so futile, is the thing God always heeds. The apostolic habit ought to be the persistent habit of each one of us.

Attitude of Daily Reaction

The way we react during the day will either hinder or help our praying. If we allow a reaction not born of a relationship to Jesus Christ, we shall have much wilderness waste to get through before we can come to God. Mists and shadows come between our conscious life and the interceding Holy Spirit. The Holy Spirit is there all the time, but we have lost sight of Him. Anything that is so continually with us, even our religious life itself, that we never really pray in the Holy Spirit may be a hindrance.

The only one who prays in the Holy Spirit is the child, the child-spirit in us, the spirit of utter confidence in God. When we pray in the Holy Spirit we bring to God the things that come quite naturally to our minds, and the Holy Spirit who "makes intercession for the saints according to the will of God" (Romans 8:27) enables God to answer the prayer He Himself prays in our bodily temples. "That you may be sons of your Father in heaven" (Matthew 5:45). The Holy Spirit cannot delight in our wisdom. It is the wisdom of God He delights in.

When we recognize that our body is the temple of the Holy Spirit we will be careful to keep it undefiled for Him. "My house shall be called a house of prayer," said Jesus (Matthew 21:13).

Lord, how I desire to see You, to hear You, to meditate on You, and to manifestly grow like You! And You have said, "Delight yourself also in the LORD, and He shall give you the desires of your heart."

Praying in the Holy Spirit

O Lord, I know Your blessing and I praise You, but it is the inde-
scribable touch as Your servant that I seek for—I know not what
I seek for, but You know. How I long for Thee!

Lord, I still move and live in a dim world, feeling You near by faith,
but I will not presume. I would hide in You in security and patience
until I am as You would have me to be.

Eight

PAUL'S PRAYER FOR INSTANTANEOUS SANCTIFICATION

Now may the God of peace Himself sanctify you completely; and may your whole spirit, soul, and body be preserved blameless at the coming of our Lord Jesus Christ. He who calls you is faithful, who also will do it (1 Thessalonians 5:23–24).

All through the Bible the separation of a people by God is revealed, and the individual members of that people have to separate themselves to God's service. We are set apart that we may set ourselves apart. God who requires the separations requires also that the person be sanctified intrinsically.

Two ideas are brought out in regard to our Lord. First, the Father separated Jesus for His redemptive work: "Do you say of Him whom the Father sanctified and sent into the world, 'You are blaspheming,' because I said, 'I am the Son of God?'" (John 10:36). Second, Jesus sanctified Himself for the work of God: "And for their sakes I sanctify Myself, that they also may be sanctified by the truth" (John 17:19).

But our Lord was holy. Why did He say "I sanctify Myself"? To coin a phrase, Jesus Christ "sanctified His sanctification," that is, He determinedly sacrificed His holy Self to His Father. Jesus Christ separated—or sanctified—Himself by sacrificing His holy Self to the will of His Father. He sanctified His intelligence by submitting His intelligence to the word of His Father. He sanctified His will by submitting His will to the will of His Father.

As the sanctified children of God we need to bear in mind that after the experience of sanctification we have to separate our holiness to God. We are not made holy for ourselves, but for God. There is to be no insubordination about us.

The majority of us are too indifferent, too religiously sentimental, to be caught up in the sweep of the apostle Paul's intercession.

Paul's Prayer for Instantaneous Sanctification

Have we a lesser idea than that God should do in us what He wants to do? Are we prepared to pray with Murray McCheyne,[10] "Lord, make me as holy a Thou canst make a sinner saved by grace"?

Some people pray and long and yearn for the experience of sanctification, but never get anywhere near it. Others enter in with a sudden marvelous realization. Sanctification is an instantaneous, continuous work of grace. How long the approach to it takes depends upon ourselves, and that leads some to say sanctification is not instantaneous. The reason some do not enter in is that they have never allowed their minds to realize what sanctification means.

When we pray to be caught up into God's purpose behind this intercession of the apostle Paul, we must see that we are willing to face the standard of these verses. Are we prepared for what sanctification will cost? It will cost an intense narrowing of all our interests on earth, and an immense broadening of our interest in God. In other words, sanctification means an intense concentration on God's point of view—every power of spirit, soul, and body chained and kept for God's purpose only. Sanctification means being made one with God, even as the Lord Jesus Christ was one—"that they may be one, even as we are one." That is much more than union; it is one in identity. The same disposition that ruled in Jesus rules in me.

Am I prepared for what that will cost? It will cost everything that is not God in me. Am I prepared for God to separate me for His work in me, as He separated Jesus, and after His work is done, am I prepared to separate myself to God even as Jesus did? It is this settling down into God's truth that we need.

The type of sanctified life is the Lord Jesus Christ, and the characteristic of His life was subordination to His Father. The only way to get right with God is to soak in the atmosphere of the life of the Lord Jesus.

The one mark of spiritual people today is insubordination. We have wild spiritual impulses that would give an opportunity to Satan as an angel of light to switch the very elect, if it were possible, away from God's plan. If you want to know the result of spiritual insubordination, read 1 Corinthians 12. There we see a portrait of spiritual lunacy—absolute insubordination to the dominant sanity of the Spirit of God. The characteristic of the Holy Spirit in a man is a strong family likeness to Jesus and freedom from everything unlike Jesus.

The best of us are all too shallow and flippant in our attitude to this tremendous secret of sanctification. Are we prepared to let the Spirit of God grip us and put us under His searchlight, and then do a work in us that is worthy of God? Sanctification is not our idea of what we want God to do for us. Sanctification is what God does for us, and He has to get us into the right relationship, the right attitude of mind and heart, where at any cost we let Him do it. Are we prepared to concentrate on the Holy Spirit's ministration?

The apostle Paul is not talking about scientific or intellectual truth. He is talking about spiritual truth, and the only way we can prove spiritual truth is by experience. People say, "I don't understand this doctrine of sanctification." Well, get into the experience first. You only get home by going there. You may think about getting there, but you will never get there till you go. Am I prepared to do what Jesus said—"Come unto me"? Am I prepared to let God make me real? Reality is the proof in my own experience that this thing is true. God grant that every worker may see the peril of not applying this spiritual logic, "Prove it." Every time we give a message that we have no experience of, the Spirit of God will bring it back to us, "Where are you in regard to this matter?"

Paul's Prayer for Instantaneous Sanctification

The Value of Calm

Now may the God of peace. . . .

By the guidance of the Holy Spirit, Paul puts the subsiding of suspicion in first place. The very nature of the old disposition is an
incurable suspicion that Jesus Christ cannot do what He came to
do. If we have the tiniest suspicion that God cannot sanctify us in
His almighty way we need to let the God of peace slip His great
calm all through our insidious unbelief till all is quiet and there is
one thing only—God and our soul; not the peace of a conscience
at rest only, but the very peace of God that will keep us rightly
related to God. "My peace I give to you," said Jesus (John 14:27).
When once we let the God of peace grip us by salvation and
squeeze the suspicion out of us till we are quiet before Him, the
believing attitude is born, there is no more suspicion, we are in
moral agreement with God about everything He wants us to do.

One of the things we need to be cured of by the God of peace
is the petulant struggle of doing things for ourselves—"I can sanctify myself; if I cut off this and that and the other I shall be all
right." No, Paul says, "the God of peace Himself sanctify you completely" (1 Thessalonians 5:23). Has the God of peace brought
you into a calm, or is there a clamor and a struggle still? Are you
still hanging onto some obstinate conviction of your own? Still
struggling with some particular line of things you want? "The God
of peace Himself sanctify you completely." If we are to be sanctified,
it must be by the God of peace Himself. The power that makes the
life of the saint does not come from our efforts at all. It comes from
the heart of the God of peace.

Some use a phrase, "to pray through." What we have to "pray
through" is all our petulant struggling after sanctification, all the

inveterate suspicion in our hearts that God cannot sanctify us. When we are rid of all that and are right before God, then God lets us see how He alone does the work.

> When we stay our feeble efforts,
> And from struggling cease,
> Unconditional surrender
> Brings us God's own peace.

The great mighty power of the God of peace is slipped into the soul under the call of supreme sanctification. Some of us are far too turbulent in spirit to experience even the first glimpse of what sanctification means. People noisy in words are not always turbulent in spirit; excessively quiet people who have nothing to express in joy and shouting may be suspicious in heart.

The Value of Massive Truth

Sanctify you wholly. . . .

When once we get calm before God and are willing to let Him do what He chooses, He gives us an outline of some of His massive truths. "And the very God of peace sanctify you wholly," preserve you in unspotted integrity. Integrity is the unimpaired state of a thing, unblameable, undeserving of censure in God's sight. Paul's intercession is for an instantaneous and insistent sanctification that will preserve a man in unspotted integrity "unto the coming of our Lord Jesus Christ." The majority of us have never allowed our minds to dwell as they should on these great massive truths; consequently sanctification has been made to mean a second dose of conversion. Sanctification can only be named in the presence of God. It is stamped by a likeness to Christ. *Wholly* means in every detail—mystical, moral, and material.

Mystical. "And I pray God your whole spirit . . . be preserved blameless." The word *spirit* here is not the same as in verse 19. "Your whole spirit" is the personality of a man imbued with the Spirit of God till all the highest mystical reaches of his personality are living in God. Where are your imaginations? Where are all the fancies that break through language and escape? Where do they live? Where are our dreams that make us afraid of ourselves?

They are in our subconscious, super-conscious, beyond the range of what we are able to grasp. The great mystic work of the Holy Spirit is in those dim regions of personality where we cannot go. If we want to know what those regions are like, we can read Psalm 139. The psalmist implies, "You are the God of the early mornings, the God of the late-at-nights, the God of the mountain peaks, the God of the sea; but, my God, my soul has further horizons than the early mornings, deeper darkness than the nights of earth, higher peaks than any mountain, greater depths than any sea can know. My God, You are the God of these; be my God! I cannot reach to the heights or depths. There are motives I cannot touch, dreams I cannot fathom; God search me, winnow out my way."

When God gives His calm, do we realize the magnitude of sanctification through His omnipotent might? Do we believe that God can garrison our imaginations, can sanctify us far beyond where we can go? Have we realized that if we walk in the light as God is in the light that the blood of Jesus Christ cleanses us from all sin? If that means cleansing from sin in conscious experience only, God almighty have mercy on us! The man who has become obtuse through sin is unconscious of sin. Being cleansed by the blood of Jesus means cleansing to the very height and depth of our spirit if we walk in the light as God is in the light.

None of us soaks sufficiently in the terrific God-like revelation of sanctification, and many a child of God would never have been led astray by the counterfeits of Satan if they had allowed their minds to be bent on that great concept of Paul's—your whole spirit—from the vague beginnings of personality known only to God, to the top-most reaches, preserved entirely, garrisoned by the God of peace.

Moral. "Your whole . . . soul preserved blameless." There are those who want to form a religion on mysticism—live according to their temperament. Every sanctified soul is mystic, but he does not live in that region only. He is soul and body as well as spirit, and what is true in the mystical sphere is true in the moral sphere. Soul is man's spirit becoming rational in the body, explaining itself.

When a little child wants to say something and has not a vocabulary, it speaks through gesticulations and facial workings. It has not the power of soul to express itself in words. Paul says not only "your whole spirit preserved blameless," but "your whole soul." Are we forming the mind of Christ? A man has the spirit of Jesus given to him, but he has not His mind until he forms it. How are we to form the mind of Christ? By letting His Spirit imbue our spirit, our thinking, and our reasoning faculties. Then we shall begin to reason as Jesus did, until slowly and surely the Spirit that fed the life of Jesus will feed the life of our soul.

Sanctification covers not only the narrow region where we begin the spiritual life, but the whole rational man, sanctified wholly in imagination and reasoning power. How do we read history? Do we discern the arm of the Lord behind it? How do we sum up the circumstances of our own lives? "The sun shall no longer be your light by day, nor for brightness shall the moon give light to you; but the LORD will be to you an everlasting light, and your God your glory" (Isaiah 60:19). The light on the inside will guide you, a reasoning soul, to understand the facts revealed by common days and nights you cannot understand otherwise. A humble, ignorant man or woman depending on the mind of God has an explanation for things that the rational man without the Spirit of God never has.

Material. "Your whole . . . body preserved blameless." Man is not only mystical and moral, but material. Never say because you have a body you cannot progress. According to the apostle Paul the body is unutterably sacred. The Bible does not say that the body is a curse and a hindrance; it says it is the temple of the Holy Spirit. "Or do you not know that your body is the temple of the Holy Spirit who is in you?" (1 Corinthians 6:19). It is only when garrisoned by the God of peace that the stupendous sanctity of the Holy Spirit preserves a man—spirit, soul, and body—in unspotted integrity, without blame, unto the coming of Jesus. Our whole body is preserved as we come into contact with all the different relationships of life. In the beginning of spiritual education we are apt to pay too much attention to one of these spheres and Satan gets his chance with others. If we pay attention to the spiritual, Satan will pay attention to the nerves.

Sanctification is an instantaneous, continuous work of God. Immediately we are related rightly to God. It is manifested instantly in spirit, soul, and body. The reason the Church as a whole does not believe it is that they will not soak in the massive truths of God. Consequently every now and again in the history of the Church, God has had to raise up some servant of His to emphasize afresh this intense, vivid sanctification of the whole spirit, the whole soul, and the whole body, preserved blameless unto the coming of our Lord Jesus Christ.

O Lord, my approach to You is dulled because of my physical dimness, but my spirit and heart rejoice in You and my flesh shall rest in hope. Touch me bodily, O Lord, till I answer in thrilling health to Your touch.

Insulate me, O Lord, from the things of sense and time, and usher me into the presence of the King.

O Lord, I am distressed at my slow manifestation of any of the beauty of holiness that might express my unspeakable gratitude for Your salvation. O Lord, cause me by looking to You to be radiant.

O Lord, I would bless and praise You. How hard I find it to praise You when I am not physically fit, and yet why should I—that means that I praise You when it is a pleasure to me physically. O Lord, that my soul were one continual praise to You.

Paul's Prayer for Instantaneous Sanctification

Nine

THIS DAY IS THAT DAY

"And in that day you will ask Me nothing. Most assuredly, I say to you, whatever you ask the Father in My name He will give you" (JOHN 16:23).

Unperplexed Realization

"That day" extends from Pentecost to the day of our Lord's return. Our Lord had just been telling His disciples that He is going to His Father, and explaining to them what this meant. As far as He was concerned it meant that He would be omnipresent, omnipotent, and omniscient. The disciples had questioned Jesus up till then, but Jesus said, "In that day ye shall ask me no question." The day our Lord was referring to was the Day of Pentecost, that is, the Day of the Spirit of God. What a wonderful day to live in!

Unquestioned Revelation

After the Resurrection our Lord breathed on these questioning, perplexed, confused, loyal disciples, and said, "Receive ye the Holy Spirit." When we read the accounts in John and Luke we find that their eyes were opened and they knew Him. Their understandings were opened and they knew the Scriptures. Their inner consciences were opened and they knew that they had received from their risen Lord the very Spirit that ruled Him.

Is it possible to sit down unperplexed while lives are being lost in so many ways right in our midst? Does it mean that we are to sit with folded hands and ask no questions? No, it means something much more sublime and practical than that. It means that in the profound regions of our lives we know that God is at work, the Holy Spirit has revealed Him, and He is taking us slowly into His counsels. "Whatever He hears He will speak; and He will tell you things to come" (John 16:13).

85

Undeflected Reflection

This does not mean that the soul who has received the Holy Spirit can demand that God tell him His secrets. It means that he is lifted to the privilege of entering into God's counsels with Christ Jesus. Great darkness, exasperating providences, but the inner secret of the Lord is with those who have His Spirit.

We know from reading John 16:2 that our Lord did not mean life would be free from external perplexities, because He says, "They will put you out of the synagogues; yes, the time is coming that whoever kills you will think that he offers God service." Through it all comes the unquestioning revelation that Christ, as He knew His Father's mind and heart, can lift any soul into the heavenly places with Him so that the counsel and understanding of God's mind might be revealed.

If we have been going on with Jesus Christ we have come to the day of unquestioning revelation; that is, we know what John meant when he said, "But you have an anointing from the Holy One, and you know all things" (1 John 2:20) and "the same anointing teaches you concerning all things" (v. 27). The meaning of that is very practical and sane—test all you hear, all you read, by this inner anointing, by the indwelling Spirit. He will test all the truth of God.

Undisturbed Relation

Most assuredly, I say to you, whatever you
ask the Father in My name . . . .

"That day" is not only a day of unquestioning revelation, but a day of undisturbed relationship between God and ourselves. Just as Jesus stood unsullied in the presence of His Father, so by the mighty

IF YOU WILL ASK

efficacy of the indwelling Holy Spirit we can be lifted up into the same relationship. "That they may be one, even as we are one." "Whatever you ask the Father in My name"—that is, in My nature—"he will give you."

When we are born of the Holy Spirit, when we are related to God and bear the same family likeness to God that Jesus bore—which we may do by the wonderful atonement of the Lord Jesus Christ—we too can have this undisturbed relation to God.

Undisguised Recognition

He will give you.

Jesus said that God will recognize our prayers. What a challenge! Had Jesus any right to say it? Have we faced it for one moment? Is it possible that the Lord Jesus Christ means that by His resurrection power, by His ascension power, by the power of the sent-down Holy Spirit, that He can lift us into such a relationship with God that we are at one with the perfect sovereign will of God by our free choice as Jesus was? Does He mean what He says?

"Until now you have asked nothing in My name." How could they ask anything in His name when He had not yet sent forth that marvelous Holy Spirit? "Ask, and you will receive, that your joy may be full." Now we begin to understand why Jesus said, "You will ask Me nothing," because the Holy Spirit in that day glorified Jesus and revealed Him to them, and brought back to their memory His words and led them into their meaning.

When clouds are around the saints, know they are but the dust of the Father's feet. And when the shadows are dark and terrible and they are afraid as they enter the cloud, they find "no one anymore, but only Jesus with themselves" (Mark 9:8) In that wonderful position, placed there at this moment, we can pray to God in

This Day Is That Day

the nature of Jesus Christ, gifted to us by the Holy Spirit, and Jesus Christ's sovereign character is tested by His own statement, "Most assuredly, I say to you, whatever you ask the Father in my name, *He will give you*" (italics added).

O Lord, You are God, Holy and Almighty, and You do all things well. Show Yourself to us this day, Lord, for myself I desire to see You. Draw me near to You that I may know You and have rare communion with You.

Lord, I praise and thank You, for my lying fallow to Your grace; for the many prayers that have surrounded me like an atmosphere of heaven.

O Lord, save us from the murmuring spirit which with the majority of us is merely skin deep, but it is harmful, hurting the bloom of spiritual communion. Keep our life hidden with Christ in God.

Ten

INTERCESSION

And Abraham came near and said, "Would You also destroy the righteous with the wicked? Suppose there were fifty righteous within the city; would You also destroy the place and not spare it for the fifty righteous that were in it? Far be it from You to do so a thing as this, to slay the righteous with the wicked, so that the righteous should be as the wicked; far be it from You! Shall not the Judge of all the earth do right?"

So the LORD said, "If I find in Sodom fifty righteous within the city, then I will spare all the place for their sakes."

Then Abraham answered and said, "Indeed now, I who am but dust and ashes have taken it upon myself to speak to the Lord: Suppose there were five less than the fifty righteous; would You destroy all of the city for lack of five?" So He said, "If I find there forty-five, I will not destroy it."

And he spoke to Him yet again and said, "Suppose there shall be forty found there?" So He said, "I will not do it for the sake of forty." Then he said, Let not the Lord be angry, and I will speak: Suppose thirty should be found there?" So He said, "I will not do it if I find thirty there. And he said, "Indeed now, I have taken it upon myself to speak to the Lord: Suppose twenty should be found there."

So He said, "I will not destroy it for the sake of twenty."

Then he said, "Let not the Lord be angry, and I will speak but once more: Suppose ten shall be found there?"

And He said, "I will not destroy it for the sake of ten." So the LORD went His way, as soon as He had finished speaking with Abraham; and Abraham returned to his place (GENESIS 18:23–33).

The great difficulty in intercession is myself, nothing less or more. The first thing I have to do is to take myself to school. My first duty is not to assert freedom, but to find an absolute master. We think that to be without a master is the sign of a high type of life. Insurgent, impertinent human beings have no master; noble beings have. I must learn not to take myself too seriously. Myself is apt to be my master; I pray to myself.

We are all Pharisees until we are willing to learn to intercede. We must go into heaven backward. That phrase means we must grow into doing some definite thing by praying, not by seeing. To learn this lesson of handling a thing by prayer properly is to enter a very severe school. A Christian's duty is not to himself or to others, but to Christ. We think of prayer as a preparation for work, or a claim after having done work, whereas prayer is the essential work. It is the supreme activity of everything that is noblest in our personality. We won't bring down to earth what we see in vision about our Master. We move around it in devotional speculations, but we won't bring it straight down to earth and work it out in actualities.

The Strength and Self-Limitation of Intercession

If anyone sees his brother sinning a sin which does not lead to death, he will ask, and He will give him life for those who commit sin not leading to death. There is a sin leading to death. I do not say that he should pray about that (1 John 5:16).

How are we going to know when a man has sinned a sin unto death and when he has not? Only through intercession. If we make our own discernment the judge, we are wrong. We have it all on an abstract truth divorced from God. We pin our faith on what God has done and not on the God who did it, and when the case begins to go wrong again, we do not intercede, we begin to scold God. We get fanatical. We upset the court of heaven by saying, "I must do this thing." That is not intercession, that is rushing in where angels fear to tread. It is fanatical frenzy, storming the throne of God and refusing to see His character while sticking true to our assertions of what He said He would do.

Beware of making God fit the mold of His own precedent. Just because He did a certain thing once does not mean He is sure to do it again. This truth becomes an imperceptible error when we subtly leave God Himself out of it. Frenzy—no strength and no self-limitation. We have taken ourselves so seriously that we cannot even see God; we are dictating to God.

The redemption of our Lord Jesus Christ mirrored in the Atonement embraces everything. Sin, sickness, limitation, and death are all done away with in redemption, but we have to remember the Atonement works under God's dispensational sovereignty. It is not a question of whether God will sovereignly permit us to be delivered from sin in this dispensation. It is His distinct expressive will that we should be delivered. When it comes to the question of sickness and limitation, it is not a question of whether we will agree with God's will, but whether God's sovereignty is active—that predispensational efficacy of the Atonement on our behalf just now.

When people come to the Atonement and say, "Now I have deliverance in the Atonement, therefore I have no business being sick," they make a fundamental confusion, because there is no case of healing in the Bible that did not come from a direct intervention of the sovereign touch of God. When it comes to deliverance from sin, it is not a question of going to God to ask Him to deliver us from sin, it is a question of accepting His deliverance. If we forget that, we take the Lord out of the Atonement and make it an abstract statement and instantly do the pharisaic dodge of putting burdens on people that they cannot bear.

Logically they are perfectly correct. It is all in the Atonement. But if it is true that in the Atonement there should be no sickness, it is also true that there should be no death. We have no business dying. We have no business having any human limitations and we should be in complete unbroken communion with God. The people who teach the present resurrection are logically consistent with the folks who say the health of the body depends entirely on our acceptance of the Atonement. To say we are in resurrection bodies now means a moral pig-sty, and makes a burlesque of the whole thing. The mistake is putting an abstract truth deduced from God in the place of God Himself.

Abraham had none of the fanatical in him. He did not stand true to what God said, but to God who said it. God said, "Offer up Isaac," and then God said, "Don't." A fanatic would have said, "I will stick to what God has said. This other voice is of the devil." Watch when some providence of God is going against what we have asserted God will always do. One of the most significant lessons is to see the rod of rebuke come on the people who insist that they know the meaning of the providential working of Christ's atonement in the times in which we live. God does give wonderful gifts of the Atonement before their dispensation. There are innumerable cases of healing. But if I make that the ground on which God must work, I intercede no longer. I cannot. I become a dictator to God. When anyone is sick, I do not pray, I say, "They have no business being sick," and that means I have destroyed altogether my contact with God.

The Sagacity and Submissiveness of Intercession

Therefore do not be like them. For your Father knows the things you have need of before you ask Him (Matthew 6:8).

Our understanding of God is the answer to prayer; getting things from God is God's indulgence of us. When God stops giving us things, He brings us into the place where we can begin to understand Him. As long as we get from God everything we ask, we never get to know Him. We look upon Him as a blessing-machine that has nothing to do with His character or with ours. "Your Father knoweth what things ye have need of, before ye ask Him." Then why pray? To get to know our Father. It is not sufficient for us to say, "Oh yes, God is love." We have to know He is love. We have to struggle through until we see that He is love and justice. Then our prayer is answered.

The nearer Abraham comes to God in his intercession, the more he recognizes his entire unworthiness. There is a subtle thing that goes by the name of unworthiness, which is petulant pride with God. When we are shy with other people it is because we believe we are superior to the average person and we won't talk until they realize our importance. Prayerlessness with God is the same thing. We are shy with God not because we are unworthy, but because we think God has not given enough consideration to our case. We have some peculiar elements He must be pleased to consider. We have to go to school to learn not to take ourselves seriously and to get the genuine unworthiness which no longer is shy before God. A child is never shy before his mother, and a child of God is conscious of his worthiness, namely, his entire dependence.

"Then he said, "Let not the Lord be angry, and I will speak but once more: Suppose ten should be found there? And He said, I will not destroy it for the sake of ten" (Genesis 18:32). Abraham does the interceding while the angels go for the final test. After the final test, prayer is impossible. Abraham knew the stopping point because he was in complete and entire communion with God throughout his intercession. When we come against things in life, are we going to cave in and say we cannot understand them? We understand them by intercession. By our intercession God does things He does not show us just now, although He reveals more and more of His character to us. He is working out His new creations in the world through His wonderful redemption and our intercession all the time, and we have to be sagacious, not impudent.

The Shamelessness and Strenuousness of Intercession

I say to you, though he will not rise and give to him
because he is his friend, yet because of his persistence he will
rise and give him as many as he needs (Luke 11:8).

Strenuousness means whipping ourselves up and jeering at ourselves till we sit down no more. We never give ourselves any encouragement; we only encourage ourselves in God. "Then He spoke a parable to them, that men always ought to pray and not lose heart" (Luke 18:1). It is a pleasant business to faint; everyone else has all the bother. "God will give it to me in His good time." He cannot until we intercede. Be at the business, use some perspiration of soul, get at the thing, and all of a sudden we come to the

place where we will say, "Now I see," but I defy you to tell anyone
what you saw until they come to where you are—

> *Oh, could I tell, ye surely would believe it!*
> *Oh, could I only say when I have seen!*
> *How should I tell or how can ye receive it,*
> *How, till He bringeth you where I have been?*

The point is that we have come to understand God. It is never
God's will for us to be dummies or babies spiritually. It is God's will
for us to be sons and daughters of God, but He does not prevent us
paying the price of being sons and daughters. He makes us sons and
daughters potentially, and then sends us out to be sons and daughters actually.

Are we prepared to go into the shameless business of prayer?
That is, are we prepared to get to the right understanding of God
in this matter? We can only get it one way—not by disputing or
controversy, but by prayer. Keep at it. We have no business remaining in the dark about the character of our Father when He has
made His character very clear to us. The Sermon on the Mount has
more to do with prayer than anything else. It means an end of self-
indulgence in the body, in the mind, in the spirit, self-indulgence
in anything and everything, and a strenuous determination to get
to understand God in this matter.

The Sacrament and Substitution of Intercession

> *Then he came to the disciples and found them*
> *sleeping, and said to Peter, "What! Could you not watch*
> *with Me one hour?" (Matthew 26:40).*

It is a great thing to watch with God rather than to put God to the
trouble of watching us in case we burn ourselves. We tax the whole

arrangement of heaven when we expect God to watch us. God wants us to come and watch with Him, to be so identified with Him that we are not causing Him any trouble, to give Him perfect delight because He can use us instead of taxing some other servants of heaven to look after us.

O Lord, my Lord, I come to You this morning with a sense of spiritual failure. Cleanse me by Your grace and restore me to the heavenly places in Christ Jesus. O that the sweet kindness of Jesus were more and more manifest in me.

O Lord, You know, in eager helpless trust I look up. O that in power and peace and purity and grace thou would shine forth in power, in grace and glory this day.

O Lord, the range of Your power, the touch of Your grace, the breathing of Your Spirit, how I long for these to bring me face to face with You; Lord, by Your grace cause me to appear before You.

Eleven

THE KEY
TO SERVICE

Therefore pray the Lord of the harvest to send out laborers into His harvest (MATTHEW 9:38).

This is the key to the whole problem of Christian work. It is simple in words, but amazingly profound, because our Lord Jesus Christ said it.

Our Master's Orders

Therefore pray . . .

Prayer is usually considered to be devotional and more or less impractical in ordinary life. Our Lord in His teaching always considered prayer work, not preparation for work. Thank God for all the marvelous organization there is in Christian work, for medical missions and finely educated missionaries, for aggressive work in every shape and form; but these are, so to speak, pieces of the lock. The key is not in any of our organizations; the key lies in our hand by our Lord's instruction, "Therefore pray."

"Most assuredly, I say to you, he who believes in Me, the works that I do he will do also; and greater works than these he will do, because I go to My Father. And whatever you ask in My name, that I will do, that the Father may be glorified in the Son" (John 14:12–13). Have the "greater works" been done? They certainly have. The men our Lord said these words to wrote the New Testament, and the reason they wrote it is that our Lord, when He was glorified, sent forth the personal Paraclete, the Holy Spirit, not only in His power—His power and influence were at work before Pentecost—but He sent Him forth to this earth personally, where He is to this hour, and through His might and inspiration produced the "greater works," namely, the New Testament.

But what does it mean for us? Have we also to do greater works than Jesus did? Certainly we have. If our Lord's words mean anything, they mean that. And the great basis of prayer is to realize that we must take our orders from our Master. He put all the emphasis on prayer, and He made prayer not preparation for the work, not a sentiment nor a devotion, but the work. There is a real danger of worshiping prayer instead of praying because we worship. It is easy to do if we lose sight of our Lord and put the emphasis not on His command but on the thing that He commands.

We pray on the great fundamental basis of redemption, and our prayers are made efficient by the wonderful presence of the personal Holy Spirit in the world. Prayer is simple, prayer is supernatural, and to anyone not related to our Lord Jesus Christ, prayer is apt to look stupid. It sounds unreasonable to say that God will do things in answer to prayer, yet our Lord said that He would. Our Lord bases everything on prayer. Then the key to all our work as Christians is, "Therefore pray."

When we pray for others the Spirit of God works in the unconscious domain of their being that we know nothing about, and the one we are praying for knows nothing about. But after the passing of time the conscious life of the one prayed for begins to show signs of unrest and disquiet. We may have spoken until we are worn out, but we have never come anywhere near, and we have given up in despair. But if we have been praying, we find on meeting them one day that there is the beginning of a softening and a desire to know something.

It is that kind of intercession that does the most damage to Satan's kingdom. It is so slight, so feeble in its initial stages, that if our reason is not wedded to the light of the Holy Spirit, we will never do it. Yet it is that kind of intercession that the New Testament places the most emphasis on, though it has so little to show for it. It seems stupid to think that we can pray and all that will happen, but remember to whom we pray. We pray to a God who understands the unconscious depths of personality about which we know nothing, and He has told us to pray. The great Master of the human heart said, "Greater works than these he will do.... And whatever you shall ask in My name, that will I do" (John 14:12–13).

Not only is prayer the work, but prayer is the way fruit abides. Our Lord puts prayer as the means to fruit-producing and fruit-abiding work. But remember, it is prayer based on His agony, not on our agony. "You did not choose Me, but I chose you and appointed you that you should go and bear fruit, and that your fruit should remain, that whatever you ask the Father in My name He may give you" (John 15:16).

Prayer is not only the work and the way fruit abides, but prayer is the battle. "Put on the whole armor of God,... Stand therefore,..." and then pray. Paul says, "Praying always... for all the saints—and for me" (Ephesians 6:11–19). Do we remember to pray on the ground of our Lord's orders for all who minister in His name? If the apostle Paul earnestly solicited prayer on his behalf that he might "make known with boldness the mystery of the Gospel," surely we should remember that this is the key our Lord puts into our hands for all Christian work; not prayer because we are helpless, but prayer because God is Almighty.

Our Master's Ownership
The Lord of the harvest. . . .

Jesus did not say, "Go into the field." He said, "Therefore pray the Lord of the harvest." That does not so much mean that the harvest is the world, it means that there are innumerable people who have

The Key to Service

reached a crisis in their lives, they are "white already to harvest." We find them everywhere, not only in foreign countries, but in neighboring houses, and the way we discern who they are is not by intellect, not by suggestions, but by prayer. Think of the countless crises in people's lives at this time, they are at the parting of the ways. "Do you not say, 'There are still four months and then comes the harvest?' Behold, I say to you, lift up your eyes and look at the fields, for they are white already for harvest." "Therefore pray the Lord of the harvest to send out laborers into His harvest."

When we read the concluding verses in Matthew's Gospel, we are apt to put the emphasis on the fact that Jesus said, "Go therefore and make disciples of all the nations," whereas the emphasis should be on "Go" because "All authority has been given to Me in heaven and on earth." Then the "going" is in perfect order, putting the emphasis where our Lord puts it. "Go therefore . . . and lo, I am with you always," that He may work His mighty works through us.

Our Master's Option

. . . to send out laborers into His harvest.

There is only one field of service that has no snares, and that is the field of intercession. All other fields have the glorious but risky snare of publicity; prayer has not. The key to all our work for God is in that one word we are apt to despise—"Pray." And prayer is "laborer" work.

The reason prayer is so important is, first of all, because our Lord told us that prayer on the ground of His redemption is the most mighty factor He has put into our hands. Second, it is important because of the personal presence of the Holy Spirit in the day in which we live. We receive our knowledge of the Holy Spirit not by experience first, but by the testimony of the Lord Jesus Christ.

The testimony of Jesus Christ regarding the Holy Spirit is that He is here, and the real living experience the Holy Spirit works in us is that all His emphasis is laid on glorifying our Lord Jesus Christ. We know the Holy Spirit first by the testimony of Jesus, and then by the conscious enjoyment of His presence.

"Therefore pray." Prayer is labor, not agony. But labor on the ground of our Lord's redemption in simple confidence in Him. Prayer is simple to us because it cost Him so much to make it possible. God grant that we may work His victories for Him by taking His way about it.

O Lord, this morning disperse every mist, and shine clear and strong and invigoratingly. Forgive my tardiness; it takes me so long to awaken to some things.

Lord God Omniscient, give me wisdom this day to worship and work aright and be well-pleasing to You. Lord, interpret Yourself to me more and more in fullness and beauty.

Dark and appalling are the clouds of war and wickedness and we know not where to turn, but, Lord God, You reign.

Twelve

THE UNREALIZED LOGIC OF PRAYER

Likewise the Spirit also helps in our weaknesses. For we do not know what we should pray for as we ought, but the Spirit Himself makes intercession for us with groanings which cannot be uttered. Now He who searches the hearts knows what the mind of the Spirit is, because He makes intercession for the saints according to the will of God. And we know that all things work together for good to those who love God, to those who are the called according to His purpose (ROMANS 8:26–28).

Praying always with all prayer and supplication in the Spirit . . . (EPHESIANS 6:18).

Praying in the Holy Spirit. . . . (JUDE 20).

Ephesians 6:18 and Jude 20 are not quite identical with Romans 8:26. In the former, man prays in the atmosphere produced by the Holy Spirit indwelling and surrounding him; in the latter, the Holy Spirit Himself prays in man. The similarity is obvious, but the point of difference is often missed in thinking about prayer. We realize that we are energized by the Holy Spirit for prayer. We know what it is to pray in the atmosphere and the presence of the Holy Spirit. But we do not so often realize that the Holy Spirit Himself prays in us with prayers that we cannot utter.

> *Likewise the Spirit also helps in our weaknesses. For we do not know not what we should pray for as we ought, but the Spirit Himself makes intercession for us with groanings which cannot be uttered (Romans 8:26).*

The great thought that we do not realize sufficiently is the interchanging action of the Divine Spirit and the human spirit. This interchanging action of the Divine and human at every stage of our religious life is vividly expressed here. The best example of the Divine Spirit working in a human spirit is seen in our Lord Jesus Christ. According to some expositors, we are so infirm that the Spirit of God brushes aside all our infirmities and prays without regard to us. But we find that our Lord recognized the difference between His own Spirit and the Spirit of God, and that His mind was always in subordination to the mind of God. "I can of Myself do nothing."

The Uncovered Truth of Our Infirmities

Likewise the Spirit also helps in our weaknesses. . . .

To ask how we are to get our prayers answered is a different point of view from the New Testament. According to the New Testament, prayer is God's answer to our poverty, not a power we exercise to obtain an answer. We have the idea that prayer is only an exercise of our spiritual life. "Pray without ceasing." We read that the disciples said to our Lord, "Lord, teach us to pray." The disciples were good men and well-versed in Jewish praying, yet when they came in contact with Jesus Christ, instead of realizing they could pray well, they came to the conclusion they did not know how to pray at all, and our Lord instructed them in the initial stages of prayer.

Most of us can probably remember a time before we were born again when we were "religious" and could pray fairly well; but after we were born again we became conscious of what Paul mentions here, our utter infirmity—"I do not know how to pray." We became conscious not only of the power God has given us by His Spirit, but of our own utter infirmity. We hinder our life of devotion when we lose the distinction in thinking between these two. Reliance on the Holy Spirit for prayer is what Paul is bringing out in this verse. It is an unrealized point. We state it glibly enough, but Paul touches the thing we need to remember. He uncovers the truth of our infirmity. The whole source of our strength is receiving, recognizing and relying on the Holy Spirit.

The Unsyllabled Torment of Our Inability

For we do not know what we should pray for as we ought . . . .

The only platform from which the holiest saint on earth is ever heard is the platform mentioned in Hebrews 10:19, that is, we have "boldness to enter into the holiest by the blood of Jesus." There is no other way. When we come into the presence of God, the human side of our praying makes us realize what Paul is trying to teach, that if we are ever going to approach God and pray acceptably, it must be by the "piece of God" in us which He has given us. Some of the qualities of God must be merged into us before our prayers can be fit for His acceptance.

We are all familiar with Luke 11:13, but we do not always remember that our Lord spoke the words in connection with receiving the Holy Spirit for prayer. Paul in Romans 8:26 beats out into gold leaf the nugget that our Lord gives in Luke 11:13. When I realize that I cannot approach God, that I cannot see as God sees, that I am choked up with things my eyes see, my flesh wants, and the empty spaces round my heart want, then Jesus says, "If you, being evil,"—we know that is our infirmity—if you ask God for the Holy Spirit, He will give Him to you (see Matthew 7:11). That is, God will be merged into me, and I can begin to think about real prayer, relying on what God has planted in me for prayer. Otherwise, we could never get near Him. The crush of our infirmities would paralyze the words on our lips. We can only pray acceptably in the Spirit, that is, by the Holy Spirit in us. All the rest is being "cumbered about."

The disposition of sin is removed in sanctification—there is no doubt about that. But Paul insists that the body is not changed, the body we had and which was ruled by the wrong disposition of sin still remains (see Romans 6:12–19). We have to use that body now and make it a slave to the new disposition, and we have to realize the need to do it more in prayer than in anything else.

The Unrealized Logic of Prayer

The Unutterable Tenderness of the Intercession

But the Spirit Himself makes intercession for us
with groanings which cannot be uttered.

The spirit of a man, whether it be energized by the Spirit of God or not, is bound to try and express itself in the body, which becomes its soul manifest. If it refuses to express itself in a rational way, it will express itself in an irrational, stupid way. When the Spirit of God energizes the spirit of a man, the man is taken up into the great mystery of the intercession of the Holy Spirit. If the Holy Spirit is allowed to dwell in the human spirit He has energized, He will express the unutterable. Think what that means. It means being quickened by the incoming of the Holy Spirit who comes in to dwell supremely, and the amazing revelation in that He intercedes in us, for us, with a tenderness exactly in accordance with the mind of God.

Have we ever allowed our minds to dwell on this element of prayer? "The sinner out of heart with self is nearest God in prayer." It is a mistake to interpret prayer on the natural instead of on the spiritual line—to say that prayer is divine because it brings us peace and joy and makes us feel better. This is the mere accident or effect of prayer. There is no real God-given revelation in it. This is the God-given revelation: that when we are born again of the Spirit of God and indwelt by the Holy Spirit, He intercedes for us with a tenderness and an understanding akin to the Lord Jesus Christ and akin to God, that is, He expresses the unutterable for us.

The Unrivaled Power of Prayer

Now He who searches the hearts knoweth what the mind
of the Spirit is, because He makes intercession for the saints
according to the will of God (Romans 8:27).

The Unimagined Interest of God. "Now He who searches the hearts knows what the mind of the Spirit is . . . ." The Holy Spirit, when He comes into the hidden sphere of our life, applies the Atonement to us in the unconscious as well as in the conscious realm. He works out in us the understanding of sin that God has; and only when we grasp the unrivaled power of the Spirit in us can we understand the meaning of 1 John 1:7, "the blood of Jesus Christ His Son cleanses us from all sin." This does not refer to conscious sin only, but to the sin that only the Holy Spirit in us realizes, and God searches our hearts to find out what the intercession of His Spirit is.

There are tremendous thoughts expressed in God's Book, and unless we have learned to rely on the Holy Spirit we shall say, "Oh, I shall never understand that." But the Holy Spirit in us understands it, and as we recognize and rely on Him, He will work it out, whether we consciously understand or not. The point for us to remember is that we must get to the place of thinking spiritually. Never depend on your personal experiences of salvation, sanctification, or the baptism of the Holy Spirit. These experiences are simply doorways into a life. We have to realize this great revealed thought underneath, that the Holy Spirit is working out in us the mind of God even as He worked out the mind of God in Christ Jesus.

The Undiscovered Intercession before God. "Because He makes intercession for the saints . . . ." Who does? The Holy Spirit in us. And God searches our hearts, not to know what our conscious prayers are, but to find out what the prayer of the Holy Spirit is behind all our conscious praying. "And the sound of the wings of the cherubim was heard even in the outer court, like the voice of Almighty God when he speaks" (Ezekiel 10:5). And slowly and

The Unrealized Logic of Prayer

surely God discerns in the life of the individual saint what He discerned always in His Son, who said, "I came down from heaven not to do mine own will, but the will of him that sent me" (see John 4:34). As we rely on the Holy Spirit we learn to brood along the line of His expression of the unutterable in us.

The Unsurpassed Identification with God. "According to the will of God." Look back over your own history with God in prayer, and you will find that the glib days of prayers are done. When we draw on the human side of our experience only, our prayers become amazingly flippant and familiar, and we ourselves become amazingly hard and metallic. But if we rely on the Holy Spirit, we shall find that our prayers become more and more inarticulate, and when they are inarticulate, reverence grows deeper and deeper, and undue familiarity has the effect of a sudden blow on the face.

There is something hopelessly incongruous in a flippant statement before God. We can always measure our growth in grace by what Paul is stating here. Am I growing slowly to lisp the very prayers of God? Is God gratified (if I may use the phrase) in seeing that His Spirit is having His way at last in a life, and turning that life into what will glorify His Son?

The Unrecognized Providence of Prayer

And we know that all things work together for good
to those who love God, to those who are the called according
to His purpose (Romans 8:28).

At first glance this verse seems to have nothing to do with the previous verses, but it has an amazingly close connection with them.

The Undefiled Shrine of Consciousness. "And we know that . . . to those who love God . . . ." Do you remember how Paul never wearied of saying, "Do you not know that your body is the temple of the Holy Spirit?" Recall what Jesus Christ said about the historic temple, which is the symbol of the body. He ruthlessly turned out those who sold and bought in the temple, and said, "It is written, 'My house shall be called a house of prayer,' but you have made it a 'den of thieves'" (Matthew 21:13). Let us apply that to ourselves. We have to remember that our conscious life, though only a tiny bit of our personality, is to be regarded by us as a shrine of the Holy Spirit. The Holy Spirit will look after the unconscious part we do not know, but we must guard the conscious part for which we are responsible as a shrine of the Holy Spirit. If we recognize this as we should, we shall be careful to keep our body undefiled for Him.

The Undetected Sacredness of Circumstances. "All things work together for good . . . ." The circumstances of a saint's life are ordained by God, and not by happy-go-lucky chance. There is no such thing as chance in the life of a saint, and we shall find that God, by His providence, brings our bodies into circumstances that we cannot understand a bit, but the Spirit of God understands. He is bringing us into places and among people and under conditions in order that the intercession of the Holy Spirit in us may take a particular line.

Do not, therefore, suddenly put your hand in front of the circumstances and say, "No, I am going to be my own amateur providence. I am going to watch this and guard that." "Trust in the LORD with all your heart; and lean not on your own understanding" (Proverbs 3:5). The point to remember is that all our circumstances are in the hand of God.

The Spirit imparts a solemnity to our circumstances and makes us understand something of the travail of Jesus Christ. It is not that we enter into the agony of intercession, it is that we intercede for the people He has placed around us; we present their cases before

Him and give the Holy Spirit a chance to intercede for them. We bring the particular people and circumstances before God's throne, and the Holy Spirit in us has a chance to intercede for them. That is how God is going to sweep the whole world by His saints.

Are we making the Holy Spirit's work difficult by being indefinite, or by trying to do His work for Him? We must be the human side of the intercession, and the human side is the circumstances we are in, the people with whom we are in contact. We have to use our common sense in keeping our conscious life and our circumstances as a shrine of the Holy Spirit, and as we bring the different ones before God, the Holy Spirit presents them before the Throne all the time. The Holy Spirit does the interceding, but we must do our part. We must do the human side while He does the Divine. So never think it strange concerning the circumstances you are in.

The Undeviating Security of His Calling. "To them who are the called according to His purpose." To talk about our intercession for another as the means of doing what the Bible says, "The effective, fervent prayer of a righteous man avails much" (James 5:16), sounds utterly ridiculous until our thinking is renewed through the Atonement and the indwelling Holy Spirit. Then it is an amazing revelation of the marvelous love and condescension of God, that in Christ Jesus and by the reception of the Holy Spirit, He can take us—sin-broken, sin-diseased, wrong creatures—and remake us entirely until we are really the ones in whom the Holy Spirit intercedes as we do our part.

Are we making it easy for the Holy Spirit to work out God's will in us, or are we continually putting Him on one side by the empty requests of our natural hearts, Christians though we be? Are we bringing ourselves into such obedience that our every thought and imagination is brought into captivity to the Lord Jesus Christ, and is the Holy Spirit having an easy way through us more and more?

Remember, your intercession can never be mine, and my intercessions can never be yours, but the Holy Spirit makes intercession for us, without which intercession someone will be impoverished. Let us remember the depth and height and solemnity of our calling as saints.

NOTES

[1] Major John Skidmore: close friend and associate of Oswald and Biddy Chambers and was involved full-time in the League of Prayer.

[2] Bible Training College (BTC): residential school near Clapham Common in southwest London, sponsored and operated by the League of Prayer from 1911 until it closed in 1915 because of World War I. Oswald Chambers was principal and main teacher; Biddy Chambers, his wife, was lady superintendent.

[3] Pentecostal League of Prayer: founded in London in 1891 by Reader Harris (1847–1909), prominent barrister and friend and mentor of Oswald Chambers.

[4] Zeitoun (zay TOON), Egypt: six miles northeast of Cairo; site of a YMCA camp, the Egypt General Mission compound, and, from 1916 to 1919, the Imperial School of Instruction, training base for British, Australian, and New Zealand troops during World War I.

[5] Bible Training Course Monthly Journal: published from 1932 to 1952 by Mrs. Chambers, with help from David Lambert.

[6] Reader Harris (1847–1909): prominent British barrister, founded the Pentecostal League of Prayer in 1891; friend and mentor to Oswald Chambers.

[7] spooned meat: liquefied food that requires no chewing or effort; baby food.

[8] Millennial Dawnism: another name for Russellism or the Jehovah's Witnesses, founded by Charles Taze Russell.

[9] mean: as used here, something or someone ordinary, common, low, or ignoble, rather than cruel or spiteful.

[10] Robert Murray McCheyne (1813–1843): Scottish minister whose short but intense life left a great impact on Scotland.

NOTE TO THE READER

The publisher invites you to share your response to the message of this book by writing Discovery House Publishers, PO Box 3566, Grand Rapids, MI 49501, USA. For information about other Discovery House books, music, or videos, contact us at the same address or call 1-800-653-8333. Find us on the Internet at http://www.dhp.org/ or send e-mail to books@dhp.org.

MY UTMOST FOR HIS HIGHEST

An Updated Edition in Today's Language

The Golden Book of OSWALD CHAMBERS

Edited by James Reimann
Authorized by The Oswald Chambers Publications Association, Ltd.

#UOCAS-9571

"The flower of God comes through this book and in my house. It is second only to the Bible and has changed my spiritual life completely."
—L.M., Pennsylvania

#UOCAS-9997

My utmost for His highest

Oswald Chambers
Special Updated Edition
Edited by James Reimann

#UOCAS-9784

LARGE P
MY UTMOST FOR HIGHEST

An Updated Edition in Today's Language

The Golden Book of OSWALD CHAMBERS

Edited by James Reimann
Authorized by The Oswald Chambers Publications Association, Ltd.

#UOCAS-0373

"It has been a long time since I have read anything which has stirred my soul as much. It became for me a personal spiritual journey where God and I hammered out some significant issues!"
—Dr. D.S., Missouri

#UOCAS-KQ587

"If you are actually serious about the Lord Jesus Christ, do not pass this by. The CD-ROM format is an especially invaluable study aid for this man's works." —MDW, Indianapolis

WITH NOTES BY DAVID McCASLAND

The Complete Works of Oswald Chambers

Oswald Chambers
AUTHOR OF
My Utmost for His Highest

#UOCAS-039X

The Complete Works of Oswald Chambers

by Oswald Chambers

Stunning! That's what people are saying about *The Complete Works of Oswald Chambers.* This treasure trove offers 1,512 pages of spiritual insight from Oswald Chambers, including two of his never-before-published manuscripts. In addition to the best-selling devotion of all time, *My Utmost for His Highest,* you get all of Chambers' 34 books, including his uplifting insights into the books of Job and Ecclesiastes, his life-changing thoughts on prayer, and a biography of his life by Chambers expert, David McCasland. Not only that, you get the entire searchable text, along with video clips of Chambers' only child, Kathleen, on the free CD-ROM*. This is a gift that will be cherished by any Christian.

#UOCAS-039X, Hardcover with *Windows® CD-ROM, 1,512 pages, $38.95

* CD is compatible with Windows® 95, 98, and 2000. It is not compatible with Windows ME, XP, or Mac OS.

Credit card orders call 1-800-653-8333 or visit us online at www.dhp.org

All prices current at time of printing, in US dollars, subject to change without notice. Prices do not include shipping and handling.

Miss Eliza's
English Kitchen

ALSO BY ANNABEL ABBS

FICTION
Frieda: The Original Lady Chatterley
The Joyce Girl

NONFICTION
Windswept: In the Footsteps of
Trailblazing Women

Miss Eliza's English Kitchen

A Novel of Victorian Cookery and Friendship

ANNABEL ABBS

WILLIAM MORROW
An Imprint of HarperCollins*Publishers*

P.S.™ is a trademark of HarperCollins Publishers.

MISS ELIZA'S ENGLISH KITCHEN. Copyright © 2021 by Annabel Abbs. All rights reserved. Printed in the United States of America. No part of this book may be used or reproduced in any manner whatsoever without written permission except in the case of brief quotations embodied in critical articles and reviews. For information, address HarperCollins Publishers, 195 Broadway, New York, NY 10007.

HarperCollins books may be purchased for educational, business, or sales promotional use. For information, please email the Special Markets Department at SPsales@harpercollins.com.

FIRST EDITION

Designed by Diahann Sturge

Antique recipe book engraving illustrations © ilbusca/iStock/Getty Images

Library of Congress Cataloging-in-Publication Data has been applied for.

ISBN 978-0-06-306646-5

22 23 24 25   ov/LSC   10 9 8 7 6 5 4

To my daughter, Bryony, fellow writer and kitchen companion

Life has dark secrets; and the hearts are few
That treasure not some sorrow from the world . . .
—L. E. L., "Secrets," 1839

But oh! the bitterest griefs of all,
Are nurs'd in tearless anguish still.
—Eliza Acton, "Yes Leave Me," 1826

I would venture to guess that Anon, who wrote so many poems
without signing them, was often a woman.
—Virginia Woolf, A Room of One's Own, 1929

PREFACE

This is a work of fiction based on a handful of known facts about the life of the poet and pioneering cookery writer, Eliza Acton, and her assistant, Ann Kirby. Between 1835 and 1845 Eliza and Ann lived in Tonbridge, Kent, and worked on a cookery book that has become known as "the greatest British cookbook of all time" (Bee Wilson, *The Telegraph*), the "greatest cookery book in our language" (Dr. Joan Thirsk, CBE), and "my beloved companion . . . illuminating and decisive" (Elizabeth David). It was a bestseller in its time, internationally as well as in the UK, selling more than 125,000 copies in thirty years. Eliza Acton had a profound influence on later cookery writers including Delia Smith, who called Eliza Acton "the best cookery writer in the English language . . . a great inspiration . . . and a great influence on me."

MISS ELIZA'S ENGLISH KITCHEN

ANN

Before Mr. Whitmarsh leaves for work, he does something quite out of character. He gives me a gift. Wrapped snug in brown paper. No ribbon, just string. But a gift all the same.

"This is for you, my Ann," he says, even as his rheumy eyes are on his pocket watch. He likes to call me "his Ann," although I think "Mrs. Kirby" would be more appropriate for a servant of my age and experience. I do more than serve, of course. Like keeping his bed warm at night and braiding the sleek hair of his motherless daughters.

As soon as the lift and press of his leather soles on the marble floor is quite gone, I prod curiously at the package. I know it's a book. I can tell by the shape and heft of it. I untie the string and pull at the paper, my mind racing and dancing. As if someone has climbed inside my head with an egg whisk and turned my brain to a fine froth.

Will it be a volume of poetry? Or a novel? Or a book of maps? And why has he bought me a gift anyway? The paper falls in clumsy shreds to the floor. Not like me to be so . . . I pause and search for the word. *Exuberant*. I smile, knowing exactly who taught me the word *exuberant*.

Mr. Whitmarsh knows I like reading for he has caught me at it. Red-handed. First, he caught me in his library examining his map collection. Then he caught me at the stove, deep in a poetry book. And after that he found me with my nose in a novel when I should have been waxing the floorboards to a shine. But isn't that why he took me so readily to his bed? And why he calls me, with such affection, *his Ann*?

A little twitch flirts at the corners of my mouth. But then the twitch sets fast. And the whisking in my head stops. For all the wrapping paper is off now, lying around my feet in scraps and rags. The book is a colossal tome that's neither poetry nor novel. Nor is it a book of maps. I turn it over, sniff its calfskin binding, feel its spine as smooth as skin. Then I run the tips of my fingers over its cover, over the raised gilding of its title. *Mrs. Beeton's Book of Household Management*.

Why would I want such a book as this? Disappointment rushes through me, making my fingers slip so that pages turn, crackle, crumple. And words flicker and spin before my eyes . . . knuckle of veal and rice . . . tartar mustard . . . turnips in white sauce . . . gooseberry pudding . . . A snorting gasping sound, most inelegant, escapes from my mouth. Mr. Whitmarsh has bought me a book of recipes! The man is more of a buffoon than I thought.

My fingers move less hastily, my gaze slows and lingers. Until I am stock-still and reading—word for word—a recipe for crimped salmon with caper sauce. A most peculiar sensation passes over me. My mind, which a few minutes ago was whisked to a foaming peak, goes very small and tight and still. Like a hazelnut.

Every word, every ingredient, is uncannily familiar. I turn the page. And read. And turn another page. And then another. Slowly it dawns on me. These recipes are mine. And *hers* too, of course. I recognize them because I cooked them. Because I wrote down my observations of them on a slate. With a stub of chalk. Day after day. Year after year.

Our recipes have been plundered, rearranged upon blank new pages, emptied of *her* elegant tilt and turn of phrase, *her* sly humor. The bones remain—cold graceless lists of instructions and ingredients—assigned now to a Mrs. Beeton, whoever she may be. Yet they belong to me and to Miss Eliza, who is barely cold in her grave.

I read on, tasting each dish upon my tongue: sweet slippery leeks, newborn peas swirled in butter, meringue as fresh and light as snow. And gradually, recipe by recipe, I'm returned to the kitchen of Bordyke House. The air smoke-thick with roasting pigeons, frying onions, softly stewing plums. The sing of it all: the water pump cranking in the scullery, the logs spitting in the range, the jangle of pewters and the rattle of cutlery, the thump of a rolling pin, the endless bubble and simmer of the stockpot.

I push away Mr. Whitmarsh's book of stolen recipes, and slowly stoop, kneel, to pick the wrapping paper from the floor. That's when I hear her. I recognize her tread—so neat and determined—upon the stone flags. She's moving toward me, her skirts swishing around her ankles. Her voice, at once purposeful and gentle, calls out: *Ann? Ann?*

I know her next words off by heart: *Today we shall be very busy, Ann.* I wait. But there's only silence. From outside I hear the faint notes of a dove, scraped thin by the wind. Then next door's cockerel starts crowing with great gusto.

And I know what I must do.

CHAPTER ONE
ELIZA

FISH BONES

Midday in the City of London, the carts and carriages rattling over the cobbles, the screech of costermongers, the jostle of barrows and handcarts, the thin-ribbed boys who are shirtless and swooping like starved birds to shovel every steaming clod of dung. It is the hottest day of the year—or so it feels to me, burning and corseted inside my best silk dress. On Paternoster Row the heat radiates from every brick, every brass bellpull, every iron railing. Even the wooden scaffolding, which props up every half-built windowless property, is stubbornly lodged with heat and creaking with thirst.

It is the most important day of my life, so to calm my nerves that are all ajangle, I observe the scene and shape it into words: The crowds dripping along the side of the road where the taller buildings fling their shadows. The straining horses that are slick with sweat. The fans stitched from peacock feathers and fluttering from carriage windows. The wilting lash of the drivers' whips. And the sun, like a vast golden orb in a dome of unbroken blue.

I pause, for the rhythm is not quite right. Perhaps *far-off bowers of blue* is more pleasant on the ear than *a dome of unbroken blue*. I mouth the words, letting them slip over my tongue and echo in my ear . . . *Far-off bowers of blue* . . .

"Look where you're going, you stupid old trout!"

I swerve and stumble, narrowly missing a cart of rotting cabbages. Suddenly I long for home, its familiarity and friendliness. I feel as though I have no place in the vast stinking skirmish that is London.

I leave the shaded side of the street with its fractious, melting throng. In the hot sunlight, the people are fewer but the stench is thicker: unwashed bodies, decaying teeth, human slops. All manner of debris lurks beneath my feet, wedged and rotting between the cobbles: bleached herring bones and cockleshells, rusting nails, spat pellets of chewed tobacco, a dead mouse bristling with maggots, the desiccated rind of oranges and gnawed apple cores fizzing with fruit flies. Everything is either dried hard or rotting softly, foully. I peg my nose with my fingers, for I have no desire to turn this noxious reek into poetry.

"Far-off bowers of blue," I say beneath my breath. A reviewer of my first poetry collection described it as "neat and elegant," and I can't help thinking that *far-off bowers of blue* is similarly neat and elegant. But what will Mr. Thomas Longman, publisher of celebrated poets, think? The thought of Mr. Longman returns me—dizzily—to the present, to my mission. I look down and see the damp silk of my dress, veined a darker shade of green, with great black puddles spreading beneath the pits of my arms. Why did I not take a carriage? I shall arrive at the most important meeting of my life drenched and sopping like a child with fever.

A brass plaque announces the offices of Messrs. Longman & Co., Publisher and Book Seller. I pause, take a breath. And in that second my life, my past, the vastness of the skies above, the tangled mass of London—all of it telescopes into a single quivering point. This is it. The moment I have awaited for ten long years. *My starry dawning* . . .

I peel the loose tendrils of hair from my neck and tuck them into my bonnet. A quick anxious rub at the damp creases in my dress and I am—tremblingly—ready. I pull on the intimidatingly long doorbell and am gestured through rooms toppling with books to a narrow flight of stairs. At the top is a single room so crammed with books there is barely space for my skirts. Mr. Longman—for I assume it to be him—sits behind a desk, examining an unrolled map, so that I am presented only with the luxuriant crown of his head.

He ignores me and I take the opportunity to observe him with my poet's gaze. He is weighted down with gold. A gold signet ring upon each hand and a gold watch chain that stretches into the black folds of his frock coat. His hair is steely gray and sits in a thick drift over the plates of his skull. When he raises his head, I see his face is florid, its rosy hue exaggerated by a cravat of lavender twill silk on which the folds of his chin rest. His eyes are set very far back in his head, beneath a scrambling pair of brows.

"Ah, Mrs. Acton . . ." He looks up at me through half-closed eyes.

My cheeks flame. "Miss Acton," I say, my voice lifting defiantly on the word *miss*.

He nods, then pushes away the maps and books and inkpots to make a channel through which he thrusts a hand. I look at his pale cushioned palm, bewildered. Am I to shake his hand, as gentlemen do? He makes no motion to take my hand to his lips, or to rise and bow. And when I shake his hand, I feel a curious excitement, a dim thrill of something I cannot explain.

"You have something for me, I believe." He rummages in a lackluster way at the papers sprawled across his desk.

"I explained it in my letter, sir. A volume of poems I have worked on diligently for ten years. My last volume was published by Richard Deck of Ipswich, and indeed you sold it from this very shop." As the words slip from my tongue—more steadily than I expected—an image swims into my head: Miss L. E. Landon reading aloud from *my* book of verse, which is beautifully bound in smoothest sealskin with my name embossed in gilt. The picture is so sharp, so bright, I see the hint of a tear in her eye, the appreciative curve of her lip, her tender fingering of the pages as if they were as delicate and precious as goose down.

But then Mr. Longman does something most baffling, most distressing. And Miss L. E. Landon, along with my published book, is swept immediately from my mind. He shakes his head, as if I have muddled my facts in some inexcusable way.

"I assure you, sir, it was stocked by Longman and Company—and many other reputable bookshops. It was reprinted within a month and—" Mr. Longman interrupts me with a loud, impatient sigh. He withdraws his hand from the desk and uses it to mop at his forehead with a handkerchief.

"I raised the subscriptions myself and received orders from as far afield as Brussels and Paris and the island of St. Helena. My readers are quite convinced I need a publisher with the universal might of yourself, sir." I hear my voice and am startled by its notes of desperation. And conceit. Mother's words rush into my head: *too hungry for recognition . . . too ambitious . . . no sense of propriety . . .*

But Mr. Longman is shaking his head more emphatically than ever. He shakes his head so strenuously, the folds of his chin bob and small drops of sweat spin from his forehead, scattering carelessly over his map.

"Poetry is not the business of a lady," he growls.

I am so taken aback every inch and ounce of me stiffens. Does he know nothing of Mrs. Hemans? Or Miss L. E. Landon? Or Ann Candler? My mouth opens, as if to remonstrate. But he swats at the air as if he knows what I am about to say and has no wish to hear it.

"Now, novel writing . . . that is quite a different matter. Novelettes, Miss Acton, are very popular with young ladies." He elongates the word *young*, making his voice rise and fall. I feel my

face scald a second time. And all my feelings of excitement and
defiance vanish.

"Novelettes of romance. Have you none of those for me?"

I blink and try to compose my thoughts. Has he even read
my letter? Or the fifty poems in my best copperplate that I delivered, by hand, six weeks ago? If not, why did he write and invite
me to meet him? To my chagrin, I feel my throat close up, my
bottom lip waver.

"Yes," continues Mr. Longman, speaking as if to himself, "I
could consider a Gothic romance."

I brace myself, biting down on my wavering lip. A spark of
something—fury? irritation?—leaps inside me. "Some of my poems have been published more recently, in the *Sudbury Pocket
Book* and the *Ipswich Journal*. I am told they are good poems." My
burst of audacity surprises me. But then Mr. Longman shrugs
and his eyes slide to the ceiling, which is low and sagging.

"It is no good bringing me poetry! Nobody wants poetry now.
If you cannot write me a little Gothic romance . . ." His palms
are open and splayed upon his desk in a gesture of helplessness.

I stare at his empty palms and feel my insides—my spirit,
my audacity—being scooped out and cast away. Ten years of
labor—in vain. The emotion, the effort, everything that has
been sacrificed in the writing of my poems, all for nothing. Perspiration runs in rivulets down the sides of my rib cage and I feel
a shortness of breath as if my throat is constricting. *The painful
beatings of a breaking heart are hush'd to stillness . . .*

Mr. Longman scratches noisily at his head and continues staring at the ceiling. The soles of his shoes tap at the floorboards

beneath his desk, as if he has forgotten my presence. Or perhaps he is deciding whether I can be trusted to write a Gothic romance. I give a discreet cough that sounds more like a harried gulp. "Sir, could I possibly have my poems back?"

He claps his hands and jumps to his feet so abruptly the gold chains of his fob watch jangle and the silver buckles on his shoes rattle. "On second thought, I have sufficient novelists at present. So do not bring me a novelette."

"My manuscript? Did you not receive it, sir?" The words limp from my throat, barely audible. Is it possible he's lost my poems? Carelessly mislaid them among his maps and papers? And now he is about to dismiss me . . . empty-handed. Not even the promise of a commissioned novelette. *I told you so*, whispers my voice of doubt. *Imposter . . . imposter . . . Surely your puny efforts at poetry have been put upon the fire* . . . I scan the room, instinctively seeking out a grate, a wisp of my verse among the ashes.

All of a sudden Mr. Longman claps his hands a second time. I look at him, wondering if this is his manner of dismissal. But he is staring at me, his eyes alight, his hands still clasped. "A cookery book!"

I frown in confusion. The man is both rude *and* obscure, I think. Who on earth does he think I am? I may be thirty-six and unmarried, my dress may be streaked with sweat, but I am no aproned household servant.

"Go home and write me a cookery book and we might come to terms. Good day, Miss Acton." His hands splash over the detritus of his desk and for a moment I think he is hunting for my poems. But then he gestures at the door.

"I do not—cannot—cook," I say lamely, moving like a somnambulist toward the door. The inside of my head is dulled with disappointment. Every bit of bravura slipped clean away.

"If you can write poems, you can write recipes." He taps on the glass face of his pocket watch and puts it to his ear with a grunt of irritation. "This infernal heat has lost me valuable time. Good day!"

I have a sudden urge to be gone, away from the monstrous stench of London, away from the humiliation of having my poems spurned for something as frivolous and functional as a cookery book. I hurry down the stairs, tears crowding in my eyes.

Suddenly Mr. Longman's voice rings out: "Neat and elegant, Miss Acton. Bring me a cookery book as neat and elegant as your poems."

CHAPTER TWO
ANN

TURNIP POTTAGE

Today is my most shameful day ever. I fall asleep by mistake and for no more than a quarter hour, only to waken with the vicar looming over me. Like a black shadow.

"Oh, Reverend Thorpe," I stutter, stumbling to my feet. I know instantly why he's here. In truth I've been waiting for this day to come.

His eyes swivel around and around, like windmills. Well-fed windmills. He's inspecting our cottage: the cobwebs in the chimney, the piles of rank rags that I'm too busy to wash, the black balls of dog hair that have collected in the corners. At least the hearth is swept clean and all the ashes taken out.

Behind him Mam is clawing at a sheet that has been knotted around her. I recognize the knots—they're the handiwork of Mrs. Thorpe. So I know Mam was found unclothed. Likely by the River Medway where she tries to wash herself and forgets to

put her frock back on. The thought makes me flinch, all the narrow boats passing by, all the men watching from the gunpowder
mills . . .

"Enough is enough," says Reverend Thorpe, one hand circling his belly that has grown soft and round on patties and pies
and boiled puddings.

"Did she go wandering? She was tied to me, but I fell asleep."
I don't tell him that all night she had me up and down, wanting
this and wanting that, pulling on the ropes, pinching me, kick-
ing me, shredding her nightdress with her nails.

"How long since she . . . ?" He jerks his head toward the
ground, toward Hell, as if to say this is the devil's work.

But I know God loves all his flock, so I answer in a most determined way, jerking my head toward Heaven. "It's five years
since she became . . . absentminded." I don't tell him that she is
worse now than ever, that after the last full moon she does not
know her own daughter.

"She must go to a lunatic asylum, Ann," he says. "There is a
new one, over at Barming Heath."

"I will tie her to me more tightly," I say, avoiding his eye.
My face is hot with shame. Did he find her or was it someone
else? Someone who took her to the rectory rather than bringing
her home. Or did she take herself to the church? All my insides
cringe into a little ball at the thought of it, at the picture of her
naked, or in her ragged underthings, sitting in church, mad as a
March hare.

"What have you eaten today, Ann?" He stares at Septimus,
who's stretched upon the hearth with one oozing eye open and

one closed. The vicar's look is wary, as if he thinks our poor skinny dog is next for the pot.

"Better than Mam would eat in the workhouse or in any lunatic asylum." I ease her down to the floor, loosening the knots on the sheet and hoping she will stay quiet. I want the vicar to go, but he presses me to answer, repeating his question three times.

"Bread and an onion, each of us, with a scraping of lard too," I say at length. I don't tell him the bread was as stale as a baker's broom. Or that the onions had sprouted stalks as long as my arm. "And a little turnip pottage," I lie, as an afterthought.

"Your mother can go to an asylum—there will be no cost and she will be well cared for. I can give your father some work tending the graveyard."

I pause, confused by the reverend's words. I can see that he might want Mam gone, but to find work for Pa too . . . Surely the man is a saint, for it's barely three years since he found a place in London for my brother, Jack, turning spits in the kitchen of a gentlemen's club. I remind him that Pa has only one leg, that he lost the other fighting for king and country.

"Yes, yes," he replies, flapping his white hands like I'm a mongrel with the mange. "God does not want your mother running naked through the fields. It is not good for . . . for . . ." He pauses and narrows his eyes. "For the morals of this parish."

Has God spoken to him? Has God complained about Mam's lunacy? Perhaps God has told him of the other night when I found Pa with his scraggy knuckles gripping Mam's neck, twisting his two hands like she was no more than a Christmas goose. He'd been in a rare temper, with the ale upon him so strong I could smell it on every reeking breath. Fortunately, the drink—and the lack of a leg—had weakened him so that he'd fallen to the floor wailing, "She remembers nothing, Ann. Not even me . . . she's lost control of every bit of herself. She ain't human no more." All the while Mam lay on the mattress, a long gummy smile on her face, no notion she'd been half throttled by her own husband.

Reverend Thorpe begins to back out of the cottage, keeping his eyes to heaven so he won't see Mam, who is crawling across the floor. Her scalp is like yellow parchment now, her hair thin and matted. I put her on the mattress, arranging her scrawny limbs so she's curled like a cat. The sheet is bunched and tangled around her with big knots at her shoulders, knees, and hips, so she looks more like a twist of dirty laundry than a human being. All at once I know it's only me that can look after her, only me that can calm her. "I promise to keep her clothed," I plead. "And I will learn to tie a firmer knot, a reef knot."

At this the vicar pauses and looks around the cottage in a very pointed way. I watch his gaze travel over the shelf that once held Mam's books: her book of prayers, her book of *Cookery Made Plain and Easy*, the *German Fairy Tales* bound in ruby linen. The shelf is empty now. Bare and empty. I wait for him to ask why we have no prayer book, no Bible. Instead he says something that stuns me, so that I cannot speak.

"Ann," he says. "You're a clever girl. A resourceful girl. You could be a housemaid. Or a nurserymaid. Wouldn't you like that?"

I blink, like a fool.

"Your mother taught you to read and write—is that not so?"

He speaks the truth, so I nod, and he says, "If you are scrupulously honest and work very hard, you could be a lady's maid. I can see that you are not averse to hard labor."

Before I can stop myself, my most secret desire blurts from my lips. The words that run through my head every night, like fluttering ribbons. "I dream of being a cook," I say. I regret my words, of course I do. But it's too late to put them back, so I busy myself picking out a twig tangled in Mam's hair.

Reverend Thorpe coughs, not a hoarse cough rattling with liquid like Pa's, but more like he has a bread crumb stuck there. "That would be ambitious indeed," he says after a while. "But perhaps in a small private family. Perhaps if you were to start as a scullery maid. How old are you, Ann?"

"Seventeen this coming Michaelmas." I try to keep my voice sure and definite, but already my mind is straying. Before me float tightly crusted pies, buttery sticky puddings, birds turning on spits, shelves of ripe orchard fruit, fat barrels of sweet raisins, sticks of cinnamon as long as my hand—and all the other things Jack has told me of.

"You are old to go into service but I shall look out for a position for you, regardless," the vicar says. "Everyone must pull their weight in God's world." I should be cross, hearing him say I'm not pulling my weight. But my mind is only half here. The other half has flown clean away, to a kitchen where I'm chopping, slicing, stirring, fixing pigs to spits, and trimming the fat from kidneys. Like Jack does in London. He says there's more food than I could ever imagine. Stockpots bigger than milk churns, Dutch ovens bigger than our cottage, larders the size of houses, mortars bigger than my own head. And then my stomach rumbles so loud I have to grip my sides for fear the vicar will think me too uncouth to work in a private kitchen.

He stoops beneath the doorframe, which is barely high enough for a donkey. "Your mother will be well fed and cared for, and you and your father shall earn some wages. So it's agreed."

A tightness pulls and tugs at the back of my eyes. Can I only be a cook if Mam is locked away in a madhouse? Is that what I've agreed to?

CHAPTER THREE
ELIZA

OXFORD PUNCH

As the coach sways and rocks I try to distract myself by looking at the scarlet poppies and great mounds of hay, radiant and disheveled. Crows rise, rags of black, from the dusty fields. But all this beauty only adds to my misery. Where once I would have exulted in finding the most accurate, the most fulsome words to describe such a scene, now every impression seems to taunt me. Besides which, I cannot stop thinking of everyone at home, waiting to hear of my meeting with the famous Mr. Longman. His words of rejection have not left me once on this long rattling journey: *Poetry is not the business of a lady . . . Nobody wants poetry now . . .* And his final, demeaning request: *Go home and write me a cookery book and we might come to terms.* Terms indeed! I have no intention of repeating that particular line. Not to anyone.

As the coach approaches Ipswich, my shame and failure settle inside me like a brick. The sky blackens, peppered now with thousands of tiny silver stars. And when our house rears up from the dark—its windows flickering with candlelight, pale moths fluttering at the glass—I want nothing more than to disappear.

The front door bursts open, spilling breathless light and voices and the tumbling sounds of a pianoforte.

"Eliza's here! She's back!"

The pianoforte stops. Candles appear, wavering in the night air. And behind them, the eager faces of Catherine, Edgar, and Anna. Even Hatty, the housemaid, is come to welcome me home.

Mother follows, squinting into the gloom. "Eliza, is that you? We have all been waiting an absolute age. Hurry! Hurry! Or all the moths of Suffolk shall be making their nests in my new curtains."

I am barely out of the coach before their pleas begin.

"What did Mr. Longman say, Eliza? Oh, please tell!" begs Catherine. "Tell us everything, from the very beginning."

"No, not from the beginning," barks Edgar. "We shall be here all night. Get directly to the point—how was Mr. Longman?"

A sharp ache catches beneath my ribs. The disappointment of my family feels so much worse than my own. Mother's will be tinged with I told you so and a quiet pleasure at my failure, but not Edgar. Not my sisters. Not Father. Their disappointment will be palpable.

"Oh, Edgar, why must you be so impatient? Anna, ask Cook to bring a bowl of her best Oxford punch and tell her to be quick about it. John is still not home and it is making me quite fretful."

Mother wrings her hands anxiously. "He was determined to be here for your arrival."

I feel a sense of relief. Telling Father of my failure is what I dread most. He has always believed in me, always supported my endeavors. It was he who provided the money when I wanted to set up a school for young ladies. And it was he who funded my first volume of verse, insisting the paper and bindings be of the highest quality. "No doubt he is delayed by paperwork or has misplaced his key," I say, keeping my voice pert to hide the relief I feel.

"How was Mr. Longman?" presses Edgar, spreading out his coattails and lowering himself into a chair. "I am prepared to wager that Mr. Longman thought your poems infinitely superior to those of that rascal Lord Byron." He rubs his hands up and down his thighs in mirth. "We shall toast you as soon as the punch bowl arrives."

"Please," I say in a thread of a whisper. "No punch. There is nothing to celebrate." I look down at my feet, at the streaks of London dirt on my boots, at the pearl buttons that are now quite black with coal dust. I have no appropriate words. Nothing to blunt the edge of their disappointment.

"Publishers no longer want poetry," I say eventually.

"Nonsense!" Edgar shuffles himself more deeply into his chair. "Is it because of your obstinate determination to use your own name?"

"Did you tell him of your last volume, of how it had to be reprinted in less than a month?" asks Catherine gently.

"Mr. Longman did not propose I publish my poems under

a nom de plume. He simply does not want them." My fingers twine themselves in the seed pearls at my neck. My throat is hot and dry. "I'm sorry."

"Well," says Mother, pausing to puff out her cheeks. "I always considered your poems too frank, slightly indelicate, if you ask me. I expect that is why Mr. Longman did not want them."

My jaw tightens. I look down and see white salted rings beneath my arms and catch the stink of London on my dress and skin. "He said no one wants poetry anymore. They want"—I stop and swallow—"novels, romances, preferably of the Gothic kind."

"Can you not write such a thing, dearest Eliza?" Catherine asks.

"This is all nonsense. You have no need of money. The poems were merely . . . merely . . ." Edgar's voice peters out, as if he isn't quite sure what the purpose of my poetry is.

"You exposed too much of yourself in that last volume," adds Mother. "There was an indiscretion that made some of our neighbors look upon me most curiously. You should never have published them under your—our—name, my dear. They were overwrought, too revealing."

"So it is well enough for Mr. Keats or Mr. Wordsworth to reveal their passions, but not me. Is that what you mean?"

"I think Mother is merely asking if you cannot be content to scribble away in private," says Edgar. "True poetry has no need of an audience, surely?"

I grope furiously for the words that will explain why I want an audience, why I want my own name upon my own *scribblings*: that it is this—precisely this—that makes me feel part of a wider, deeper world, a richer world in which I am connected to others, a world in which I matter. How can I achieve this if I *scribble* only for myself? If I am blank, nameless?

Mother tilts her head to one side and nods. "There is something a little ostentatious about seeking publication. For a lady, that is . . . ungodly even."

I stiffen, a burning behind my eyes. Mr. Longman's words float before me . . . *Poetry is not the business of a lady* . . . But for Mother to introduce God, to suggest that God's hand is at play, is too much. I stare angrily at her, but she has her eyes piously to Heaven.

Anna—sweet, kind Anna—reaches for my hand, squeezes it. "There are many other publishers, dearest Eliza. You must not despair."

I nod gratefully but cannot speak. My heart is too choked with the words of Mother and Edgar, mingling unpleasantly with those of Mr. Longman. And beneath all my anger, beneath my justifications for an audience, hovers the perpetual doubt. *Imposter. Imposter.* But also something more, something hazy and obscure. A feeling of loss. Ebbing and flowing through the anger, the disappointment, the doubt. For what am I now? A spinster from Suffolk with a single small book of verse to my name . . .

I stare at the silver punch bowl and my reflection glares back: a swag of dark hair, streaked with gray. A lattice of lines creeping around my eyes. Arcs appearing at the corners of my mouth. I am thirty-six. And I am nothing.

I excuse myself, mumble that the coach journey has exhausted me, and bolt toward the stairs and up to my room, desperate to be alone. I want to plunge my head into my pillow and forget everything. I light a candle and lie on my bed, wondering if I should have taken a fortifying glass of Oxford punch. The smell of warmed spices and port wine seeps below my door, wrapping its fug around me like a shawl of softest lambswool. A glass of punch would have helped me sleep, I think. Helped me blot out the words of my family. But perhaps not the words of Mr. Longman, which are altogether more tenacious, more shameful. Had I been a gentleman, I would never have been sent packing with a frivolous request for a cookery book. He spoke to me as if I was little more than a servant. Not even worthy of a novel. Or a book of botany, or lepidoptera.

I sniff at the spiced air, as if for consolation, when all of a sudden my thoughts are sent scattering. From below comes a long, high wail. Like the piercing shriek of a barn owl. I sit up, startled. The house is alive with rising voices, slamming doors, a rushing heave of wind through the hall and up the stairs. As if a fire has slipped under its skin.

All thoughts of Mr. Longman, of poetry, of myself are gone. I grab the candlestick, run to the landing, and look over the banisters. Everyone is gathered in the hall, caught in a broad beam of lamplight. And such a ruckus! Father is back and turning in flustered circles. Anna and Catherine are sobbing, Edgar is shouting, Mother has her head in her hands, Hatty is watching with an open mouth.

Booted feet race up the stairs toward me. It's Father, his white hair standing in wild peaks, his cravat hanging loosely at his neck, his eyes flaring behind his wire-framed spectacles.

"What is it?" I ask, confused and frightened in equal measure.

"We are finished, Eliza! Finished!" He turns and runs down the stairs to the drawing room, with me—bewildered—at his heels. He catches sight of the punch bowl, its contents now carrying a thin pale scurf, and staggers toward it. He draws out the silver ladle and drinks directly from its lip, so that punch streams into his collar.

"We have lost everything." He takes another mouthful, his hand shaking. Crimson liquid runs down his neck, staining his shirt, his cravat, the lapels of his frock coat.

"How?" I stare at him, assuming he's mistaken or drunk or with fever of the brain. Every week the *Ipswich Journal* lists a dozen or more bankruptcies, but none of the ilk of my father, a gentleman, a bachelor of law from St. John's College, Cambridge.

"It's not my fault, Eliza. I was overcharged for the leases of the Golden Lion and the King's Head. Grossly overcharged. And the eight bushels of coal that were stolen left me severely out of pocket. I had no choice but to borrow." He plunges the ladle back into the punch bowl and lifts it to his dripping mouth.

"Borrow from whom? Can we not repay them?" I stare at Father, and it's as if I'm staring at a stranger, a man I've never known.

"My debts are too huge . . . they'll declare me bankrupt, imprison me with common criminals. We are finished, Eliza!"

Just as I reach to take the ladle from him, Catherine bursts into the drawing room. "Eliza, come quickly! Mother is in a swoon. Oh, what are we to do?"

CHAPTER FOUR
ANN

SEASONED GRUEL

I think of the vicar's words as I work our little patch of land that is no bigger than a tinderbox. Mam is bound to me with a rope that is three yards long. Together we hoe and dig and try to plant a few leeks. I say *together*, but mostly I am coaxing and cajoling. *Mam, will you not kneel now? Mam, please do not pull so on the rope. Mam, stop your griping!* All day long I am *Mam this* and *Mam that*.

Presently she begins to gnaw at the rope with her four teeth, which have become so loose I fear she shan't have them much longer. When I try to pry her mouth from the rope, I see her tongue has a mossy coating. I sniff at her breath. Her mouth and gums carry the thick, low reek of sickness, but there's no money for a doctor. All the money Jack sent has gone for Pa's new crutch that must be made with the sturdiest wood. The vicar says Pa can only work the graveyard if his crutches are of the very best quality.

"Mam, will you not sit still?" The rope cuts deep into my arm every time she strains at it. She raises her bony hand as if to strike me. I flinch and am about to call for help from Pa—who is asleep upon the mattress—when I hear a familiar voice singing in the lane. My heart leaps. I know that voice anywhere. Always so chipper, so full of good cheer. A minute later and he's swaggering through the gate like the cat that got the cream.

"Who is it, Ann?" Mam's eyes are full of terror, darting this way and that. But I'm so happy to see Jack, I rush toward him, forgetting the rope. Mam is pulled roughly behind me and starts clawing at my back.

"For God's sake," says Jack, all the song and swagger gone from him as he sees Mam and me lurching and tumbling. "What's with the rope?"

I untie the rope and bind it instead around her wrists so that her hands stop their fevered scrabbling. Then I tell Jack how she has taken a turn for the worse, running away, taking all her garments off right down to her underthings, no longer recognizing kith or kin. By the time I've finished, tears are pouring down my face and I can only gulp and choke.

"Mam? Mam?" Jack watches her squatting in the mud. "I'm back from London with a few coins for you and Pa. I've walked two days with a drover and his goats, just to . . . Mam?"

But she is staring at him, her eyes frozen with fear. "I don't know you," she says, and starts struggling with the ropes around her wrists. And when she cannot loosen them, she tries to jump across the earth, heading for the lane. I pull her back and hold her tight to me, weeping and stroking her scalp until she lies still against me. Her bones are as thin as a bird's and she smells like no mother should. It strikes me then that we have swapped parts, utterly and completely.

"Oh, Ann," says Jack, shaking his head. "Why must she be tied up like a donkey?"

I wipe at my eyes with a muddy fist. Finally, I whisper, "The vicar wants her put in an asylum. He doesn't like her wandering around not properly dressed. He says it's not good for the morals of his parish. So I must tie her up."

"Morals!" snorts Jack. "Since when has a churchman had *morals?*"

"Hush," I say. "He's a godly man and well-intentioned, Pa says so."

"There's only one place you'll find God and it's not in a church or a vicar."

"So where is it?" I pull myself and Mam up, and Jack helps maneuver the both of us inside.

"In a crust of bread," says Jack without the shred of a smile. "Better still, in a good meal. I've always found him most present in a good hearty supper."

His answer—and his voice so full of scorn—unsettles me. For didn't Mam raise us to trust in the Lord? I'm on the verge of telling him he's wrong, that sitting alone in church with the carved angels and the smell of burning candles makes me feel better, when I decide not to think about such things any longer. Mam is as quiet as a mouse now, all the terror gone.

"Tell me stories of London, of your work," I beg. I have Jack to myself until Pa wakes up or Mam starts her griping or Septimus sets off with his barking, and I don't want to waste time talking about God or church or anything else for that matter.

"I'm in the roasting kitchen now, skinning and trussing," Jack says. "There are two ranges as big as this mattress, and spits that can roast a whole sheep."

"A whole sheep . . ." I have a notion of tender roasted mutton, flavored with woodsmoke and forest herbs. Saliva floods into my mouth. I put an iron pot of oats and water on a trivet over the fire, which is low and half-hearted. "Tell me about the fine food you prepare."

"Well, last week a gentleman returned a soufflé and Master Soyer let us taste it."

"What's a soufflé?" I sigh, for that is how the word sounds. Soft and sweet as a summer breeze. I repeat the word in my head: *Soufflé. Soufflé.*

"You beat eggs as light as air. And you make a batter of cream and butter, very fresh and the butter as bright as possible and cut very small. Then you flavor it. Master Soyer likes to use an Italian cheese or sometimes the finest bitter chocolate. And into the oven, where it rises so tall you cannot believe it. And when you bite in, it's like having cloud upon your tongue." Jack smacks his lips together.

I stir absently at the gruel and wish we had a few currants to sweeten it. And as I think of currants, all manner of other dried fruits swim before my eyes. I've seen them at market in Tonbridge. Great mounds of wizened shining prunes and raisins, orange peel crusted white with sugary syrup, rings of apple like the softest, palest leather.

"There's a larder just for game. Snipe, woodcock, pheasants, grouse, guinea fowl . . . and a meat safe where great haunches of beef and venison are stored. And suckling pigs and whole sheep. And a stove where nine stewpans can be bubbling all at once." Jack pauses and his eyes roll up to the ceiling, which is cracked and stained and has bindweed creeping at the corners. "You should see Master Soyer. In his red beret, with a diamond ring as big as an acorn. It doesn't matter how hot the soup is, he plunges his finger in, diamond and all, and passes it across his tongue. And then he's shaking in this and that—more salt, more pepper, more cayenne. Until it is just so."

"How grand," I murmur, thinking of the drama of it all, and how a kitchen is like a puppet show, a fairy tale, and how good it must feel to have none of the violent hunger that comes on me and Pa and Mam when food and money are scarce. And how good it must feel to be in a room that is always warm.

"There are plenty of girls in the kitchen. But only pretty ones. The master says he wants no *plain* cooks in his kitchen." Jack prods the dying embers with a poker and yawns.

I concentrate on the gruel, pushing the spoon hard against the iron pot. For a second I feel as if a huge door has been slammed in my face. For I am plain indeed. And for how long have I nursed my little dream of working alongside Jack? Oh, months and months. Every night I go to sleep thinking of Master Soyer in his kitchen whites with me at his side, whisking, slicing, beating, tasting. That'll teach me, I think. Dreams should be dreams and nothing more. I stir at the thin gray gruel with extra vigor. Mam is sleeping now, curled up on the mattress beside Pa. As peaceful as a pair of cats.

"Tell me more." My voice comes out like the squeak of a mouse. Jack narrows his eyes and looks at me very close, but then he nods his head and starts describing all the grand dishes that have swept beneath his nose on their journey from the kitchen to the gentlemen diners. Pigeons wrapped in the leaves of vines. Oysters in crisp pastry cases. Whole Gloucester salmon in aspic. Yarmouth lobsters cooked in wine and herbs. Glazed tarts of pippin apples. Paper-thin layers of buttery pastry spread with greengages, apricots, peaches, cherries, served with great gouts of golden cream.

"Well," I say, "it's gruel for us tonight, with a smidgeon of salt and pepper." Whereupon he reaches into his pocket, pulls out a twist of greased paper, and opens it. Immediately I smell the tang of heather honey.

"For you, Ann." In his grimed palm sits an oozing chunk of honeycomb as big as a plover's egg.

I clap my hands in delight, my tongue waggling with greed. As we eat our gruel I make the clots of chewy wax last as long as possible, pushing them around and around my mouth, pressing them against my molars, sucking on them 'til they slip sweetly down my throat. When my bowl is wiped clean and the honeycomb quite gone from my teeth, I tell Jack about the vicar wanting me to get a *position*, and thinking me *resourceful* and *clever*.

"And if Mam won't go to his asylum?" asks Jack. But I don't answer him. And I say nothing of Pa trying to strangle Mam when I have left them for barely an hour. Jack puts his bowl on the floor so that Septimus may lick it clean. "And what do you want, Ann?"

"I want to be . . ." I pause, and then the words rush from me. "A cook."

"A cook?" And he is doubled up, laughing so hard the tears stream from his eyes.

"Yes," I reply, hurt. "A *plain* cook."

He points at his empty gruel bowl and starts laughing again. Then he wipes his eyes and says he's sorry and that even he—after three years of kitchen service—has only just moved up from turning spits. I want to remind him that I can read and write, and he cannot. That I can dream. And hope. But I hold my tongue. For what is the use?

My eyes turn, of their own accord, to the shelf where Mam's books once sat. And that is when I know I'm all alone. A strange forsaken feeling comes over me. As if I'm standing on the very edge of the earth. Utterly alone.

CHAPTER FIVE
ELIZA

BROWN BREAD PUDDING

I remove my books from their shelves, one by one, pausing to caress a particularly handsome spine or a binding of embossed Italian leather. Wordsworth, Keats, Shelley, Coleridge—I wrap each volume in a sheet of old newspaper and consign it carefully to a tea chest. I linger on the highest shelf: the collected works of Ann Candler, seven volumes of Mrs. Hemans's poems, and three of L. E. Landon's. Every now and then I flick through the pages, gorging on an old familiar verse, and feeling wings sprouting on my shoulder blades.

When my small library is packed away, I grope beneath my mattress for a final volume . . . neat, elegant, and tightly bound in silk of sapphire blue. I sit on the edge of my bed and stare at it: *The Poems of Eliza Acton.* How slender and flimsy it seems. I run my finger down its spine, then lift it to my nose, inhaling its dry odor of dust and parchment. I open the book and feel the same sense of satisfaction as when I held it in my hands for the very first time, struck by how the neat orderliness of printing had transformed the inky sentiment of my verse. Molded it into something with greater clarity. Bestowed upon it a weightiness and significance. And detached it from me, the final severing of an umbilical cord. The feeling had pleased me then, and it pleases me now. But as I look more closely, my insides curl and cringe . . . *My first affections, and my last, were thine—thine only— fare thee well!*

How youthful those words seem now. Perhaps Mother was right. They are overwrought, brimming with exaggerated emotion. Or so it seems, a decade on. My new poems are better, defter, more mature. And yet Mr. Longman . . . An image of him comes to me, his plump ringed fingers patting at his pockets, the ticking of his gold pocket watch echoing in the swelter of his office, his vast polished desk that had sat between us like the Great Wall of China. He has yet to return my poems. Lost, no doubt. Drowned in the deluge of manuscripts—biographies, books of science, poetry, Gothic novels—that come daily from the sweating fists of hopeful writers everywhere.

I slip the volume into the tea chest and look around my bedchamber: the empty grate, the damask curtains that have been taken from their hooks and folded in neat squares, the old Turkey rug rolled up and propped against the mahogany washstand. We are taking only the bare essentials: beds and linen, two tallboys, the elm kitchen table and the mahogany dining table with matching chairs. Everything else is to be sold at auction:

the prints and paintings, the crystal, the silver plate, the feather mattresses, the wall clocks, the rugs and books. All except my collection of books that I fought to keep, offering up every piece of jewelry in its place. Much to the surprise of my sisters who declared themselves *flabbergasted* that I should prefer books to my triple string of pearls or my diamond ear drops on gold wires or my brooch of amethysts and rose quartz.

"Eliza! Eliza!" Mother's voice rises from the floor below.

I place the lid on the tea chest, ready to be nailed down, and pick my way downstairs. The entire house is awry, with the heaving of furniture; the rolling of rugs; the lifting of portraits and maps from the picture rails; the dismantling of curtains; the wrapping and crating of china, books, mirrors, and every piece of ornamentation from my past. All to grace the homes of others now. We are to leave for our new rented accommodations after dark, when no one will see us. Like thieves in the night.

Mother appears, her fingers chewing at the jet crucifix at her neck. "Cook is in a terrible state. Do hurry down to the kitchen, Eliza." She turns away and barks instructions at a boy standing idle in the hall.

"The kitchen?" I have not been belowstairs for months and months. The kitchen, larders, and scullery are the domain of Mrs. Durham, the cook, who does not like visitors. Our previous cook was more openhearted; and as a girl I would cut pastry into oak leaves for decorating the crusts of pies or punch my small fists into mounds of dough. But Mrs. Durham is decidedly un-welcoming. Only Mother and Hatty are permitted to take the

back stairs now. Or Father, should he wish to check the contents
of his wine cellar. But the wine has gone early to auction. And
Father has fled to France.

Cook is sitting at the table surrounded by glass jars, tins of
salt, loaves of sugar, baskets of eggs and onions. And at her feet, a
circle of sacks—of flour, chestnuts, hops. "Is none of this wanted,
Miss Eliza?" Her eyes are pink, and her face washed through
with the tracks of tears.

"It's all been so sudden, Miss Eliza. And to see the advertisement in the *Ipswich Journal*, even before we hears it from the mistress herself." She pulls a fraying handkerchief from her pocket
and blows noisily into it.

"But you're coming with us to Tonbridge. We shall need a
good cook for our . . . boardinghouse." I frown at the word, new
in my mouth. *Boardinghouse. Boardinghouse.* I don't like the feel
of it in my throat, or the sound of it in the air. I shake my head.
But it hangs there, like unripe fruit clinging to a windblown
branch. "Only you and Hatty are being retained," I add, unsure
if Mother has explained anything. "Other servants we must find
in Tonbridge." If we can afford them . . . which is unlikely.

Cook nods and blows her nose again. "What am I to pack? I've
received no instructions . . . The jelly molds? The cut-glass finger bowls? And what of all these spices? They're worth a pretty
fortune." She waves a juddering arm across the table, at the tins
and glass jars and earthenware pots. All at once a shaft of thin
northern light swoops over them, jolting them into luminous
life: bubbled glass jars of briny green peppercorns, salted capers,
gleaming vanilla pods, rusted cinnamon sticks, all leaping and

glinting. The sudden startling beauty of it, the palette of hues—ocher, terra-cotta, shades of earth and sand and grass—the pale trembling light. All thoughts of running a *boardinghouse* vanish.

I reach for a jar, lift its cork lid. The scent of bark, earth, roots, sky. And for a second I am somewhere else. "The mysterious scent of a secret kingdom," I murmur. The jar contains little pellets, brown, spherical, unexotic. How marvelous that something so plain can have such an enthralling perfume, I think.

"Oh, Miss Eliza. Always the poetess! It's only allspice." Cook gives a wan smile and gestures at the ceiling, where long bunches of herbs hang from a rack. Rosemary, tansy, sage, nettles, woodruff. "And what of these? All summer I was collecting these and they still ain't properly dry."

"May I lower it?" Not waiting for an answer I wind down the rack until the drying herbs are directly in front of me—a farmyard sweetness, a woody sappy scent, the smell of bruised apples and ripe earth and crushed ferns. Briefly, quite unexpectedly, I'm thrust back in time . . . pine needles scratch my skin, light gushes through overhead branches, soft words fill my ears. Quickly I wind up the rack. "Do you have family that could use these herbs, Mrs. Durham?"

She brightens. "Now there's an idea, Miss Eliza. And Mistress says all the books must be sold too, but not my own recipes surely?"

"We have cookery books?"

"Only a few." She lumbers to the pantry, returning with an armful of books. "There's one here in French that I do believe you brought back from your travels, Miss Eliza."

I pick up the volume, its corners worn, oily rings staining its leather bindings. *Le Cuisinier Royal* is stamped upon the tan spine. A second unwanted memory twitches inside me. I drop the book and begin leafing through another: *A New System of Domestic Cookery by a Lady*. I pause at a recipe for pickled oysters, scan it, and frown. What messy strangled prose this *lady* uses. Some of it is barely comprehensible. None of it conjures the exquisite sensation of a fresh oyster—briny and sharp, a rock pool at dawn—upon the unsuspecting tongue. "Tell me, Mrs. Durham, do these recipes make sense to you?"

"Truth be told, Miss Eliza, I can't make head nor tail of it. I'm not a good reader at the best of times."

I read another recipe. The grammar is poor, the recipe unenticing, the entire thing flabby with half-formed opinions. "If I read this aloud, will you tell me what this good *lady* is attempting to say?"

"And why would you be asking?" She looks at me through half-closed eyes.

"It makes no sense to me, but perhaps that is because I have no expertise in the culinary arts. Unlike you, of course, who are so accomplished a cook we simply cannot imagine a future home without you."

Mollified, she nods. "Normally I use my own recipes, what I've collected over years and years of being a cook."

I begin reading: "'Brown bread pudding. Half a pound of stale brown bread grated, ditto of currants, ditto of shred suet, sugar, and nutmeg: mix with four eggs, a spoonful of brandy, and two spoonfuls of cream. Boil, in a cloth or basin that exactly holds it, three or four hours.'" I feel an inexplicable stab of annoyance. If anyone wrote a poem as imprecise and inarticulate as this recipe, they would be derided and mocked. "Surely she doesn't mean half a pound of nutmeg? And what size is a spoonful? How are we to tell if she refers to a ladle or a salt spoon?"

Mrs. Durham sucks in her cheeks and rolls her eyes. "My own recipe is much better," she says. "Half a pound of nutmeg would take forever to grate and it would cost a king's fortune too. And there's no mention of washing the grit from the currants, nor taking off their stalks." She clicks her tongue disapprovingly.

"And why does she say to boil for three *or* four hours?"

"Think of the waste, Miss Eliza. All that extra fuel needed when it might only take three hours and you've been boiling it for four hours." She clucks again and shakes her head. "Bad recipes to be sure and yet every kitchen I ever worked in has a copy of that book."

I scan the recipe a third time. Something gnaws at me. Something other than the implicit wastage and the irritating imprecision. My mind ticks through the ingredients: *bread, currants, suet, sugar, nutmeg, eggs, brandy, cream.*

"How do you imagine this brown bread pudding would taste, Mrs. Durham?" I close the book and, without thinking, tuck it beneath my arm.

"If it was me, I would be adding other ingredients. Salt to bring out the flavor . . . just a pinch, mind you. And candied peel perhaps. And the zest of a nice fresh lemon stirred into the suet."

"Very good, Mrs. Durham. Very good," I say softly. She is right, of course. This mysterious *lady's* recipe is dull as well as poorly written, inexact, and scruffy in its presentation.

Cook swells beneath my praise and begins bustling around the kitchen, taking the herbs from the rack and binding them in twine.

"Take anything you wish," I say, eager to escape with the cookery book. Mr. Longman's words ring in my ears: *Go home and write me a cookery book and we might come to terms.* Was I too hasty with my scorn?

"And these?" Cook holds up a clutch of books. "I don't use any of 'em."

"I'll take them," I reply, and hurry to my bedchamber, relieved the lid to my tea chest hasn't yet been hammered down. I slip the books inside, place a folded shawl on top, and go down into the fray.

A BASIN OF BROTH THICKENED
WITH ARROWROOT

I'm at church a month later, when the vicar glances my way and nods his head at the vestry.

"Ann . . ." His voice is a whisper, even though everyone has left.

"Yes, Father?" I try to look godly, hiding the pleasure from my face. Church has become the happiest part of my week, now that I may go alone and listen to the hymns and smell the white lilies on the altar and watch the colored light coming through the stained glass in the arched window. All the while knowing that Pa won't yet have taken any ale and is securely bound to Mam. And then there is the walk home, through fields of corn and poppies. And although I must hurry, I always make time to nibble on hawthorn and dandelion leaves or collect a few berries. As I used to when I was little and Mam—in her church best—would show me which leaves to eat and which blackberries carried the devil's spit and must be avoided.

"I think there may be a position for you, as underhousemaid." He rubs his thin white hands together and I see the bones moving beneath his skin. "A new family is taking up residence here . . . I couldn't recommend you to anyone familiar with your situation, of course." He stops and gazes right over my head, looking for heavenly guidance, I think to myself. I know only too well that no one wants a girl with madness in her blood. Nor do they want a girl whose father is a known drunk and whose mother roams the fields half naked. But a new family is like a fresh clean canvas. They won't know of my shame.

"Where are they from, Father?" I ask, trying to stop my fingernails from jumping to my mouth in excitement. No one wants a girl who chews her nails.

"They have moved here from Ipswich. Might you be interested, Ann?"

"Yes, Father. If I can be assured my parents won't be alone."

He is still sky gazing when he replies. "Leave that to me. Can you get to Tonbridge this week? Mrs. Thorpe has an outgrown dress she is generously willing to lend you for your interview."

My eyes go very wide, for Mrs. Thorpe has never once smiled at me, let alone spoken to me. And then I wonder how her dress might look and my eyes stretch even wider—Mrs. Thorpe has a bosom so ample you could trot a mouse on it. I look down at my flat chest and see the vicar's eyes traveling in the same direction. As if he is reading my mind.

"You can darn, Ann?"

I nod.

"Good, good." And he rubs his hands again as if he has a chill. "A meek and pliable girl like yourself should suit them nicely."

"May I ask the family's name, Father?"

"Their name is Acton." He points at the vestry door, dismissing me in the way gentlemen do. I drop a curtsy and as I bob up he says, "Do not disappoint me, or the good Lord, Ann."

"No, Father," I say, but I'm not thinking of the good Lord, for my head is full of other thoughts. Who is to look after Mam while I go to Tonbridge? The walk alone will take me thirty minutes there and thirty minutes back. In that time, Mam could have removed every shred of clothing and run naked all the way to Tunbridge Wells. Or Pa could have strangled her to death or beat her senseless with his crutch. I want to ask the vicar who will take Mam to the new lunatic asylum but I'm too late. The vestry door has closed with a clang and the iron key grates in the enormous iron lock.

A wind begins to blow up from the fields, shaking the leaves on the trees and making the hedgerows sway. Above me the heavens turn black. Needles of rain slice at my face. I gather up my skirts and break into a run.

At home there is no sign of Pa. The cottage is empty; even Septimus is gone. A feverish panic fills me. Where is Mam? My heart is galloping like a wild mule, and all thoughts of wearing a crisp white apron and stirring a dairy bowl with a long-handled spoon vanish. What was I thinking? Of course I can't go into service!

I stop and listen. And above the sounds of the wind, I hear

someone moaning my name, very soft and sad. I rush to the back of the cottage and there is Mam, bound to a tree.

"Ann, Ann," she wails, her hands pulling at her ears. I hurry to her side and scrabble at the knot, for he has bound her well and truly.

But then she turns on me, vicious, her eyes bulging like a frog's.

"You're not my Ann," she shouts. "Go away, you rogue!" A spew of vile language pours from her crusted tongue, words fit only for a drunken sailor. As her curses rain upon my head, I comfort myself by saying, "The Acton family, a respectable family," under my breath, over and over.

By the time I've untied the knots, rain is coming down in fat angry drops. "Mam, we must go inside," I say, all gentle and pleading, for she has such a fury on her now.

"No!" she shrieks. "I must wait for my Ann." And she lashes at my face with her uncut fingernails that are as sharp as blades, and ragged too.

"I am your Ann," I plead.

"Liar!" She spits in my face, and as I step back she says something that strikes me cold. "Ann is dead. Dead, dead, dead!"

That is when I know Mr. Thorpe is right and I must get myself out of here before I too go quite mad. I put my arms tight around her and maneuver her to the cottage. I can feel her sopping skirts against me as I pull her along and I thank the Lord she carries as little flesh as I do.

Later Pa returns from the tavern, his eyes a milky yellow, but only a trace of ale on his breath. "Ann," he says and I notice his voice has the softest of slurs. "I cannot go on like this. Mr. Thorpe, God bless him, says if I stop the drink, he will give me a small stipend for keeping the graves clear of brambles and nettles."

"So who will look after Mam while you're working?" I ask, keeping my voice light and steady.

"Ah, there's the rub." His eyes fill with silver tears that he tries to wipe away with the backs of his hands. "The lunacy is upon her stronger than ever." He blinks very fast. "She doesn't recognize us anymore. She has become little more than—an animal."

I try to speak, to tell him he's wrong. But a lump the size of a quince has risen up my throat.

"The vicar says there's no cure for madness. And he says you have brains, Ann. Proper brains. He says he has found work for you. Not in an alehouse or on a farm, but in a private house with ladies of delicacy. Gentlewomen."

I look away, fixing my eyes on the door, on the filthy muddy fingerprints that circle the latch and must be scrubbed away before they dry hard. I hadn't found the words to tell Pa what the vicar said. To repeat all that talk of *jobs* and *positions* would have doomed it, made it all vanish in a puff of smoke. "Yes," I whisper. "I was going to tell you myself, but . . ."

I glance at Mam. She's sitting on the floor watching us blankly, as if she's someone else now, someone empty and gone. Not Mam at all. I put my arms around Pa and feel his wiry beard on my cheek. He smells of the tavern—drink and tobacco and woodsmoke—and clothes that need a good washing and airing.

"It'll be heavy work—carrying coal and water, scrubbing floors and beating carpets. But no more than here. And you'll be properly fed." He indicates the pot on the fire that we both know contains nothing more than broth of peelings thickened with a pinch of arrowroot. From his mouth comes a long rasping sigh, so thick with defeat my heart goes out to him.

"I'll be paid, Pa. I'll send the money home." I nuzzle my nose into his beard, thinking that I'll also get a good night's sleep at last, without ropes digging into my flesh or Mam's knees and elbows jousting with me every hour.

"Mr. Thorpe is a good man, a godly man," he says. I follow his gaze across the room to where Mam sits, all docile. And for a minute I wonder if we are both making a terrible mistake. Shouldn't I be here, looking after my mad mother and crippled father? What if this Acton family is no better? There's always a story or two in the village of some poor girl who has been beaten or locked up by her master. Or worse. Like the girls who return with bellies as round and full as a new moon.

"Pa, what do you know about this family that Mr. Thorpe wants me to work for?"

"I believe you'll have two mistresses, a widow and a spinster. There is no man of the house." And when he says that I know he's thinking just as I am.

CHAPTER SEVEN
ELIZA

CRAB APPLE JELLY

In spite of the fish vans that clatter through the town on their way to London and the hop pickers who arrive daily by wagon, Tonbridge does not have the hustle and bustle of Ipswich. This pleases Mother, who crows constantly about Tonbridge's *superior* inhabitants and its *superior* visitors. And it is these that she has her ruthless gimlet eye upon: the well-dressed ladies and gentlemen who come to take the waters of our neighboring spa town, Tunbridge Wells, and are in need of *superior* rooms.

Our rented home is newly built and has its name—Bordyke House—carved into the lintel. As befits a *superior* boardinghouse, it is spacious, well furnished, and situated well away from the town's open drains. And yet it feels all wrong, like a poorly cut coat. Perhaps this is because Edgar has set sail to make his fortune in Mauritius, and Catherine and Anna have taken up positions as governesses—all of us fleeing gossip and disgrace—so

it is only Mother and I rattling around here. Or perhaps it is because no amount of *superiority* can disguise our future as the
landladies of a boardinghouse.

We are in the morning room—yellow walls, armchairs upholstered in a shiny fabric featuring oversize yellow pineapples—
when I finally muster the courage to suggest my plan to Mother.
For three weeks I have worked on it. Night after night. Poring
over cookery books by candlelight. Reading. Rereading. During
the days, as Mother busied herself arranging the furniture and
placing advertisements for boarders, I loitered at the bookdealer's,
ordering books we could ill afford.

"Mother, do the lawyers have any claim on our remaining
possessions?"

"I think not, my dear. I hope not. But we must make enough
money to be independent." She looks up from her ledger. "We
are woefully short at present. I have placed three advertisements
for boarders and spoken to the vicar and the headmaster of Tonbridge School. We are in debt to the tune of . . ." She pauses
and scrutinizes her ledger. "Twenty guineas, perhaps more. The
finances are muddled. Or I am muddled. I cannot tell which."

"Can we afford to keep Mrs. Durham?"

"We must have someone to cook for our boarders."

"But we have no boarders. And this house is substantial—and
costly."

"Well, my dear, I cannot cook and nor can you."

I take a deep breath. "Mr. Longman asked me to write a cookery book."

Mother looks up, startled. "You never mentioned that. What a rude man!"

"I've decided to accept his commission, if it still stands."

"But you cannot cook, Eliza. You have never cooked. Besides, *ladies* do not cook."

"I'm determined to make a contribution to the household costs."

"You wish me to dismiss Mrs. Durham and put you in her place? In the kitchen? Like a common servant?" Mother's mouth settles in a stubborn pout.

"Yes," I reply shortly. "I shall teach myself cookery and then I shall write the book Mr. Longman has requested."

"You wish to practice cookery on our paying guests?"

I lower my voice and look down at my hands. "You forget, I have spent time in Italy and . . . in France."

"But you were not cooking!" The word *cooking* bolts from her mouth as if she cannot get shot of it fast enough. "Whatever else you were doing, you were not working in a windowless kitchen belowstairs." She pauses, then screws up her eyes and stares at me. "Or were you?"

"French food made a great impression on me." For a second, a creamy vanilla pool collects sweetly in my throat. As if my body remembers where my mind will not. Then mother squares her jaw and the taste slides away. "I've been studying cookery writers and I can do better. Some of them are barely literate. The measurements are imprecise, the wording is inelegant. They lack clarity, and even the recipes themselves are unappetizing."

I glance at Mother—she is wringing her hands, her lips and jaws working soundlessly.

"I shan't be a cook. I shall be a cookery *writer*. It is perfectly seemly." From beneath my gown I produce *A New System of Domestic Cookery by a Lady*, and offer it to her.

She flicks through the pages, her nostrils flaring. "Your folio of verse was bad enough. But this"—she taps a fingernail on the cover—"this is . . . unbecoming. If you wish to contribute financially, I think you should find a position as a governess. With your experience a place in a prominent family should be quite possible."

Something cools and hardens inside me. I'm not the person who once ran a school, who inspired intelligent girls to excel, who accompanied wealthy young ladies on their grand tours. No—I am someone else entirely now and there can be no return. Sometimes I wonder if my past experiences have rendered me, in some obscure way, feeble. Frail even. For the merest thought of being in a schoolroom again fills me with exhausted dread. How much more pleasant a kitchen seems . . .

"At least let me write to Mr. Longman and agree on terms."

"And you would publish anonymously of course, like this alleged *lady*."

A small sigh escapes my lips. I know Mother will be shamed by my—our—association with kitchen work, but I cannot forget my book of verse, *Poems by Eliza Acton*. I cannot forget the many times I ran a fingertip over my name, not from conceit or from pride but because it showed me who I was. Because, in some strange way, it placed me in the world. "Only if Mr. Longman insists," I say after a lengthy pause.

She drops the cookery book in my lap and returns to her ledger. "You are always so bellicose, Eliza. No wonder you have no husband." She picks up her pen and prods at a column of figures. "The saving on Mrs. Durham will be ten guineas a year. I suppose we can try it . . ."

"Thank you! Thank you!" I leap from my chair with such exuberance *Domestic Cookery by a Lady* flies into the air.

"Well, I can't have you mooning over poetry at your age. But you'll need help in the kitchen, a scullery maid. She can sleep in the eaves with Hatty."

"I want someone quiet. And clever." The thought of an ill-educated garrulous girl with dirty fingernails and not an ounce of common sense, in my ear all day, suddenly seems unendurable. I must have a modicum of seclusion and solitude, I think to myself.

"You can choose the girl yourself." Mother swivels her arched eyebrows in my direction. "What if it turns out that you have no skill for cookery?"

I don't answer her, for my thoughts are elsewhere . . . the exotic spices arriving daily from the East Indies and the Americas, the crates of sweet oranges and bitter lemons from Sicily, the apricots from Mesopotamia, the olive oil from Naples, the almonds from the Jordan valley . . . I have seen and smelled these delicacies at market. But does any English person know how to cook with such foods?

I think back to my time in France and Italy, of all the delicacies that passed across my tongue. And then to the gardens I've seen in Tonbridge with their raised beds of sorrel, lettuce, cucumbers, marrows, pumpkins. Already the banks are starred bright with blackberries and rose hips, with damsons and sour sloes, the bloom still upon them. Trees are weighted down with green apples and yellow mottled pears and crab apples flushed pink and gold. Soon there will be fresh cobnuts in their husks, and ripe walnuts, and field mushrooms, and giant puffballs.

I have a sudden craving for crab apple jelly. A craving so sharp, my tongue aches. I turn back into the room. Mother's head is bent low over her ledger again.

"My first attempt at cookery will be crab apple jelly," I announce.

"Do you have the slightest idea how to make a jelly set fast?"

"With sage," I add, as an afterthought. Yes, sage, I think. Such a muscular earthy herb—perfect for the cruel tartness of those tight little crab apples.

"Eliza? Did you hear me?"

CHAPTER EIGHT
ANN

EXCELLENT PORTABLE LEMONADE
(WITH LAVENDER)

Today is my interview. I'm all dressed up in Mrs. Thorpe's cast-off frock, which is billowing around me, far too big and roomy for a scrawny creature like me. Mrs. Thorpe has spoken to me for the first time, saying I will double in size once I'm working in Miss Acton's house. She also told me that I must call Miss Acton *ma'am* and reveal nothing of my *bad blood*.

I help Pa rope himself to Mam. She's very quiet today, as if she knows I'm up to something. I walk the half hour to Tonbridge, trembling like a leaf and my mouth as dry as sawdust. My nerves are made worse by Mrs. Thorpe's frock, for I'm afraid of damaging it and must lift the trailing skirts very high. She made it plain she was only lending it because her husband is a godly man and the frock is worn to a thread and fit only for the rag-and-bone man.

When I find Miss Acton's house, my shakes get worse, for the

house is very big and very grand. I slip through the carriage entrance, past a brewhouse, a washhouse, and a coach house. Fresh
straw has been strewn over the cobbles, although there are no
horses or carriages and all the doors are shut fast.

I'm standing in the yard, smoothing at my hair and at
Mrs. Thorpe's skirts, when a door bursts open. Out steps a lady,
very tall, with dark hair that is swept up and twisted with pins.
"Can I help you?" she asks.

"I'm Ann Kirby, come to speak with Miss Acton." My voice is
all up-and-down squeaky.

"I am Miss Acton," she says, which surprises me because
Mrs. Thorpe says gentlewomen sit in their parlors, out of the
sun. She asks me to follow her inside, and as I walk behind her I
get a good eyeful of her frock, which is pale blue and of the softest fabric, with real lace at the collar. She has no jewels—nothing
at the ears or neck—and I wonder if this is to preserve me from
temptation. Mrs. Thorpe told me never to stare at a lady's jewels
in case I'm thought a common thief.

"We will talk in the kitchen," she says. I nod my head but cannot speak, for my mouth is stiff with fear.

The kitchen is very roomy and lofty, four times as big as
our cottage. Copper pans hang from the ceiling and fluted copper molds in every size run over the walls. In the middle is an
enormous table all covered with fancy utensils—which I think
might be sugar nippers, and pastry prickers, and biscuit cutters,
and butter molds, just as Jack has described to me. They are so
beautiful, all embossed and shaped and shining, I want to look
at them forever.

"This is where we shall be spending our days," she says. And I am so confused by her words I just stare at her, speechless. Who is *we*? I look around for the cook, but she must be in the garden or gone to market.

"Tell me where you've worked, Ann." Her voice is soft, very gentle, and kindly, so that I forget my nerves. But then she says something that throws me even more. "Forgive me, I have not offered you refreshment. How rude of me! Would you care for a glass of fresh lemonade?"

I shake my head, for it's not her place to be pouring drinks for *me*. I will wait for the cook to return, I think.

But she presses me, saying, "I made it myself this morning. I've been experimenting and this version includes a little crushed lavender."

I don't want her to think me rude, so I nod and whisper, "Yes, please, ma'am." Just as Mrs. Thorpe told me.

She pours a tall glass. And then I realize she's waiting for me to drink it. Mrs. Thorpe didn't mention anything about drinks, so I'm unsure what to do.

"Drink!" Miss Acton commands.

I take a sip, and it's like nothing I've ever tasted. Sweet and sour and sharp and blossomy all at once.

"What do you think?" she asks. I stare at her, forgetting that Mrs. Thorpe told me never to stare.

"Well, speak," she says, but I don't think she's cross because there's a little smile on her lips.

I don't say that her question makes me tremble, that Mrs. Thorpe told me I must never have an opinion. And nor do

I tell her that the lemonade tastes of something I can't put into words, of Mam shredding lavender flowers and mixing them with the crushed leaves of verbena and lemon balm . . . Tears prick at the back of my eyes, and I reach for the table to steady myself.

"Are you unwell?" Miss Acton comes to my side and helps me into a low chair, where I sit, hot and ashamed.

"You need more lemonade," she says, and pours another glass. Then she stoops beside me and holds the glass right by my face so I can see the pale cloudy liquid and smell the lemons and lavender all over again.

"Perhaps the heat has affected you, in that worsted dress." She puts the glass on the floor and leaves the room. And I know full well she's gone to write a letter of complaint to Mrs. Thorpe, that I have done everything wrong—and shown myself to be puny and rude and a disgrace. No doubt my *bad blood* has shown itself.

I drink the lemonade, and it's like coming from a gray dream and feeling the world lift and rise around me. Calming. So that when I hear her step in the hall, I jump up and stand very straight beside the sink. As if I'm ready for work.

"You're better," she declares.

"The l-lemonade, ma'am," I stutter. I want to make amends by telling her how delicious it is but when I pause, Miss Acton leaps in.

"It made you unwell? Oh, that is terrible!" She frowns very severely and peers into the earthenware jug. "I think the lavender was a mistake. Perhaps cold milk and a dash of sherry would improve it . . ."

"No, ma'am," I say, quite desperate now. "It is the most delicious thing I have ever tasted and brought back such memories I was quite overcome. I'm very sorry, ma'am. I'm normally strong as an ox, ma'am."

She looks at me, very keen and solemn. This is it, I think. She'll ask me to leave now, on account of my impertinence. But she doesn't. She throws back her head and laughs, and I see her long pale throat with wisps of dark hair jigging around her ears.

"I think you and I shall get along very well," she says once she's stopped laughing. "Tell me, where else have you worked?"

I'm baffled and bewildered by her notion of us *getting along*, but Mrs. Thorpe prepared me for this question, so I answer quick as a flash. "I've been looking after my parents who've been in delicate health until now. My father fought against Napoleon, ma'am. I can carry coal and water, and I can clean grates and black stoves, and polish and dust and run a hem. And I can scrub vegetables and peel potatoes and chop kindling and lay fires."

"Can you read and write?" she asks, pushing a book toward me.

I nod, whereupon she asks me to open the book and read.

I turn the cover and see it's a book of recipes. All at once I feel a thrill run over me, as if there's a fire under my skin. But the fire blows up too quick, and turns to panic. "Ma'am, I have not read for some years."

"Go as slowly as you like," she says, all the time smiling in a most encouraging way.

I open the book and begin reading, very slowly and concentrating very hard. "'To dress a hare,'" I read. She nods and smiles and her eyes are warm and generous. "'Wash her in fair water, parboil her, then lay her in cold water. Then lard her and roast her. For sauce, take red wine, salt, vinegar, ginger, pepper, cloves, and mace, and put these together. Then mince onions and apples and fry them in a pan. Then put your sauce to them with a little sugar. And let them boil together and so serve it.'"

When I finish reading, there's a short silence until my stomach growls with hunger. My face scalds again, but Miss Acton just laughs and asks me where I learned to read so well.

"My mam taught me," I say. "She was most particular that I learn to read. My brother would not take to his letters, but I liked nothing more."

"You must have an excellent mother," she says, and her smile flows right across her lovely face.

I feel suddenly very tired, as if the reading has taken all the life from me.

"I think you will do very well," she says. "We cannot pay much, but would you accept five shillings a week?"

I am so blinded by this question that I freeze, like an idiot. It isn't that I don't believe her—although the house is so very grand they are surely rich as Croesus—but more that I am flummoxed at her question. Mrs. Thorpe said I would be informed of the wages and that I was to curtsy and say, "Thank you, ma'am." But I remember this too late and Miss Acton is speaking again, all flustered and concerned.

"The wages will rise, of course, as you become more familiar with the workings of the house. Perhaps we can stretch to a little more. I can see that it's not a vast wage, but . . ."

"Five shillings is very kind, ma'am," I say quickly, before she takes it away and writes to Mrs. Thorpe that I am full of cheek.

"Excellent. Would you like to see the room where you shall sleep? You will be with our housemaid, Hatty, who has come with us from Ipswich."

I look at her in alarm. Another question Mrs. Thorpe said nothing of.

"I'm sure it's very nice, ma'am."

"Good," she says and she puts her hand on my arm as if to steer me, gentle like, to the door. And the feeling of her hand upon my arm makes me come over peculiar, for no one has touched me with affection for so long. With Mam it's all tying and binding, or else she's shoving and prodding at me. And with Pa it's no different—either I'm bearing the weight of him or tugging at him, with the stir of his drunken breath in my face. But Miss Acton is so very clean, so warm and pure and orderly.

"There is one final thing," she says, as we enter the yard. My eyes go wide and stiff again, for surely now she has seen the truth of me—the *bad blood*.

"Yes, ma'am."

She pauses and her hand flutters at her throat. "We must find another way for you to address me."

"Yes, ma'am," I say, panicked. For I don't know what she means.

She laughs again, as if I've said something very funny. "You may address Mrs. Acton as 'Ma'am,' but would you be comfortable calling me 'Miss Eliza'?" She reaches out and touches me on my arm again with her long pale fingers, very quick and very light.

"Yes, ma'am," I say, shaken. She laughs and I see what a dunce I am. "Yes, Miss Eliza," I say, speaking in the voice I use on Mam, my Napoleon voice. It bursts from me of its own accord and when I hear the force of it, I clap my hand over my mouth. But Miss Eliza only nods and smiles. And her blue eyes sparkle like dewy forget-me-nots with the sun flashing over them.

I dance all the way home, through the stubbled cornfields and the copse of oak trees, everything bathed in soft green light. It's only when I turn the final corner that I remember Mrs. Thorpe told me to mention Jack—and how he works in the grandest kitchen in London. Oh, what a fool I am! My tongue was so tied by the beautiful Miss Eliza with her lemonade, and her kitchen all neat and gleaming like paradise, that Mrs. Thorpe's command flew straight out of my head. I decide not to tell Mrs. Thorpe. And nor shall I tell her how Miss Eliza touched me, like a friend. I put Mrs. Thorpe out of my head—along with her trailing dress which is scratching and prickling at every seam—and hurry to the cottage, hoping Pa has kept his promise and stayed off the drink and not murdered Mam.

CHAPTER NINE

ELIZA

VERY GOOD LEMON CREAMS

The eggs are still warm and stuck with feathers as I count them from the basket. I pour grated sugar from the earthenware jar, then take a freshly whetted knife and pare the rind from two lemons. The world slips away. I feel my eye, my nose, my palate yielding, and I think how satisfying it is to scrape at a lemon, to lose myself in its sharp bright song.

I have started to see poetry in the strangest of things: from the roughest nub of nutmeg to the pale parsnip seamed with soil. And this has made me wonder if I can write a cookery book that includes the truth and beauty of poetry. Why should the culinary arts not include poetry? Why should a recipe book not be a thing of beauty?

My thoughts come quickly and smoothly in the solitude of the kitchen, and as I beat the eggs I find myself comparing the process of following a recipe to that of writing a poem. Fruit,

herbs, spices, eggs, cream: these are my words and I must com-
bine them in such a way they produce something to delight the
palate. Exactly as a poem should fall upon the ears of its readers,
charming or moving them. I must coax the flavors from my
ingredients, as a poet coaxes mood and meaning from his words.
And then there is the writing itself. Like a poem, a recipe should
be clear and precise and ordered. Nothing stray or flabby or inexact. And yet the recipes I follow now are like the very worst
poems—sloppy, scrappy, disordered.

When Mr. Longman wrote to me with his terms, he divulged
a little more about the mysterious *lady*, author of the successful
but deeply frustrating *Domestic Cookery*. The *lady* (a Mrs. Maria
Rundell) has been dead some years. But before dying she sold
half a million copies of her cookery book, a fact underlined twice
by Mr. Longman in his letter. As if to say that is what he expects
from my modest efforts. Half a million readers!

I scan Mrs. Rundell's recipe a third time, with a flutter of irritation. Why didn't the wretched woman arrange the ingredients
in a simple list? It would be easier, I think, to list them myself
rather than reading and rereading the recipe over and over.

I shall write my recipes differently, I decide. I shall list the
ingredients separately—and with precise measurements. Yes—
with the most minute exactness! Surely women have enough to
juggle in their heads without having to memorize lists of ingredients as they work? And it is women I shall write for. Mr. Longman has been quite specific on this point: "Aspiring ladies from
the growing merchant classes wish to display their domestic

qualities at dinners and the like. They require assistance in the guidance of their cooks or so that they themselves may be coaxed into the kitchen for the pleasure of their husbands or to enable their husbands to entertain and impress important persons."

I sigh deeply, for Mr. Longman has yet to return my folio of poems despite my asking twice, despite my accepting his cookery book commission. I cut the lemons in two, then squeeze each half into the mixing bowl, crushing them until not a drop of juice remains—and until all thoughts of Mr. Longman have gone. My mind slides to Ann Kirby. Such an odd little creature. Plain. Freckled. Bony. Her collarbones jutting from a winter dress that positively ballooned around her. And her shoulders stooped and rounded, as though she'd spent her short life heaving sacks of coal. And yet able to read . . . and so very responsive to my lavender lemonade. As if she has a thread of poetry running through her. Her face, in all its childish hesitancy, revealed traits I like: honesty, curiosity, intelligence. There was something else about her too. A poignancy I can't explain. A feeling that we are united in some odd and inarticulate way. Mother objected, of course, demanding to know my reasons for hiring a girl who has never been in service. She stopped her complaints when I told her how very inexpensive Ann was, how her letter of recommendation came directly from a vicar.

"Wonderful news, Eliza dear!" Mother's trill interrupts my thoughts. "Our first boarders arrive on Monday. Colonel and Mrs. Martin, from Spitalfields in London, come to take the waters for his gout. Will you be ready for them?"

A nervous excitement spikes inside me. "I'm attempting jugged hare and lemon creams for luncheon, and spiced beef with dandelion leaf salad for dinner, followed by apple charlotte." I suck at my finger where lemon juice has made its way into a knife cut, and silently curse my clumsy hands that have slipped upon the bread rasp, the paste jigger, the nutmeg grater, the herb cutter. "If the dishes are good, I shall repeat them on Monday."

"Goodness, Eliza—your hands! They are chopped raw! Who will marry you with hands like that?"

I roll my eyes. "I'm not expecting any offers of marriage."

"But what if Colonel Martin has an eligible brother?" Mother pats her hair with her fingertips.

"I would rather be a hated old maid than marry a gouty old man who needs nursing."

"Oh, Eliza! An old maid has less value than a clod of dirt. Surely you want respect and dignity? Perhaps Colonel Martin will have a son who does not have gout." She sniffs and looks me up and down. "The blacksmith's wife is with child and apparently she is forty-three. Forty-three! Her hair is completely white, while yours is still a lovely shade of chestnut."

"If you leave me in peace, I can work on my cookery book which will give us an income quite independent of Colonel Martin and his possible sons and brothers." I crack an egg on the bowl's rim and watch the yolk and its white slip free. Not a shard of shell escapes, and for a second I feel inordinately happy at this minor accomplishment.

"And do you plan to devise your own recipes? Or are you simply plundering the work of others?"

"I'm teaching myself to cook and then I shall write to all our friends and acquaintances and ask them to donate their favorite recipes." My knuckles whiten beneath the whisk and the yolks spin a little faster around the bowl.

"So that all and sundry will know you have become a—a cook?" splutters Mother.

"And I shall create my own recipes," I continue, keeping my voice steady and even. I don't tell her I'm already combining, pairing, mixing things in my mind—fruits with spices, fresh fish with herbs, meat with wild leaves and cream—for I doubt she would understand.

"Well, my dear, when you write to *our* friends and acquaintances, I propose you tell them that we need a varied menu for our boarders. There's no reason to say any more than that." She folds her arms staunchly over her chest. "At least that is respectable."

"No, Mother. If I use their recipes I will credit them in my book. Unless they'd rather be anonymous." I keep my gaze on the eggs, lifting the whisk high into the air, then plunging it back into the bowl until my arm aches. "You must have things to prepare for Colonel and Mrs. Martin," I say at length, wishing she would go away.

"Hatty is settling into Tonbridge very well," she says. "But I think she will be happier when the scullery maid arrives and she has a friend."

I think of Ann . . . scrawny little Ann, rendered speechless by my lemonade. "And so will I," I say. "So will I."

CHAPTER TEN
ANN

ACTON GINGERBREAD

I arrive at Bordyke House on Sunday night, but there's no sign of Miss Eliza. Instead, an uppity housemaid takes me to the room that we're to share, up in the eaves.

"You may call me Hatty," she says, looking at me like a starving cat come across a mouse. "I've been in service before and this is my third job and I've come with the Acton family all the way from Ipswich, so I'm in charge here."

"In charge of me?" I ask, looking around the little attic room. There are two beds, very narrow but properly raised from the floor, with sheets and blankets. The window is small and looks over the carriage entrance. There's a washstand with a basin and jug, a chest where I'm to store my belongings, and a chamber pot with a faded green bird on the side.

"Of course," she says. "Where's your box? Ain't you been in service before?"

I feel so ashamed I open my mouth to lie, to say my box is coming later. But the lie won't come. I shake my head, mumble, feel my face scalding. Am I the only girl who has nothing of her own? Not even a change of clothes or shoes . . .

"No box? Every girl has a box."

"It's all in my bag," I point to the dirty canvas bag that contains my hairbrush, a set of rags for my monthlies, a cracked heel of soap, and a whittled stick for my teeth. "When can I meet the cook?"

"There ain't no cook here," says Hatty, with a little superior smirk. "There's only Miss Eliza and she won't be giving orders up here, will she?"

I frown, the shame of being without a box pushed aside by my confusion. Mrs. Thorpe was most definite about me working for a cook. "No cook? Who prepares the food?"

"Miss Eliza," says Hatty; and before I can close my mouth, which is hanging wide open, she tells me to get into bed because the first boarders arrive tomorrow and Ma'am wants us up at half past five.

As soon as I'm lying in bed, Hatty starts whispering, asking me questions about my family. Questions Mrs. Thorpe says I must never answer. "Why are you so late into service, Ann? Are your mother and father still alive, Ann?" I mumble and mutter until she starts on questions I can answer without telling any lies.

"How many of your brothers and sisters have died, Ann?"

"All seven except me and my brother, Jack." I don't say that four of them died of the sweats in a single weekend. I don't want to think about that now.

"Have you a fancy man, Ann?"

"No."

"Why not?"

"I don't know. Have you?"

"Yes, a boy in Ipswich. He works for a draper and can get any fabric you want. Also cotton thread in any color. D'you know everyone in Tonbridge, Ann?"

"No, not really. Just the vicar and his wife."

"Don't you have any friends here?"

"My brother, Jack, but he's in London."

Eventually Hatty falls asleep, right in the middle of an instruction about how I'm to do exactly as she says unless I'm in the kitchen with Miss Eliza. I listen to a scurrying creature in the rafters and try not to cry. Mr. Thorpe took Mam away today. To the new asylum, where he says everyone is very godly. Tomorrow Pa will work in the graveyard, I will work at Bordyke House and Mam will—what will Mam do? Mr. Thorpe says she'll have her own nurse who'll calm her when she has the terrors and protect her modesty when she tears at her clothing. Eventually I stop thinking about Mam, Pa, home, and I start thinking about Miss Eliza who is really a cook and not a lady at all. And I wonder why Mrs. Thorpe didn't explain this to me. When my thoughts stop churning, I listen for the scurrying creature but it's gone. I wish Hatty would snore, or toss and turn, or shout out in her sleep. Like Mam and Pa do. But she just lies there very still.

The next morning I creep down to the kitchen. Everything is neat and tidy, clean and polished and in its place. The glasses stand in lines upon a shelf, ranged in size from those no bigger than my thumb to those I suppose are for jelly or wine, cut to dazzle and with trailing plants etched around the rim. Above them are earthenware flagons and pewter jugs, not like Mam's, but with great curving handles. The earthenware has no cracks or chips and the pewter has a gleam that ours does not. Freshly oiled oak spoons, with carved handles, stand upright in enameled pots. On the table are three willow baskets: one contains two dozen brown hens' eggs, another has half a dozen white pullets' eggs, and a third—lined with red cloth and fresh straw—contains speckled eggs no bigger than my thumbnail. The eggs of plovers or quail, I think to myself with a rush of hunger. I haven't eaten an egg since Mam got ill and we sold our hens.

But then I catch sight of a newfangled range and fear pours into me. I put my finger to it and it's warm as toast. I'm gawping at the range and wondering why I didn't notice it before when Hatty appears and asks me why I haven't raked the ashes.

"Oh, Hatty," I whisper. "I've never seen one of these." I expect her to look all smug but she doesn't. Instead she kneels down and says Ma'am likes the cinders separated from the ashes and reused.

"You must put the ashes on the black currant bushes in the garden," she adds. "But first you move the fenders and the fire irons, throw in the damp tea leaves to keep the dust down, then it's the raking and sifting. After that you clean away the grease, then black and polish the stove." She opens a door at the bottom of the range and points inside. "The lead and turpentine and brushes are in there. But always do it early while the range is still warm so that a good shine comes up. Then you whiten the hearth and lay the fire. Miss Eliza likes coal for the range. Have you used coal before?"

I shake my head. At home we use gorse and cow dung from the common, which makes our cottage stink half to death, although Reverend Thorpe has said Pa can take the furze and pine cones from the graveyard now he's working. But I don't tell Hatty that, not only because I'm ashamed but because she might ask why the vicar is so particular about my family. And I'm not sure she'll believe Pa's answer—that he is a godly man. So I keep my lips tight shut.

"Are you still using a tinderbox at home?"

I nod.

"The Actons use matches. I'll show you how to strike one."

I've never struck a match before and when I scrape the stick, it flares red and blue, and shoots sparks everywhere, and a foul smell like a rotten egg bursts into the room.

"I shall be glad not to clean this range anymore," says Hatty, before telling me I must rise extra early on Fridays to clean the flues.

"And you do everything?" I ask, thinking of how big the house is, all the rooms and fireplaces and windows that must be kept clean.

"In Ipswich, there were seven of us and a butler. But something terrible happened—I'm not allowed to speak of it—and now there is just you and me. But Ma'am has promised more servants once the boarders arrive. Which is today, Ann!" And she claps her hands and beams at me, as if the boarders are a great gift to us all. "An army colonel and his wife with their own housemaid—so I won't need to empty and scrub their chamber pots. And perhaps they'll bring a boy." She winks at me when she says "boy," and I feel a flush travel up my neck and across my cheeks.

By the time I've finished the stove—which seems to take hours and hours and leaves my hands black as pitch—the clock strikes eight and Hatty changes her apron and says she must go to Ma'am. "Don't forget that I'm in charge and you're to do exactly as I tell you," she adds, all bossy again, as if she has slipped inside another skin. "Oh, and you can break your fast with bread and dripping from the larder, but not too much, mind."

I've been so busy I've barely thought of Mam. Or Pa on his first day in the graveyard. And I've certainly not thought of breakfast. But when Hatty leaves—having instructed me to scour the shelves in the scullery—I think of Mam out walking with her nurse in the asylum gardens that Mr. Thorpe says are flush with flowers. I told Mr. Thorpe that Mam doesn't like strangers or new places, but he said I was to put my trust in the Lord. And so I do. Even now, as tears spill from my eyes.

"Why, Ann, you are weeping," says Miss Eliza, who appears as silent and sudden as a barn owl.

I wipe my eyes and shake my head. "Oh no, Miss Eliza. I have ash in my eye," I say.

"No doubt it feels very strange for you here. But if you feel an ounce of sadness, you will tell me, won't you?"

How to answer? Without telling yet another lie? I nod and say nothing, just look at my feet as Mrs. Thorpe told me to. But I cannot keep my gaze upon my boots, with their water stains and frayed laces and the soles that are coming away from the uppers. So I raise my head and see her observing me from her forget-me-not eyes, with their long dark lashes.

"We shall be busy today," she says, putting her hand to her pale throat and stroking it in an absentminded way. "What are your thoughts on a stewed shoulder of veal with potato bou-lettes, followed by a baked plum pudding?"

Her question confuses me. What is a *boulette*? And how am I expected to have thoughts on a menu? "It sounds very good," I say, pressing my palm against my stomach to stop the growling.

"I think it's perfect for a colonel with gout," she says. "And perfect for our first day together, as the recipe is not too compli-cated. Why don't you start on the plum pudding?" She sees the terror in my eyes and gives a reassuring smile. "Find a loaf of stale bread, and then remove the crusts and grate it finely. Ev-erything's in there." She points to the larder. "My mother only has China tea for her breakfast which Hatty will make. You and I shall have a slice of cake a little later and I hope you will deign to give me your opinion on the flavoring."

As I go to the larder, fear grips my insides. Why aren't I carry-ing coal and water—as Mrs. Thorpe said I would? Mrs. Thorpe made no mention of cooking. Worse, she made no mention of *giving opinions on flavoring*. And then it strikes me. Mrs. Thorpe has mentioned Jack. And Miss Eliza has misunderstood, think-ing my brother has taught me all he knows. I'm about to rush from the larder and tell Miss Eliza everything—that my mother is as mad as a cuckoo, that my father is a cripple with a fondness for ale, that Jack does nothing but turn spits and skin rabbits, that I have done little more than plant potatoes and scrub chamber pots and other dirty work—when I notice the air is dizzy with syrupy sweetness. The scent comes from a bowl of fleshy purple berries, dusty with bloom and crawling with drunken wasps. For a moment I can't think straight. I want only to breathe in the perfume of these peculiar berries.

"Have you found the bread? It is next to the Turkey figs," calls out Miss Eliza. I stare at the little dusty fruits, with their splitting crimson seams. Jack has told me of figs and how his gentlemen diners eat them stewed with port wine and cream. But I imagined them small and wrinkled, like currants.

I find the bread and the grater and a knife. But when I scrape the bread against the grater, I'm clumsy and grate my fingertip so that blood drips into the bowl and soaks into the bread.

Miss Eliza asks me to weigh the crumbs and note the weight on a slate. "I'm very particular when it comes to weighing and measuring," she says. "I must have order and precision in everything. That way we keep the chaos of life at bay—don't you agree, Ann?"

I wish she would stop asking what I think, for it flummoxes me when I have a throbbing finger and so many other things to think about. But this question is particularly flummoxing because her life *is* ordered and beautiful and I don't see a bit of chaos anywhere. Chaos, I want to tell her, is when your mother doesn't know who you are and cannot control her insides and takes the knife to her own hair for no reason. And when your father must be pulled from your mother before he murders her. And when you have a stomach that hasn't been filled for several days. And when your memories are nothing but dying brothers and sisters and a father shaking and shouting in his sleep every night. But then I think of how her kitchen is like paradise, clean and neat. And perhaps this is what she means. And perhaps this is why I have always dreamed of being a cook, of taking edible things in all their messiness and turning them into tasty dishes. So I say, "Yes, Miss Eliza."

After that, we don't talk much until she brings out a ginger cake from the larder.

"An old family recipe," she says. "I've been experimenting with the quantities of cloves and Jamaica ginger. Tell me what you think." And she pushes a slice toward me. I try not to gobble it, for I am starving.

"The most important thing with this cake is to beat in every ingredient, one by one, with the back of a wooden spoon," she says. "Simply throwing everything in together and then beating produces a most unsuccessful cake. I know because my first attempt was as heavy as a brick—quite indigestible!" She gives a rueful smile and asks if I think it needs more ginger.

I feel the crumb, dense and dark, melt on my tongue. My mouth floods with warmth and spice and sweetness. As I swallow, something sharp and clean seems to lift through my nose and throat until my head swims.

"I can see you like it." Miss Eliza watches me and smiles.

And then I blurt something out. Something I know Reverend

Thorpe and his wife would not like. But it's too late, the words jump from my throat of their own accord. "I can taste an African heaven, a forest full of dark earth and heat."

The smile on Miss Eliza's face stretches a little wider and her eyes grow brighter. And this gives me the courage to ask a question that's nothing to do with my work. "What is the flavor that cuts through it so keenly, so that it sings a high note on my tongue?"

She stares at me with her forget-me-not eyes. "It's the lightly grated rinds of two fresh lemons!"

"It's very good." I want to say it could take a spot more ginger, but that would be rude and not my place. And Miss Eliza is so pleased I've spotted the lemon rind that she doesn't press me for my *opinion on flavoring.*

The rest of my day is spent helping Hatty prepare for the arrival of the boarders and then helping Miss Eliza as she makes dinner. I can tell she's nervous because she moves in a quick anxious way and becomes a little red around the face. "My first real diners," she says several times, and more to herself than to me. She has me chopping rosemary, sage, and thyme for the veal. Then I measure and weigh ingredients for a sweet sauce she is making to accompany the plum pudding. The sauce is from a recipe that vexes her, for it has no weights so she must guess them. I pour a wineglass of Madeira; weigh out butter, sugar, and flour; then juice a lemon and grate a spoonful of nutmeg. Miss Eliza dips a salt spoon in and out of the veal stew, tasting and adding a little more cayenne and mace and extra salt grains, and talking to herself in a low voice. In the warmth of the kitchen, with my hands busy and the smell of fresh nutmeg blowing up from the table, I forget about Mam and Pa. And for the first time in years I feel joy. And the feeling is even better than sitting in the quiet of church with the drone of Mr. Thorpe and all the painted golden angels looking down on me.

CHAPTER ELEVEN
ELIZA

ROAST CALF'S LIVER WITH LEMON PICKLE

There is something about Colonel Martin and his wife that I do not like. A coldness at the backs of their eyes. Mother is all over them like melted butter on a dish of parsnips. When I say they lack warmth, she snaps at me, accusing me of having airs and graces that I'm no longer entitled to.

"You can stay in the kitchen," she says haughtily. "But be discreet. I can't have our boarders thinking we're unable to afford a proper cook."

I bridle at her words, for haven't my meals been as good as any *proper cook's*? "It's a good thing I prefer it in the kitchen," I reply tersely. While the Martins take their carriage every day to Tunbridge Wells, I cook and write. Mainly recipes, some of which I compose over and over, for I am determined they be not only accurate and precise but neat and elegant. Sometimes I put my recipes aside and practice a line or two of poetry. It is this—the

constant switching between verse writing and recipe writing—
that keeps my mind sharp and my ear attuned. So that I catch the
rhythm, the cadence, of every line, be it verse or cookery book.
But as the days go by, the words come so swiftly, so smoothly, I
know something else is at play. The first time this thought strikes
me, I look up and see Ann. And another peculiar thought comes:
it is she, Ann, that is causing this surge of inspiration.

I had expected some disarray from her intrusion into my solitude. Instead her presence has set me alight. She is such a slither
of a girl. Like a thinly flaked almond. Her shoulder blades jutting
like stunted wings. Her large luminous eyes lighting up from
pockets of darkness, like church candles. Her boots peeling away
from their soles . . . And yet she has a palate capable of distin-
guishing the subtlest of flavors. And it seems to me that her looks
and gestures show meaning in the smallest and commonest of
things. I cannot explain it but I feel it beneath my skin—and
suppose it to be a wave of misplaced affection that must be kept
hidden from Mother's prying eyes.

In spite of this, we quickly settle into a daily routine. We prepare meals for Colonel Martin and his wife, starting at first light
so that we have time to make a dish two or three times if need
be. Then Ann cleans up and I write. On our first day together I
went to the drawing room to compose a recipe for a short crust
paste that we had repeatedly undercooked, then charred to a cinder, wasting a pound of best beef kidney suet in the process. My
nerves were on edge and the words refused to come, not helped by
Mother snapping about the reek of burned grease. So I returned
to the kitchen and wrote at the pine table while Ann scrubbed

and swept around me. The slop of water, the scrape of broom over stone, the scatter of sand and salt, soothed me, and now I pen my recipes only in the kitchen. Afterward I take a fractious luncheon with Mother in the dining room, and then Ann and I spend our afternoons preparing dinner. If the dishes are not too painstaking, my mind is able to swim between verse and recipe.

A few days after the arrival of the Martins I decide to submit a new poem to one of the more literary annuals, *The Keepsake*, which has the most embellished and loveliest of covers. I send my poem by express mail coach, with a feeling of . . . accomplishment . . . satisfaction. Afterward, as I scribble a short recipe for roast calf's liver with lemon pickle, I see the poetry in my words and feel a tenuous thrill. A recipe can be as beautiful as a poem, I think. Useful and beautiful. It doesn't have to be a graceless list of barked instructions. *Take a fine white sound liver . . . steep it overnight with good vinegar and a sliced onion and branches of savory herbs laid over it . . . roast it on a clear fire . . .*

For the first time since Father fled to Calais, I feel a sense of purpose, a sense of being myself. As if I have been given some tacit permission to *exist*. Perhaps I'm not intended to live out some dim and broken life. Perhaps creating recipes can sustain and nourish me, just as writing verse does. Perhaps I can be more than an *old maid*.

I'm so wrapped up in my work, in keeping tightly to the kitchen and my bedchamber, I barely notice the Martins and I forget entirely their peculiar lack of warmth. Only later do I wish I'd paid more attention, been a little less consumed by my own resurrection. But by then it is too late.

CHAPTER TWELVE
ANN

A JUG OF WATER

For three days, Miss Eliza gives me instructions and I follow them to the letter. I scrape the sugar from its loaf, scrub the vegetables of mud and insects, scour the sink with sand, and spread the tea leaves for drying. I fetch water and firewood and fish from the market. I slice and sift and grate and pluck. I stoke and sweep and black the range. I wash and dry and polish. And when I get a second to myself, I eat. I eat pie crusts burned to a crisp and fit only for the pig. I drink cream that has curdled and is intended for the cat. I steal spoonfuls of oversalted sauces so that my tongue withers in my mouth. I eat the leftovers and lick the cooking spoons and even wipe my tongue around the batter basin. I cannot help myself for my insides are gnawed half to death from hunger and I've never seen so much food. Miss Eliza is very absorbed in her work and doesn't notice if a crumb goes missing or a wooden spoon is licked clean. Sometimes she stops and stares at me. But not because she's caught me chewing at a blackened pie paste from the pig bin or on Colonel Martin's leftover crust of bread. More as if she's wondering why I'm in her kitchen. Or who I am.

Every now and then Ma'am appears with words of praise from the boarders. And me and Miss Eliza swell with pride. Only once does a kidney pie return, half-eaten. Miss Eliza sees me ogling it, no doubt with drool upon my lips. She pushes it toward me and says I may eat it if I wish. The gravy is so meaty, so rich with rosemary and bone marrow and red currant jelly, the whole world shrinks to nothing but my mouth. Afterward my stomach is hard with the cramps. And bloated tight. I must remember not to guzzle, I think.

One evening, just as I'm collecting up the peelings for the stockpot, Ma'am rushes in. "Hatty has been taken sick. Ann, you must go to the dining room and see the Martins have everything they need. Oh, Eliza, we are so woefully short of servants. This will not do!"

"Put on Hatty's slippers and change to a clean apron," Miss Eliza tells me. "Then go straight to the dining room and pour the Martins their water. And be careful not to spill any."

She tucks a sprig of drying lavender into the neckline of my dress, saying it'll disguise the kitchen smell of me, and gestures me out with a flap of her hand.

I go to the dining room, feeling most unsure of myself. Colonel and Mrs. Martin are sitting at a round table, covered with a linen cloth on which has been laid heavy silver cutlery, glasses of various sizes, striped napkins, a little dish of toothpicks, and some silver cruets. Mrs. Martin eyes me very strangely, as if she thinks I'm come to steal her jewels. Then she examines her hands in great detail. Colonel Martin looks at me and his eyes travel up and down me, as if he is measuring me by eye for a new frock.

No one has told me how to speak to boarders. So I pick up the water jug and say, "Water?" It comes out more abrupt than I planned, for the line of glasses has flummoxed me. Which one is for water and which is for wine? Mrs. Martin ignores me and continues to look at her fingernails with great concentration. But Colonel Martin points to a plain straight-sided glass and nods in a kindly way. As if he knows this is my first time waiting at table. I start pouring the water, very carefully and very slowly. And then I freeze. Something is moving up the back of my leg. Chewing, squeezing at my thigh. I stay very still, my heart pounding, my hand gripping the jug, which is poised and trembling above the cruets. A voice in my head tells me to move away, to walk around the table and fill Mrs. Martin's glass. But I don't. Because another voice springs into another bit of my head, telling me not to cause offense, not to hurt the feelings of our boarders. I'm saved from indecision by the colonel.

"To the brim, girl. To the brim!" He motions at the glass with his fat, veined hand. His other hand—for so it is—stays on the back of my thigh. His fingers have stopped searching into my flesh, so I wonder if it's all a mistake. An accident. Perhaps he doesn't realize his hand is on my leg. Perhaps if I was to shake off his hand—like a man brushes off an insect or a dog shakes off a flea—he would realize and be embarrassed, and return his hand to his own leg.

I know my arm is shaking—indeed all of me is trembling, like water after a stiff breeze has rolled over it—so I pour very slow, concentrating on the lip of the jug, keeping it centered over his glass even as it wobbles in my grip.

All of a sudden I feel his fingers again. Crawling up the back of my thigh, and moving in rough circles over my behind. Then he squeezes so hard the jug lurches in my hand and water leaps from the spout in a great rush, all over the table. It happens so quick, and the combination of my limbs set rigid and the hammering of my heart and all the little voices in my head, mean I lose my nerve and stand, deaf and dumb, like a pillar of salt, even as the water seeps into Ma'am's best linen.

"Oh, clumsy girl!" Mrs. Martin looks up, a darting, glittering look.

"Now, now, Jane," chides Colonel Martin, whose straying hand is conspicuously stroking his whiskers. "I suspect she is new to the establishment." He takes his napkin from his collar and dabs at the spilled water. Then he waves it at me and asks me to bring a fresh one from the kitchen.

Still, I cannot move. The voice in my head tells me I must apologize but my mouth refuses to open.

"Get along, girl! A fresh napkin!" Mrs. Martin's glowering words bring me swiftly to my senses, so I snatch the napkin from the colonel and scamper to the linen chest in the hall.

When I return, Ma'am is talking to Mrs. Martin about the weather. I pray she hasn't noticed the wet tablecloth, but she bustles off, saying she is going to the cellar for their wine. I bob a clumsy curtsy and offer Colonel Martin the new napkin. He points at his collar, as if he wants me to tuck it in for him. Then he leans his chest away from the table and I shake out the napkin, all fingers and thumbs. Keeping my arms outstretched I try to fold the corner of the napkin into his collar, fumbling like a blind man and waiting to feel his hand on my leg. But his hands are in his lap, so I edge a little closer and push the napkin right into his collar. My fingers scrape his neck, which is red and hot and doughy. Just as the napkin is securely in place and I'm about to step away, I see something from the corner of my eye. His manhood has come free from his breeches and is standing stiff and pink beneath the table. I shrink back, my face flooding and burning with heat.

At that very moment, Ma'am returns with a bottle of wine. Colonel Martin tugs the napkin from his neck, cool as a cucumber, and drops it on his lap. "Is she new?" He jerks his head at me. My whole body trembles. What if he complains about me? What if Ma'am sees the water stain on her best linen? Mrs. Martin looks at me through eyes screwed so tight they're like peppercorns.

"Ann is usually in the scullery, Colonel," says Mrs. Acton. "But our regular serving maid is indisposed. I do hope she hasn't caused you any trouble? I do hope everything is to your satisfaction?"

"Oh very much so," says the colonel.

"I'll get a decanter," says Ma'am and she is gone, leaving me alone with the terrible colonel and his peculiar wife.

"Over here!" The colonel beckons me to him. I move very gingerly, for now I know why Hatty has been taken sick. "My napkin has fallen to the floor and my gout restricts my movement. Could you . . . ?" He points at his napkin, lying crumpled beneath the table. I glance in the direction of Mrs. Martin, but she is staring very hard at the window.

I kneel down and pick up the napkin, being very careful where I look. Then I stand up, throw the napkin on his lap, and run to the kitchen.

Chapter Thirteen
Eliza

Pigeons Roasted in Vine Leaves

I wake early, my eyes snapping open. In those first blurred seconds I wonder why my blood seems so wildly alight in my veins. Then I recall the previous evening—the success of my most ambitious dinner yet. Colonel and Mrs. Martin ate everything, mopping up the veal gravy with slabs of bread and requesting second helpings of plum pudding. The colonel smacked his lips with satisfaction and declared my Madeira sauce "the best wine sauce I have ever tasted with a sweet pudding." I know this because Mother hovered anxiously at the dining room door, eavesdropping.

I stretch and smile to myself. I didn't tell Mother the sauce recipe was almost entirely mine: the orange zest, the extra egg yolk, the little touches that made it so distinctive. Ann suggested the nutmeg, and she was right. It provided an extra depth and spiced sweetness . . .

The sun pushes its warm saffron rays though the shutter slats so they fall in stripes across the counterpane. For a moment I feel quite inexplicably happy, a feeling of lightness—a bird-in-the-air feeling. And why shouldn't I? My recipes are working. I can cook as well as I can write. The poems I sent to *The Keepsake* are among the best I've ever written. The kitchen, which I thought to be my jailer, has inspired me in ways I never imagined. Even the ill-composed recipes of former cooks have inspired me, enabling me to sniff out a great dish of my own. Like a dog that smells a body buried in the snow and coaxes it back to life with its warm breath.

And then there's the sheer joy of writing recipes that sing! I smile again and wonder if perhaps I should pen poems about cooking or food or eating. But no—that would be hopeless. Mr. Longman would laugh in my face. I can hear him now . . . *No, no, no . . . Poems are the preserve of fine feelings . . . And no one has fine feelings in a kitchen, Miss Acton . . .*

How strange this world is—that no woman must admit to the pleasures of the table. She must prepare the table, of course. But without feeling. And she must eat of it—if only to live— but without expressing any pleasure in the process. For us of the fairer sex, food must be merely functional.

This chain of thought returns me to our boarders: What shall I treat the colonel and his dour wife to today? Pigeons. And tiny peas fragrant as flowers. The last peas of the year. And the small-est potatoes I can find, poached, then buttered and sprinkled with coarse salt. I stretch out beneath my sheet and it comes again—the bird-in-the-air feeling, the swallow-on-the-wing feeling. Only this time I hear its song too: *I am, I am, I am.*

I get up, push back the shutters, and let the light flood in. I have a sudden urge to fill my room with autumn branches— rose hips, scarlet-and-gold leaves, the last bright greenery of the year. But then I look around my room and my joy slips clean away. The uncluttered spinsterish emptiness of it . . . reminding me that spinsters are living confessions of failure. And that little chiding voice pipes up. *Your poems, your writing . . . all conceit and pride and immodesty.* No doubt my poems will be returned to me today . . . *Imposter . . . Imposter . . .* My wings clipped. Again. My punishment for craving an audience.

When I get to the kitchen, Ann is on her knees, scrubbing hard at the oil stains on the flagstones. The dewy soles of her boots hang loose and darkly damp, and on the table is a basket of rose hips. The girl must have been up since before dawn. My eye slips to the range, but it's been newly blacked and laid, and the hearth is swept clean.

"You've picked rose hips?"

"Yes, miss. I thought you might be wanting to make a syrup. Mam always made it in September when the hips were fresh." She looks up, her eyes like two dark holes.

A sharp lump rises in my throat. I swallow it and say, "As soon as you've served breakfast to the colonel and his wife I want you to go directly to William Gale's shoe shop, and get yourself some boots."

Ann gapes at me.

"I know you haven't been paid yet, but I will buy your boots. Think of them as a gift."

"Oh, I c-can't do that," she stammers. "I can't accept such a generous gift, Miss Eliza."

"Well, I insist. Would you disobey your mistress?"

"What about Hatty?"

"She doesn't need new boots and you do."

"I mean, won't she be serving Colonel and Mrs. Martin today?"

I tip the rose hips into a large bowl, tasting them on my mind's tongue . . . folding in thyme . . . or rosemary . . . or would a hint of something more exotic work? A stick of cinnamon? The quick dip of a vanilla pod? I try to recall the rose hip syrup Mrs. Durham used to make and a rich French rose hip preserve—with apples? elderberries?—I tasted a decade ago.

"Will Hatty be serving today, miss?"

I sigh at her intrusion. Summoning flavors from memory and combining them imaginatively on my tongue requires concentration. One interruption and the flavor—so fleetingly recalled—is lost entirely. "I know you weren't expecting to be in the dining room, but we're a small private establishment and we must all pull together. Even Mrs. Acton must overcome her prejudices and help serve at table."

"I—I don't think I'm so good at it," Ann mumbles into the soapy flagstones.

"Well, let's wait and see if Hatty is recovered. Did you see her this morning?"

"I was up before she was, Miss Eliza. I haven't seen her." She buries her face in the scrubbing brush.

"The Martins won't be down before nine, but you can set the

breakfast table. The porcelain cruets at breakfast and don't forget the sugar bowl."

"And dinner?"

Her question pleases me. "I am thinking the exact same thing,
Ann. Your culinary curiosity is such a delight! A brace of pigeons
came last night and is hanging in the cellar. I'll need you to pluck
them." How shall I prepare them? Juniper . . . sage . . . possibly
an apple sauce. Or could I use the rose hip jelly?

"It's not my place, Miss Eliza, but . . ." Ann stands up, hopping
from one foot to another as if she is perched on hot cinders.

"You know how to pluck game birds, I presume?" My tone
is brusquer than intended, but I need to concentrate and Ann's
hopping is distracting me.

"Yes, b-but what about pigeons wrapped in vine leaves? Only
I saw a vine in the garden and . . ." Her voice peters out as she
disappears into the scullery with the pail of dirty floor water.

I stare at her departing back. But I don't see her. I see an image
from my past, formless at first, then filling out with color, smell,
sound . . . the pruned twigs of vines alight and burning . . . an
iron grill, roughly hammered . . . someone pulling the innards
from birds—larks, gulls, pigeons . . . a basket of fresh green vine
leaves . . . An ache rolls up beneath my ribs.

Ann returns, the pigeons swinging from her scrawny hand,
and looks at me with alarm. "Are you all right, Miss Eliza?"

"I ate meats roasted with vine leaves in France." I regret my
words immediately for I have no desire to relive those fren-
zied days. Before Ann can ask any further questions, I say, "But
enough of that. Why do you suggest vine leaves?"

"My brother, Jack, has seen it. He works for a Monsieur Soyer who comes from France."

I look at Ann for a long time, my fingers slowly circling my temples as I try and remember Mrs. Rundell's instructions for preparing pigeons. "When they're plucked, remove the heads, and cut their toes at the first joint. Then fetch me some vine leaves, the largest you can find."

Ann disappears into the scullery, the soles of her boots flapping so generously I see the blistered skin of her feet. The girl has no stockings on! I wonder what sort of mother sends her daughter into service with broken boots and no stockings. But as I think this, a shutter closes in my mind, as if it is too cramped to dwell on thoughts like this. "And yarn," I call out. "When you are measured for new boots, ask Mr. Gale for stocking yarn."

My mind veers back to roasted pigeon. And from pigeon, I travel effortlessly, unrestrainedly back to France . . . the pots of rillettes fragrant with garlic, the boned forelegs of ham yellowed with bread crumbs, the blood puddings curled up like snakes, the terrines and pâtés, the sausages from Lyons and Arles, the jowls of salmon cooked à la génoise, the hundreds of cheeses resplendent beneath their glass bells, the perfumed melons and honeyed apricots and . . . I shake my head, returning my runaway thoughts to roasted pigeon . . . each must be stuffed with a pat of butter, but should the pat be rolled in minced parsley or cayenne?

CHAPTER FOURTEEN
ANN

FRESH BREWED COFFEE

After my *encounter* with the colonel, I tossed and turned all night. Hatty slept sound as a board. No sign of sickness. No sweats or moans. No squatting for hours over the chamber pot. Not even the smell of sickness on her breath.

But the next morning, as I'm wrestling with vine leaves in the garden and praying I won't be called on to serve at table again, she arrives all harried, her hair flying from beneath her cap, her fingers fumbling at her apron strings.

"You haven't forgotten I'm in charge, have you?" She crouches beside me, a sizzle in her eye.

"I thought you were sick?"

"Of course I ain't sick." She gives a most careless toss of her head.

"So does that mean you're in charge of the colonel?"

She looks at me, triumphant. "He showed you his pork sausage and chestnuts, didn't he?"

As relief rushes through me, all my fear and loneliness fall away. "Is that why you ran off?"

"Yes! I know his sort. Likely that's why they arrived with no maid. And so now I must scrub out their pots and lay their fire and hang their clothes and carry their water—everything!"

I frown, confused. "You pretended to be ill so that I would have to see his—his sausage?"

"They like it when that happens," she says, her face flushed and shining with the drama of it all. "It's part of their little game. And we must egg him on before he gets his comeuppance."

I snip at the vine leaves in a fog of *not understanding*. What is she talking about?

"Without the boarders we won't get no wages, so we must wait until he pays his bill. Then we'll teach him a lesson. For now, keep your eyes above table and don't be frightened." Her nose gives a little twitch and I'm reminded of Septimus when the smell of meat is in the air.

"I've seen my pa's," I say, not wanting to be the little innocent, the dumb village girl. "And my brother's."

"But not like that, surely?"

"Course not! But I've seen bulls and dogs."

"But not at table, you fool."

She has a point. "No, but if Ma'am were to see, surely she would ask him to leave?"

"Oh, he's too clever for that. They only flash their sausages at little frightened serving girls."

"And what of poor Mrs. Martin?" I ask, feeling a prickle of sympathy for his wife, that she must sit there while he fiddles with himself and have no idea of his dirty ways.

Hatty snorts. "She's no *poor Mrs. Martin*."

"Why doesn't she put a stop to it, then?" I ask, puzzled, and thinking of all the times Pa and I had to tie Mam up to stop her undressing in public. And now she's locked up in a lunatic asylum, while Colonel Martin is dining out and taking the waters with gentlemen and ladies from London.

"It'll suit her to turn a blind eye. Anyway, I'll be serving from now on." She stands up and sighs, as if her earlier boldness is slipping away. So I ask her what exactly she plans to do for his *comeuppance*, as she calls it.

"I can't tell you." She puts her finger to her lips. "But there's nothing to be afraid of now I have a plan."

Then she leans in and gives me a quick hug. A small thing but it makes me forget the colonel altogether. I'm still smiling when I return with the vine leaves.

"Ah," says Miss Eliza. "I see time with nature makes you joyful."

I don't know what to say, but she's smiling brightly and I'm still grinning like a buffoon, so I nod and think to myself, *I have a friend . . . I have a friend . . . and no more serving at table either!*

"Colonel and Mrs. Martin want coffee today, and you shall make it," she announces. "Warm the coffee berries in a stewpan high over the fire and keep turning them."

I've never seen a coffee berry, but she has a stone jar of them; and as they roast over the fire, a wonderful smell—dark and brooding—fills the kitchen. When she crushes them in her special grinding box, I long to taste this berry that smells of the forest, of leather and honey. And something else . . . which I think is hazelnuts, like those Mam once picked and cracked between two rocks.

All the time, Miss Eliza is telling me what a disgrace it is that no one can make coffee in the right way. "There's no economy in cheaper berries . . . and they should always be roasted and ground at the very last minute." She gives a final heave of the handle on her grinding box and adds, as if it's an afterthought, "The milk must be boiling and the cream must be very fresh and cold."

I'm still thinking of Mam cracking hazelnuts when Hatty comes for the coffeepot and winks at me in a most obvious way. She disappears in a whirl of banging doors and steam, and I feel a shiver of excitement—whatever is she up to?

As I clean out the stewpan, Miss Eliza pours some of the thick dark liquid into one of her porcelain cups that is no taller than my little finger. She stirs it very slowly and then asks, "With what do you think Monsieur Soyer would stuff his pigeons?"

I think very hard and wish I'd asked more questions of Jack when he last came. "Perhaps just some butter," I say eventually.

She smiles at me, one of those smiles that sweeps over me and makes me think I am walking on a cushion of warm rosy air. "I shall roll a nut of new butter in cayenne, I think. Or we could

stuff them with small mushrooms and offer them with a mushroom sauce. And shall we serve them on crisp fresh watercress?"

I never know if she is talking to me or to herself, but I nod
anyway. She's about to finish her coffee when she sees me staring at it. "Would you like a sip?"

Mrs. Thorpe's voice crowds in upon my head: *remember your
place . . . remember your place.* I ignore it. "Yes please, miss."

She pushes the little porcelain cup toward me and watches as
I taste. Bitter, rich, slightly grainy on my tongue. An image of
what a coffeehouse might be like comes into my head . . . all the
gentlemen in their colored stockings, the rustle of newspapers,
the smell of pipe tobacco, the heads buried in talk and books.
Jack has told me of coffeehouses, and theaters, and the carriages
of gentlefolk that race through the streets of London. And now
my mind is racing in the same way.

"What are you thinking?" asks Miss Eliza. And I tell her I'm
imagining a coffeehouse. She smiles and says, in her gleaming
voice, "Let's see if the good colonel finds our coffee to his liking.
He is from London, so no doubt he's accustomed to the very
best."

I wonder if he's waving his sausage and chestnuts in Hatty's
face this very minute. Then I think of Mrs. Martin, and how she
must sit there while he does it, feigning ignorance. Something
sickly shifts in the pit of my stomach.

When Hatty brings the coffeepot back to the kitchen and
says the colonel sends his compliments to the chef, Miss Eliza
does a few dainty steps around the table.

Later, when I'm taking the ash to the black currant bushes, I pass the colonel and Mrs. Martin climbing into their curtained carriage. I stare at her large round rump disappearing up the steps and wonder if she feels the shame I felt when Mam disrobed in the fields. Or the feeling of helplessness when I knew I could not stop her. How would Reverend Thorpe advise Mrs. Martin? I wonder . . . But after she has settled herself among the carriage cushions, she turns to the window and sees me standing there with the ash gusting into my face. She shoots me a look of venom, then her lip curls and she turns away. Leaving me feeling small and despised.

I summon back the taste of Miss Eliza's coffee. And as it broods upon my tongue, I feel my mood restored. Jack was wrong when he said God is in a crust of bread. God, I think, blasphemously, is in a sip of coffee.

CHAPTER FIFTEEN
ELIZA

A COMPOTE OF WILD BULLACES
WITH THICK CREAM

When the letter comes, I slip it into my bodice, tie on my bonnet, and tell Ann I'm off to collect bullaces. I cannot open it under Mother's prying, disparaging eyes or Hatty's meddlesome stare. Besides, I want to open my letter in a country lane, where only flocks of finches will bear witness to this momentous occasion. Because this is my moment of truth. If *The Keepsake* wants my poem, I shall persevere. And perhaps I shall become a published poet after all. If not, my life in verse is over.

When Bordyke House is no longer in view and the town—with its sprawl of mills and tanneries and brick works—is left behind, I tear open the envelope. My eyes race across the few lines . . . *A most charming poem . . . We would be delighted to print it . . . Many of our regular poetesses publish either as "A Lady" or "Anonymous" . . .*

But married or maiden names are, of course, acceptable . . . We are un-able to offer a fee of any kind . . . Yours sincerely.

I raise my face to the sky and sing, "Yes! Yes! Yes!" A startled pigeon beats its wings and flaps in an upward direction, as if carried by the current of my voice. I glance along the wooded path, see that no one is in attendance, and chant aloud, "I *am* a poet!" My words have such weight and heft I could reach out and pluck them from the very air. Finches flit from the hedgerow, and in their chirpings I seem to hear an echo of myself: *I am . . . I am . . . I am.*

There is such a spring in my step, it's as if I walk on whipped meringue. *Charming,* I think. My poem is deemed *charming.* When the exultation fades, I look at the letter again. But on a second reading I am struck by something else entirely. *Anony-mous? A Lady? My married name?* E. Acton, I think. Ernest . . . Edmund . . . Edward . . . Edgar. Should I take my brother's name, Edgar Acton? Anger and indignation flare inside me. Why must I creep around in disguise? Why must I efface myself? "Eliza Ac-ton," I say aloud. As if in affirmation the finches start up their noisy chorus . . . *I am . . . I am . . . I am.*

When I return to the kitchen, I cannot hold my tongue. I go to the scullery, where Ann is scouring the pots and pans, and put my basket of bullaces beside the sink. "Ann, do you like poetry?"

She blinks, takes a fresh handful of sand from the bucket, and starts scouring the fish kettle. "I've not had much time for it."

"No, no, of course not," I say hastily. "But would you like to learn?"

"Learn poetry, miss?" She repeats my words as if she's a bit slow-witted this morning.

"I've had some good news." I pause, drumming up the courage to say the words aloud to another human being. Then they rush from me, without any finesse. "I'm a poet!"

"You, miss? A poet?" Her voice is so full of veneration, I could fall to her feet. Except her feet are in a puddle of cold water, shiny with grease.

"An annual called *The Keepsake* wants to publish one of my poems." I can barely keep the pride from my voice.

"That's very good, miss," she says, resuming her scouring.

"Yes, it is," I agree. "And I'd like to teach you poetry, Ann."

She nods, then asks what I'd like done with the bullaces.

Normally, this would send my mind into a tumult of flavors and tastes. But I'm too intoxicated by my own poetic success. I bat at the air and say, "Oh, something will come to me, don't worry!"

"How about a simple compote, miss?"

I'm so taken aback at her using the word *compote*—and at how unexpectedly right it sounds on her lips—that I'm lost for words. All my poetic pride ebbs away.

"With thick cream and a dusting of cinnamon," she adds.

"Indeed," I say. And my voice comes out flat, as if her talk of bullaces has taken all the glow from my moment of glory.

CHAPTER SIXTEEN
Ann

A SIMPLE SPONGE CAKE

A few days later I'm sent to the post office to collect two packages. One is large and heavy, with corners that have burst through the brown paper, so I know it's books. The other is thin and flimsy, but the address has been written in a very fine hand with flourishes and inky tails on all the letters. I hurry home and find Miss Eliza in the kitchen, writing in a little notebook. Whether she is writing poems or recipes I can't tell, for her face is very still and calm, but when she sees the thin package her face falls and all the light goes from her eyes.

She opens it while I'm busying myself with my cap, which has slipped half off my head. I watch her from beneath my lashes and feel a great relief when her eyes brighten again and her beautiful lips curve into a smile.

"My collection of poems, returned at last," she says.

I wait, hoping she will start to read aloud from them. But she doesn't. She flicks through them and, as she does so, her smile fades. From the hall comes the sound of Ma'am's heels on the flagstones and, quick as a whip, Miss Eliza slips her poems beneath the breadboard.

"I come bearing good news," says Ma'am, patting at the jet crucifix she wears always at her neck. "Colonel and Mrs. Martin are delighted with their rooms and with your cooking. They want to extend their stay for another week."

My heart falls as I think of Hatty, who must now endure still more of the colonel's hands upon her *arse* (as she calls it) and his endless fumblings below table. And how can she deliver his *comeuppance* if he extends his stay on and on? But then Ma'am says something that makes me anxious.

"Mrs. Thorpe is paying us a visit this morning and I'd like you there, Eliza. Not lurking in the servants' quarters."

Miss Eliza nods and agrees, but I'm swilling with nerves. Does Mrs. Thorpe have news of Mam? Or Pa? Or worse . . . far worse . . . Has the asylum refused to keep Mam? Has she run away and not been found? All these thoughts rush through my head in a great torrent.

Ma'am points at the unopened parcel still sitting on the table. "Not more books, surely?"

Miss Eliza picks up the package, unties the string, and pulls the paper off. Even as my mind spins, I notice her fingers working at the twine—so long and white with their nails of the palest pink, like rosebuds.

"Do you not have anything to do, Ann?" says Ma'am. "If there's no kitchen work, you can dust the drawing room and make it fit for Mrs. Thorpe."

I have plenty of work, but I get the feather duster from the scullery and as I do so I hear Miss Eliza explaining each new cookery book.

"This one is by a *professed cook* . . . and this one is from a Mr. Henderson . . . but what I find so objectionable is the great quantities these cooks require. Listen to this . . . a simple sponge cake." She starts to read aloud. "'Take twenty-four eggs' . . . How many private families need a cake on this scale? These are for feast days and nothing more!" She slams the book closed.

Whereupon Ma'am asks, in a strained voice, "Why must you purchase these books if you cannot use their recipes, my dear?"

"I learn from them," says Miss Eliza. "I've drawn up a list of people who might donate a favorite recipe. I have a lady who is renowned for her Jewish dinners and—"

And then Ma'am interrupts Miss Eliza, in a voice as cold as iron. "Surely you don't intend to include Jewish food? English families will not want Jewish food—of that I am certain!"

I shuffle past them, my head bowed and my fingers wrapped tight around the feather duster. The air is so thick with tension you could run a blade through it. I dash upstairs to the colonel's rooms, where I know Hatty is airing the beds.

"Hatty," I hiss. "What does 'Jewish' mean?"

"It's a religion," she says, not sounding very sure of herself.

"Do they eat differently from us?" I ask, baffled.

She pounds her fists into a pillow, then looks at me all quizzical. "I don't know about that. You ask the oddest questions, Ann Kirby."

I scurry to the drawing room and swipe at the window frames with the feather duster. My head feels like a butter churner and, for a second, I wish I was back at home, planting out some turnips and thinking of nothing more complicated than how to keep Mam from straying.

CHAPTER SEVENTEEN
ELIZA

FILLETS OF PERCH WITH CRISP FRIED PARSLEY

Mrs. Thorpe's superiority radiates from her garments, her shoes, the ivory drops at her ears, the violet silk sash at her waist, the lace that sits so confidently at her bosom. Her gestures—the flaunting of the wedding-ringed finger, the lifting of her *married* chin—all consign Mother and me to a lesser life, a diminished life. They remind us that she is a player in the drama of life, while we are merely spectators.

"What a pleasant aspect this room has." Her eyes swivel around the room, taking in the brass fenders, the heavy velvet drapes, the mahogany cabinets with their clutch of leather-and-gilt books, the Brussels carpet. "All rented, is it?" Her head jerks backward and forward like a strutting pigeon.

"We have leased Bordyke House fully furnished," nods Mother. "It suits us very well, doesn't it, Eliza?"

"And is Ann Kirby to your satisfaction?" Mrs. Thorpe drums

her fingers on her skirts, as if anxious to move on to more interesting topics.

"She has barely been with us long enough to tell," says Mother.

"I like her," I say with a great effort at serenity. "She is without insolence or malice and she's very keen to learn."

"Quite, quite." Mrs. Thorpe gives another roll of her fingers. "I hear you are a poetess, Miss Acton?"

For a second I contemplate telling her I am indeed a poet. But then Mother fills the silence with her picked-clean voice. "My daughter was a poetess, but now she has an important writing commission from an important London publisher."

Mrs. Thorpe's lips tighten into a pout, as if she cannot quite decide what her response should be. "Oh, do tell. A novelette perhaps?"

"We cannot talk of it now." Mother presses a forefinger to her lips, a picture of reluctant secrecy. "But rest assured you will be the first to know."

I feel a flash of gratitude. Mother has tried—in her own uncertain way—to redeem me, to redeem us both. To show Mrs. Thorpe that we are more than shriveled husbandless ladies running a rented boardinghouse. Naturally, she couldn't own up to my writing a cookery book. But still her words have bound us closer.

"How are Ann Kirby's parents?" I ask.

Mrs. Thorpe's eyes widen and her jaw swings. "I have no idea. I cannot be expected to discourse with every member of my husband's congregation. Naturally, Ann Kirby always attends his sermons. They are known the length and breadth of the county."

She coughs, then adds in a splutter, "His sermons, that is. His sermons are renowned."

"I wouldn't want to lose her." I smile stiffly at Mrs. Thorpe. "Was there anything in particular you wished to discuss with me?" I can feel Mother's furious eyes upon me, but the tug of the kitchen is stronger: my new books, the fresh perch gleaming in the larder, the trugs of field mushrooms and damsons and pippin apples still with the dew upon them, the curly green parsley I shall fry until crisp . . .

"I am merely here to welcome you to Tonbridge, to offer the hand of friendship, Miss Acton." Mrs. Thorpe's head wobbles on her shoulders, a flush rising up her neck.

"Please forgive me, but I have matters to attend to." I leave the room with Mother's blistering fury at my back. I half run to the kitchen, light with relief even as I feel the guilt of betrayal. My departure is rude, a failure to reciprocate Mother's uncharacteristic gesture of support. But a few minutes of Mrs. Thorpe's eyes scraping over us and our *rented* furniture is more than enough. And how can I be a writer, a cook, a poet if I am expected to make conversation with every smug snooping woman who appears in our drawing room?

In the kitchen, I find Ann preparing a bowl of damsons, halving them with a fruit knife and easing out the stones. This is the third batch of damson jam we have prepared this week and yet none has been quite good enough, either too stiff or too liquid or without the right notes of sweetness and acidity. I wonder if it is me at fault or the damsons, too watery from the August rains perhaps.

"These are beautifully ripe and very fresh, Miss Eliza," Ann says, as if reading my thoughts. She passes me one and I squeeze it briefly between finger and thumb so that a runnel of juice drips over my hand.

"Let's cook this batch for a little longer." I lick absently at the juice on my hand. It tastes of hedgerow and sunshine and autumn leaves.

"D-Did Mrs. Thorpe say anything of my family?" Ann stops her work mid-damson, her knife aloft, juice skimming down her wrists and into the rolled-up sleeves of her dress.

"Were you expecting news?"

"No, Miss Eliza. But might I be allowed a half day this week? To visit my father?"

I pause. She's entitled to a half day each week . . . But how am I to feed the colonel and Mrs. Martin on my own?

"I appear to have become rather dependent on you, Ann," I say at last. "If you can help with breakfast and be back before four o'clock, I can manage."

"Thank you, Miss Eliza." She slices open the last damson, removes the stone, and places the fruit in the long-handled pan, batting away a drowsy wasp.

"Why do you ask for time to visit your father but make no mention of your mother?"

She wipes her hands on her apron, her tongue running quickly over her top lip. "My father is at home alone."

"So you have a father at home and a mother who is away and I have a mother at home and—" I stop abruptly. Mother and I have agreed that John Acton is not to be mentioned, that our clean start in Tonbridge could be jeopardized if his bankruptcy is known of. Boarders might be deterred from taking rooms. Butchers and bakers would deny us credit. And who knows what would happen if the landlord were to hear. Everyone—including our servants—must believe Mother is a respectable widow, living with her respectable daughter. Hatty knows, of course. But Mother has bribed her into silence.

"I'm sorry for your loss." Ann turns quickly back to the damsons. But she's not quick enough and I see the tremble in her top lip.

For a moment I say nothing: let her think, like everyone else in this town, that he is dead. But there have been too many lies in my life, and my yearning for a friendship—just one—untainted by half-truths and concealments gets the better of me. "He's alive, living in Calais. But he mustn't be spoken of."

"I'll never mention him." To my surprise Ann thrusts her small, knuckly hand at me. "Pa says to always shake hands on a promise." Her cheeks flush pink as if her gesture was too hasty and she now sees its inappropriateness.

I take her hand, as if it were a butterfly and I might crush it. I feel the cool skin stretched over the small bones, the knuckles like glass beads, the roughened fingertips, the scabs and cuts and calluses. Why haven't I noticed them before? Something tips and lurches queasily inside me. I steer it away and disappear to the larder, returning with the perch and a scaling knife.

"Would you like to hear what I've learned from my new books

about buying fish, Ann? Every housewife should know how to choose a truly fresh fish. Look first at the eyes." I point to the perch's head. "The eyes should always be bright, the gills a fine clear red, the body stiff, the flesh firm yet elastic to the touch, and the smell not disagreeable." The perch glitters, its scales like old gold.

Boiled Eels with Sage, German-Style

Today I'm called on to serve Colonel and Mrs. Martin at table again. Hatty has hurt her shoulder turning the mattresses and Ma'am doesn't trust her not to spill hot coffee on her best Irish linen.

I put on a clean apron and quickly buff up my new boots, which shine like oil and hug my feet so neatly there's no more dampness between my toes nor wind whistling around my ankles. Then I tell myself the colonel is a dirty old man—about to get his *comeuppance*—and nothing to be frightened of.

I keep my head bowed and take the silver coffeepot and cream jug to the table. Mrs. Martin sits very straight, as if all her muscles are stiff and clenched in expectation. She must get terrible indigestion, I think, and without meaning to, I look up and meet her glare hard upon me. Her eyes, like cold black marbles. Even the air around her is trying to escape, so that she sits in a little rigid space surrounded by the poison of her own thoughts. I'm concentrating on placing the pot very carefully on the woven mat, when the colonel says, "You can pour my coffee, one third cream."

I hear the rustling silk of Mrs. Martin's dress as she shifts upon her chair. "I can pour, my dear." Her voice is tight and clipped.

"We are paying good money to be here, Jane. I will not have you lift a finger." The colonel flaps his red gouty hand at the coffeepot. The other hand is nowhere to be seen. No doubt beneath the table fumbling at his breeches. I hold the spout above the cup and am on the brink of pouring when I see the slow crawl of his gouty hand. He's shifting it toward the sugar bowl which is perilous close to the edge of the table. It strikes me then that he must have put it there, for Hatty and I always place the sugar bowl at the very center, next to the silver cruets. Quick as a flash I see his game. I push the sugar bowl back to the middle of the table. Then I take the coffeepot, and his cup and saucer, to the side table—where there's nothing to distract me—and pour it there. When I serve his cup, all neatly poured and not a drop in the saucer, he is furious. Angry globs of spit bubble at the corners of his mouth.

Mrs. Martin glowers. "You may pour mine at the table," she says. "No cream." Then she turns to the colonel and adds, "This is how Roman slaves poisoned their masters, is it not?"

I am so confused and afraid that I don't speak. I just stand there, as if I'm a tree putting down roots. All of a sudden words stream into my head, as if God sent them. "Ma'am, I beg your pardon, but the lip of the pot is misshapen and this is Mrs. Acton's best linen tablecloth. Besides, if I had wanted to poison the coffee I would have done so in the kitchen."

They both stare at me, with outraged eyes. Then Mrs. Martin does something most peculiar. She gets up, takes the colonel's coffee to the window—which is open to let in the air—and pours it onto the street.

"You will serve my husband's coffee at the table." She puts the cup, smeared with dregs, in front of him. His hand is still beneath the table, his wrist and elbow moving in a most robust way, as if he's struggling with the buttons of his breeches.

I do as I'm bid and pour the coffee. Very slowly. Keeping my eyes tight upon the spout. I try to think of Hatty's words about not being frightened, but my arm is shaking terrible and coffee starts to splash from the cup into the saucer. And then from the saucer onto Ma'am's best Irish linen.

Mrs. Martin is sipping at her cup, her eyes fixed on the oil painting of a girl and a dog that hangs above the fireplace. All at once she puts her cup down and jerks out her elbow so that the saltcellar is knocked to the floor, landing right at the colonel's feet.

"Pick it up," she commands and the glittering beam of her black eyes bores into me. And that is when I know she doesn't deserve one ounce of my sympathy. I think of Hatty's words—about keeping my eyes from *it* and not showing a morsel of fear for them to feed upon—and I pull my puny frame up to its full height. I want to turn on my newly booted heel but I don't: I know I must keep my job, that their words will always have more weight than mine.

I go down on my hands and knees, and crawl beneath the linen tablecloth. It smells of rotting fish and something I take to be gentleman's cologne. Eyes tight closed I grope for the saltcellar, curl my fingers quickly around it, and come back up, very calm and still. I replace it beside the pepper pot and then I say something I will regret forever.

"Would you care for some more of the *unpoisoned* coffee?"

"The what?" gasps Mrs. Martin. She starts fanning at her face with her fingers as if she's about to go into a swoon.

The colonel's face is a livid red, his eyes bulging and popping in their sockets. I look away, startled at my own cheek. But an odd hoggish sound comes from the colonel's mouth and I know I've gone too far this time. And then he brings his hand from beneath the table and strokes at the air. "Now, now, Jane," he splutters, breathless. "Let's not disrupt this most enjoyable breakfast. Baked mackerel is on its way."

"Bring my husband's mackerel, girl. In plenty of butter." Mrs. Martin has stopped her feigned swooning and her voice is curt and snappish. She flaps her hand at me, but I dare not look her in the eye.

I run to find Hatty, who is in the washroom pressing pillowcases in a swirl of hissing steam. She agrees I've gone too far. "But you showed him," she adds proudly. "You showed him how fearless you are and no doubt that will stop his dirty ways."

"Will I lose my position?"

"Likely they'll say nothing—they rarely do—but you must say nothing too. And we must get that tablecloth soaked in brine before Ma'am sees it."

"Why does Mrs. Martin have no shame of him?"

"Not to us, because we are no one. She'd be ashamed if society ladies found out. But they won't, will they?" Hatty gives my hand a little squeeze. "I'm teaching you the ways of the world and they ain't always pretty. Now, you take over these and I'll take 'em their mackerel. And watch your lip next time, Ann Kirby, for we can rarely beat 'em at their own game."

Later, as Miss Eliza and I struggle with an eel, I think of Hatty's words and they fill me with an unspoken savagery. The eel is as long as my arm, writhing and twisting upon the table. I grip its slippery body as Miss Eliza peers at her recipe book.

"'Split the skin at the neck and remove in a single motion,'" she reads. "But first we must secure it to a board with a fork."

The eel thrashes madly as Miss Eliza stabs at its head with a toasting fork, shuddering and grimacing as if she's been asked to stab a child. "This is unspeakably cruel," she gasps. "Boiling it first would surely be more humane."

"I will do it, Miss Eliza," I cry. "It's only a pond creature!" And she throws me the fork with great eagerness, no doubt thinking I've killed a writhing eel before. I haven't, but Hatty's words have made my blood pump like liquid fire. I grit my teeth, think of the colonel, and plunge the fork into its body, so the eel stops its thrashing and lies quite still.

Miss Eliza steps back and looks at me in awe. "Why, Ann . . . and you so small and slight." She laughs in relief. "You are barely much bigger than this beast."

I blink at her, my body shaking beneath my bibbed apron.

"You are full of surprises," she says. "I will leave you to skin it. Then can you open it, clean it, and cut it into finger-length pieces. I think sage will pair well, don't you?"

I don't tell her it was pure fury, and nothing more, that caused me to kill the eel so effortlessly. As her footsteps recede, I curse myself—for now she thinks I have a true skill at murdering eels, so I must skin it perfectly. I place my hands upon the eel and am wondering how best to open and empty it, when all of a sudden the eel twitches and its head rears up. Panicked, I jump back against the wall of the scullery. Why will this blasted eel not die! I grab a brass skillet and hit the eel. Over and over I hit it, 'til the sweat is running into my eyes. When I stop, a strange calm falls over me. My shoulders are where they should be, not up by my ears. The coil in my stomach has gone. And I feel drained, like a wrung-out cloth. But there's no time to rest. The eel lies, lifeless, on the board and now I must skin it. I pierce the neck with a knife tip and try to grip a flap of skin. The eel slips and slides from my grasp, leaving its slime upon my fingers. Tears of frustration and exhaustion prick the backs of my eyes. Suddenly I long for Mam, for how she was. What am I doing here, fighting with eels and dirty old colonels with their devilish wives? I should be looking after Mam . . .

Just as I'm thinking this, Miss Eliza returns and sees the eel has slipped half across the table.

"We'll tackle this beast together," she says, standing so close I can smell the fresh-picked sage on her fingers, the lavender from her laundered clothes, the lemony cleanness of her skin.

"You hold and I'll pull." She takes the loosened skin from the eel's neck and eases it down. It peels off clean like the pelt of a well-hung rabbit.

"Next time we will boil it, like a lobster, with culinary kindness," she says. Then she turns to me, stooping her head so it's the same level as mine. "Ann, are you happy here?"

I nod, but tears fill my eyes. No one—since Mam a decade back—has ever asked me if I'm happy. I sniff and tell her it's just my monthlies giving me pain.

She studies me with great concentration. Then says I must go and rest and she will bring me something warm to lay against my stomach. Immediately I regret my hasty lie. Although what was I to say? That my mam is a lunatic? That Colonel Martin likes to frighten servant girls with his sausages and chestnuts? That I have ruined Ma'am's best tablecloth? The truth is I've never felt happier than I am in Miss Eliza's kitchen. The near-constant bubbling of the stockpot, the endless eggs in straw-lined baskets, the trays of mulberries drying above the stove, the quinces and medlars laid out in lines. Just seeing it all and knowing—every single day—that I won't go to bed aching with hunger. But it's more than that: it's *her*. Her very presence makes my heart leap like a spring salmon. I will bear anything to stay beside her. And nothing the colonel can do will frighten me away.

"The cramps have passed," I lie.

"Good! Bring me a fresh knife with a keen edge and let us clean the beast together," she says, and the lines slope away from her brow, leaving it as smooth as china again.

CHAPTER NINETEEN
ELIZA

RICE PUDDING

When I take Mother her morning tea, she is sitting up in bed against a mountain of pillows and cushions, her nightcap flopping from her head like a pale wilting flower. Instantly I know something is wrong: there are violet crescents beneath her eyes, her lips are thin and tight, her shoulders braced.

She holds up her arm to prevent me speaking. "Colonel and Mrs. Martin spoke to me last night. I have barely slept a wink."

I think immediately of the money we've borrowed. If the Martins fail to pay us, we shall all be fleeing to Calais. "They cannot pay?"

"Don't be silly, Eliza!"

I stare at her. "Well, what?"

"Ann must leave. They were most insistent. She has to leave immediately."

"Leave?" I repeat, stupefied. "And for what?"

"Her impudence is inexcusable. We cannot have a servant who threatens our livelihood, Eliza."

"What has she done?" I reach out to steady myself on the bedpost, for Mother's words are ridiculous.

"She said our coffee was poisoned. Mrs. Martin was so upset, she was plagued with stomach pains all day. Luckily the colonel convinced her that Ann was joking. A joke in very poor taste, I might add. But it will not do, Eliza. It will not do!"

"Surely you do not believe them?"

"Why would they lie?" She leans back against the cushions, her eyes closed, her face set hard. "I have heard so many tales of servants like this . . . they loathe their mistresses and find any way they can to sabotage them. If we allow it, we will go the way of France, where the servants chopped the head from every master and every mistress."

"How can you say this without hearing her account of events?" I shake my head, confounded. There's not a whiff of Ann in all this talk. But Mother carries on.

"I have seen you with that girl, Eliza. I have seen how you dote on her. I do not find it . . ." She pauses as if searching for the right word. "Wholesome," she says, at length.

I swallow, and make myself count to three before I respond. My knuckles are blanched white from gripping the bedpost and I am so angry, red sparks tumble through my head. "She is a good servant, Mother. The best I have ever known. I cannot complete my book without her."

"Without our boarders, there will be no book. Who do you imagine is paying for the kitchen, the ingredients, your precious time?" She opens her eyes, looks at the ceiling, sighs. "The Martins are adamant. They are powerful people in London."

"Hatty can serve and we can keep Ann in the kitchen." I steady my voice but it's impossible to miss the note of pleading. "Out of sight and out of mind."

"If Ann Kirby has been rude to our first boarders, why will she be any different with the next? The baths at Tunbridge Wells are a small place. There will be gossip. We cannot afford to make another blunder, not after your father . . ." Her voice tails off. She drags the back of her hand over her eyes and sighs again. "If we lose boarders like this, we shall be forced to take in schoolboys. Is that what you want? To spend your days producing rice pudding for unruly boys?"

I chew my lip. And from some distant place come lines of poetry, whirling through the past to hover in the present:

> Darkly, darkly, Misfortune's wing
> Is o'er thee rolling its heavy cloud;
> Slowly, slowly, 'tis gathering . . .

"And if we have no schoolboy boarders, we are destitute!" Mother's voice snaps at the air.

"I shall speak to Ann. And if the fault is not hers, I suggest we ask the Martins to leave." I straighten my shoulders and turn to go, feigning a defiance I do not feel. A bitter blend of self-loathing and self-pity rolls slowly through me. I should have defended Ann more vigorously, I think. But Mother is right: we need the goodwill of our boarders. Without them, we shall be forced to crawl on our impoverished knees to Edgar in the jungles of Mauritius, or to my married sister, Mary, to live at the mercy of their charity. And yet without Ann how shall I write my book?

Ann is stoking the fire in the stove. She turns as I enter, her face flushed from the heat of the flames. "Shall I make you some tea, Miss Eliza?"

"What has happened between you and the Martins?"

She looks away, chewing on her lower lip.

"You must tell me the truth. I cannot have a servant who lies to me." My hands are pressed so tightly together, an ache begins to spread from my wrists up my arms. Ann's small head is bowed and I notice that the nape of her neck is a mottled pink. In the silence I hear her gulp, then the fire spits and sparks spray from the open door of the stove and die, one by one, upon the hearth.

"The colonel has peculiar habits," she whispers. "He likes to sh-show himself."

"Show himself?" I repeat. "Whatever do you mean?"

"The parts of him that no one but Mrs. Martin should see."

"He has had you in his room?" I am so shocked my mouth hangs, open and slack.

"No, miss. He does it at breakfast or at dinner. He sh-shows himself to Hatty too, but she is m-more used to it than me."

"At table?" The idea is so ridiculous I want to laugh out loud. But Ann's face is crimson with shame. And I know all about shame. "So you threatened to poison his coffee?"

"No." She stops and I see her eyes welling with tears. "I can leave today, Miss Eliza."

And then I do something that no mistress should do with her kitchen maid. I take her in my arms and hold her to me, stroking her hair, patting her back. "I am so sorry, Ann. I am so very sorry," I whisper. And in my mind's eye, I am imagining her as Susannah. My Susannah.

CHAPTER TWENTY
ANN

BREAD AND AN ONION

I walk the half hour home through a damp white mist, my thoughts turning over and over. I am grateful for my dry feet, so snug in my new boots. Or are they my boots? This is how my mind is working, question after question. What will Hatty be told? What am I to say to Pa? How is a girl meant to deal with a man like the colonel? I think on Ma'am's words as she ushered me from the back door: *He did no one any harm and yet your insolence has hurt us all.* And it's the truth of her words that cuts me to the quick. For my departure has hurt Hatty and Ma'am and Miss Eliza, who must now find another scullery maid. And it's hurt me and will hurt Pa and Reverend Thorpe, who found me the position, and Mrs. Thorpe, who lent me her old frock. I feel their disappointment like buckets of water on my back.

Most of all I think of Miss Eliza. How her hair smelled of lemons, the sob that caught in her throat so she could not speak. I will never find another mistress such as her. My chest heaves and the tears rise up in me again. Why have I been such a fool? Is it such a sinful thing for a man to want to show his private parts beneath a breakfast table?

The smell of bruised apples reaches me of a sudden. And in that moment I am back in Miss Eliza's kitchen, rich with cooking odors: the nutty smell of roasting coffee berries, the syrupy scent of fruit upon the stove, the pierce of a fresh-cut lemon, the sweet warmth of a split vanilla pod, the earthy heat of a crushed clove. And her, showing me how to separate a yolk from its white, or how to hold a blade, or how to skin a tomato. A tear rolls down my nose. Then another and another.

When I reach the cottage, my heart is so heavy I nearly turn away. Perhaps Pa will be at the graveyard and I will have time to pull myself together. Septimus comes bounding to the door. I scratch his ears in the way he likes, then I kneel down and push my face into his neck.

"Who's there?" Pa's voice slurs toward me and my heart sinks as heavy as a stone.

"It's me. Why are you not at the graveyard?"

"Ann?" I hear his crutches crashing against the wall as he staggers and swings through the darkness of the cottage. I peer into the gloom. The cottage reeks, as if a rodent has died and been left to rot in a corner. I push the door back and remove the rag that hangs in front of the window. Pa coughs and curses.

"What has happened?" I whisper.

"Nothing, Ann. Nothing." He clutches at my arm and I see

his hand is streaked with mud and his nails rimed with earth. A good sign. He must have done some work in the graveyard.

"But 'tis hard on my own . . ." His breath is heavy with the stink of ale.

"Are you going to the graveyard today?"

He shakes his head and gives a long rattling cough that makes his whole body judder. "I'm not well," he says, easing himself clumsily onto the mattress.

"This place needs cleaning." I look around the cottage. There's a pile of gnawed bones in a corner. The grate is empty but for a charred log and, beneath it, a thin layer of ash. The mattress has no bedding on it and hay spews from the single pillow. Mam's things have gone and the room seems bare and decaying.

I find the dead rodent—a rat—behind the grate, flies crawling over it. I wonder if I can make a meal from it but decide it's too far gone, so I carry it out by its tail and throw it as far away as I can. I turn the mattress over, sweep out the ash from the hearth, swish a leafy branch into the corners to catch the cobwebs. I fill a bucket from the stream and scrub the cottage floor and wipe the walls, changing the water several times until my arms ache from the filling and carrying and my fingers are numb with cold. My stomach growls, but there's no food in the place, not even an old potato. I pat my pocket, checking for the five shillings Miss Eliza gave me.

"I must go and buy some bread," I say. "It'll be bread and an onion for supper, like the old days." Pa nods and coughs, liquid gurgling on his chest. "Before I go, tell me how Mam is."

"And how would I know that?" he answers, his voice hoarse from the coughing.

"I—I supposed Reverend Thorpe would have kept in touch with the asylum . . . to see that she was well settled . . ." My words peter out, hollow and half-hearted. Why did I think such a thing? Reverend Thorpe is a busy man with an entire parish to look after. And all this time I have been thinking only of how to dress an eel, or how to spice a pork chop, or whether four or five eggs makes the lightest Madeira cake. I feel such a rush of self-hatred all the strength leaves my legs. I crumple down, next to Pa. The mattress is damp—whether from the mist or his sweat or spilled ale I cannot tell. For a second Pa looks surprised. Then he reaches for my hand and grips it.

"Why are you here, Ann?"

I look into his pink eyes and can't think how to explain. After a full minute's silence, I tell him I must buy some food and visit Mam. "Do you have an address? For the asylum?"

He shakes his head. "Ask the reverend." He lets go of my hand, lies down, and curls into a ball, like a baby.

"Will you come with me? You can lean on me." And when Pa shakes his head, I know something is amiss, that he's surely lost his position. Like me.

"Did Reverend Thorpe give you any money?" I ask softly. "For the work you did?"

He shakes his head, then coughs so fierce his body quivers from head to toe.

"You should see a doctor. I have some money from Miss Eliza."

Pa shakes his head and croaks into the pillow, "No, please no."

I find a scrap of blanket and put it over him. As I kiss his bearded cheek I feel the damp heat of him, as if he has a fever. I wonder if he has the white plague—and my heart drops into my feet. Why did Mrs. Thorpe not say anything? Why has no one told me of his illness? I'll visit Mam, I think. Which means I must go to the rectory and ask Mrs. Thorpe for the address. Even if it's the last thing on earth I want to do.

ROAST WILD DUCK WITH CUCUMBERS

The butcher's boy brings eight mutton kidneys and two wild ducks to the back door.

"The mallards 'ave 'anged for six days," he says, "and I'm to tell you the kidneys is fresh as daisies." The ducks hang upside down from his bloodstained hand. He gives them a jaunty swing, making the light catch, flash, on their bottle-green heads.

"I hope there are no maggots crawling around in those ducks." I haven't the disposition for Hatty's shrieking indignations today. The girl hasn't an ounce of Ann's practical stoicism and my nerves are already in tatters.

"Tell the maid what picks 'em to use a deep bucket, otherwise your house will be full of feathers with every gust of wind." He wipes some drool from his nose with his cuff and turns back to his barrow.

I take the ducks to the scullery, stepping with irritation over the night's chamber pots that are lined up in front of the plate room. Why hasn't Hatty emptied them? The scullery reeks and the sink is choked with unwashed pans sitting in a puddle of oily water. Beside the sink, unscrubbed turnips and parsnips sprawl amid clods of mud. The sugarloaf has been left unwrapped and is alive with wasps. The egg baskets are empty. The dishcloths have been discarded in a damp mound. Crumbs snap and crunch beneath my feet.

The kitchen is no better. I need a brisk fire for the ducks, but Hatty has not roused it and both the log basket and the coal scuttle are empty. My teeth grind and gnash with furied frustration. But without Hatty, the wretched colonel and his gimlet-eyed wife will have no dinner, so I silently seethe and reread today's recipes: mutton kidneys à la française and roast wild duck with cucumbers à la poulette. The cucumbers are the last of the season and have toughened skin and overlarge seeds, but it can't be helped. The recipe I'm using appears to be for a banquet and requires twenty cucumbers. I must scale everything back: butter, parsley, veal stock, flour. I've just started paring the cucumbers, when Hatty flies in.

"Miss Eliza, I must speak with you!"

I am on the verge of scolding her for her slovenly ways when something in the wild look of her stops me. I put aside the paring knife and twist my lips into a congenial smile.

"About Ann," she continues, her hands fidgeting at the brim of her cap.

I nod and keep my face blank. No one must know of the swill of guilt and anger that has kept me tossing and turning these last two nights.

"Ma'am is talking of placing an advertisement, but it ain't right. This"—she pauses, sweeping a scrappy arm around the kitchen—"is Ann's position and no one else's."

I'm about to explain that Mrs. Acton—mistress of this house—has made her decision and we must abide by it. But Hatty starts hopping from one foot to the other in great agitation. "Why did no one ask me, Miss Eliza? For it was my fault . . . all my fault." Her hands are back at her cap, tugging at its scalloped edge as though she wishes to draw it directly over her face.

"Explain yourself," I say gently. Beneath my ribs, something leaps. As if a galloping breeze has fallen upon a dying fire and caused a flame to catch.

"The colonel was always at it, under the breakfast table, wanting to show us his—his . . ."

"Yes, yes." I wave an impatient hand at her. I need more than this if I am to convince Mother that Ann should be returned to us.

"I told her some gentlemen do this and they like it when the maids are scared. I think she had a mind to be particular brave after that. Most of us girls have a mother or an older sister who explains the ways of certain gentlemen." She pauses briefly for breath, then runs on, words spilling out of her: "And new girls that have none of these will likely be instructed by the cook or the housekeeper. But Bordyke House don't have either. So, you see, it's not Ann's fault, miss."

A lump appears in my throat, forcing me to cough in as delicate a manner as I can muster. But the lump is lodged fast, so I must speak through it. "Have you had much experience of gentlemen"—I pause on this word that now seems so evidently misapplied—"like this?"

"Oh yes, miss. And worse. Taking rougher liberties and the like. My ma warned me of their ploys and tricks so I knows when to step away and how to escape without 'em losing face, but Ann—"

"But Ann has no mother." I reach for the paring knife and the cucumber. My hands must be busy. I must peel and cut and slice. "This knife is blunt, Hatty. Sharpen it, please."

She strikes the blade against the whetstone. "I don't think Ann Kirby knows much about gentlemen, miss, and anyways it was not she that spoke of poisoning the coffee, but Mrs. Martin herself."

The lump in my throat cools, hardens, so that I can only croak, "Oh?"

Hatty gingerly puts a fingertip to the blade, then lays it on the table in front of me. "Yes. Her hand was shaking and she didn't want to spill coffee on Ma'am's newly pressed Irish linen. It's a devil to get out—only the hottest water will shift it, and hours of brine scrubbing so that your hands is quite raw."

As I gouge the seeds from the cucumbers, Hatty explains what happened between Ann and Mrs. Martin. My mind turns over, question upon question. As I salt and steep the cucumbers and slice the fat from the kidneys, I think of how we have mistreated

Ann. None of this would have happened if she'd had a mother, if she'd been in service with a *proper* cook, if she'd worked for an establishment with a *housekeeper*.

"She did not say any of this to me," I say, batting at the metallic odor of butchery and blood drifting from the sliced kidneys. And yet I know the fault to be mine. For I did not press her. And I did not sufficiently defend her to Mother. I put the knife down, wipe my hands on my apron, and go to the drawing room, where Mother is reviewing the household accounts.

She sits hunched over her ledger but straightens up when I enter. There is a small smile playing over her lips that strikes me as peculiar given our present circumstances.

"I have good news," she says. "Very good news!"

"There can be no good news while Ann Kirby is not here!" I burst out.

She looks peevish and the smile slips from her lips. "That's as may be, but you forget yourself, Eliza."

I am not inclined to waste time on explanations or justifications, nor do I feel like hearing her *good news* which most likely involves some small saving she has made. "Hatty has told me the truth about Ann and the Martins. We have treated her most unfairly and I want her returned."

Mother frowns, then closes the ledger and pushes it away.

"I wish to pay her more and to hire a scullery maid to work under her." I pause and wipe the back of my hand over my forehead. How tiring, how humiliating it is to have conversations like this with my mother at my age. In a final rush of fury, I add,

"If she is not returned to me, on my terms, then I shall produce my cookery book elsewhere!"

"Let us not fight, my dear. If you were married and had your own household, you would be free to make your own decisions on servants, furnishings, bills of fare . . . Indeed all aspects of domestic management would be yours and yours alone." She looks at me in a very pointed way, as if this twisting conversation is leading somewhere and I am too truculent to see it.

"I know I'm an old maid—to be pitied and loathed in equal measure—and that I must submit to your will," I say through clenched teeth. "But I want Ann back. I shall serve the Martins myself if necessary." I turn on my heel, for the room has become airless and oppressive, as if our combined presences are too big for it.

"Patience, my dear! Your temper is most unbecoming. Wouldn't you like your own household? With every Ann Kirby you might want?"

"Of course." I turn back into the room. "But your gibes are hurtful—as you must surely know. And I wish to discuss Ann Kirby, not my lack of matrimony."

"My dear, you may have Ann back. Colonel and Mrs. Martin are now unable to extend their stay, but have generously offered to pay us the full amount."

A lightness sweeps over me, followed at once by a feeling of panic. What if Ann has found a new position? What if she refuses to return? "And the extra wages? The undermaid?"

Mother twists her wedding ring with a conspicuous flourish.

"You must find the money, Eliza. I have heard of cooks who turn a tidy sum selling feathers and bones to the rag-and-bone men or selling beef dripping from the back door. Even rancid fat can be sold for soap, I'm told."

"You expect me to do that?" I ask, startled. For this is exactly the sort of thing that would shame Mother. More shaming, I suspect, than having a common cook for a daughter.

"No, no, no!" She throws her hands into the air. "Ann Kirby must do that. She must earn her own extra wages. At least until we are financially stable."

"You know full well that we use everything, that I am the thriftiest housekeeper in all of Kent," I say coldly. But Mother ignores me.

"Don't you want to hear my good news?" The smile returns to her mouth, as if she cannot suppress it. "We have a new boarder coming. A single gentleman in possession of a fortune."

Now I understand why she looks so pleased with herself.

"He's an old friend of your father's. John's business may have crumbled, but Mr. Arnott's enterprise stretches to the ends of the earth." She pauses, as if for effect, then adds, "And he is a widower!"

An image of Mr. Arnott forms in my mind: old, stooped, balding, jowls that fall in doughy rolls around his neck, a stomach of pork fat that flops over his breeches. "And he's come to take the waters at Tunbridge Wells? Gout? Kidney stones?"

"I did not like to pry, but be practical, Eliza. At least keep an open mind." She gives her ring another sharp turn. And it's as though I can read the pattern of her thoughts: he is elderly and sick and rich, and the prospect of being a wealthy wife is bettered by one thing only—being a wealthy widow. The shamelessness of her machinations makes my innards shrivel.

As I leave, she calls out after me, "You have not inquired about the nature of his enterprise!"

But I'm in no mood to ask. Besides, I have ducks to roast; cucumbers to braise; buttered kidneys to toss in parsley, thyme, and cayenne.

And after that I must find the address of Ann Kirby. Before it is too late.

CHAPTER TWENTY-TWO
ANN

A PIECE OF BREAD

Mrs. Thorpe doesn't comment on my hair, which is blown wild around my face, or compliment me on my new boots now covered in dust and mud, or ask why I'm not at Bordyke House. Nor does she invite me in, not even to the scullery. So we stand in the backyard while the stable boy and the butcher's boy come and go around us, and she has one eye on them and one eye on the kitchen maid, who is taking delivery of a bunch of dead rabbits.

"I have no idea where your mother is," Mrs. Thorpe says, impatient. "I'm very busy, as you can see."

"Please, ma'am, Reverend Thorpe might know," I say, persistent but with my eyes cast meek and humble to the ground. "I was told he took her there."

"Took her where?" She doesn't wait for an answer, but turns away and shouts, "I hope those rabbits are fresh and young? I will not have rabbits beyond four months, Florence. Do you hear me? Four months!"

I look at Florence, a poor bitten-down creature as thin as a gnawed bone. But something in me sings, for Miss Eliza never shouted at me, never spoke to me as if I were dirt scraped from the floor. And with that little bit of knowledge I feel myself swell and grow.

"Where can I find Reverend Thorpe, ma'am?" I look her straight in the eye, as bold as brass.

"My husband may be anywhere—he's in great demand. If you wait here, Florence will bring you a piece of bread and then you can be on your way."

"No thanks, ma'am. I need to see my mother. Reverend Thorpe took her away and I have no address."

Mrs. Thorpe blows out a huge angry breath. "I. Have. Told. You." She flaps her hands at me, as if I'm a stray dog. Then she pauses, narrows her eyes, and fixes them on mine. "Why are you not at Bordyke House, Ann Kirby?"

My cheeks go hot, and all my boldness vanishes. "I'm dismissed," I say, my head bowed so that I'm like a cringing dog.

"Dismissed? I bent over backward to get you that position!"

Her anger is like a tongue of cold fire.

"Just like your father, Ann Kirby! My poor dear husband had to dismiss him too. On his first day of work! We have done everything for you Kirbys and this is how you repay us." She shakes her head and turns away as if she can't bear the sight of me. I feel smaller than a beetle. As if I've been gobbled up by my own shame.

She walks toward the rectory but I cannot move, even with the butcher's boy gawping at me. Then at the door, she turns back. "Kent County Lunatic Asylum, that's where your mother is. Safely under lock and key. Where all you Kirbys should be!" And she's gone, the back door slamming behind her.

"But where is that, ma'am? Where is that?" I cry, but I know she can't hear me behind her big closed door. Tears shove at the backs of my eyes, but I won't let them out. Not in front of the butcher's boy. I squeeze every muscle in my face as he steers his cart toward the street, the iron wheels clattering over the cobbles. But then he shouts over his shoulder, "Ain't far from here, missy. Barming Heath, near Maidstone. Fifteen mile or so."

"Fifteen miles?" I echo. I can walk fifteen miles easy, only I have no directions.

"You can follow the river or you can ride with Jones the miller," he adds. "He has a lady friend who works there. Visits regular, he does."

Hope skips inside me. "Thank you!" I say. "Thank you!"

CHAPTER TWENTY-THREE
ELIZA

AN APPLE HEDGEHOG, ICED
WITH ALMOND SPIKES

I scrub the taint of kitchen from me—onions, gravy, boiled bones—and put on my good stout boots. With my plaid shawl around my shoulders I walk to the rectory, a distinct spring in my step. The despicable Martins have paid and left. The colonel had the audacity to enter the passageway to the kitchen after their last breakfast—for which he demanded cold beef, Cochin eggs, crumb muffins, *and* baked mushrooms to *fortify them for the journey ahead.* I found him lurking, like the miscreant he is, and assumed he was checking we had dismissed Ann Kirby.

"I wish to compliment the chef," he simpered. "We suppose him to be French. Is that so?"

I snorted into my neckline, before remembering myself. "You are right, sir. She is an excellent chef and I shall pass on your kind words."

"Oh? A plain cook? In which case our conjectures were entirely wrong." And he turned so quickly I thought he might trip over his own varnished shoes.

Needless to say, his compliments to the *French chef* have added a bounce to my step. As did this morning's post which included two annuals: the *Literary Gazette* and *Friendship's Offering*. Having no boarders to cook for and not wanting to arrive too early at the rectory, I was at liberty to read. I settled myself in the drawing room and feasted on the words of Mrs. Hemans; Mrs. Howitt; Miss Jewsbury; and, oh, marvel that she is, L. E. Landon. When I read her verse, I seem to observe myself in a looking glass of words. As if she sees inside me, understands me. I found myself repeating lines aloud, committing them to memory that I might quote them later, that I might educate Ann on England's finest poems.

Her poignant words return to me now . . .

> *With what still hours of calm delight*
> *Thy songs and image blend;*
> *I cannot choose but think thou wert*
> *An old familiar friend.*

For that is how I feel about my fellow lady poets. They are like intimate friends of mine, appearing when I am most in need.

By the time I arrive at the rectory my head is swimming with verse lines from L. E. Landon, a stanza from the formidable Mrs. Howitt that refuses to leave my tongue, my own feeble attempts. A melee of words, images, illuminations that raises my spirits even as it reveals the inadequacies of my own verse. I lift the brass knocker—the maned head of a lion—and bring it down so firmly it echoes through the house. The shuffle of feet, the grate of a turning key, and the door opens on its well-oiled hinges. A bobbing housemaid with frightened eyes hurries off to announce my arrival.

When Mrs. Thorpe appears, it is with ill-concealed astonishment. The muscles beneath her cheeks and around her thin mouth twitch. As if she cannot decide which facial pose to adopt. Eventually she welcomes me with a watery smile.

"I'm here for Ann Kirby's address," I say. "We have had a misunderstanding and now I must ask her to return."

My words, as ever, are too blunt. Mrs. Thorpe's eyes become cold and clouded, like the dulled eyes of a dead trout. "You were so clever to find her, Mrs. Thorpe," I add with obsequious haste.

Her expression softens. "Let us take some tea together, or perhaps you would prefer coffee?" She brings a carved silver bell from the folds of her skirt and jerks at it. The little housemaid appears, bobs, disappears. Mrs. Thorpe leads the way to a drawing room—wallpaper patterned with rosebuds, an oil painting of Mr. Thorpe above the fireplace, a pair of chairs upholstered in green leather.

We discuss the weather, the havoc wreaked by this year's late frosts, the London East Enders who have arrived to harvest the hops, the difficulty of finding good servants. The latter is my cue and I pounce, like a cat upon its prey. "A simple, foolish misunderstanding," I explain, looking demurely into my tea, where stray leaves float like drowned insects. "Entirely my fault and

now I must retrieve her, if I am not too late." And God forbid
that I'm too late, I think, with another heave of regret.

Mrs. Thorpe puffs up at my words and puts her teacup upon
the table in such a way that a shaft of light catches, holds, spar-
kles on her wedding ring. After a short silence—her hand carefully preserved in its shaft of light—she says, "Yes, it's possible
she's joined a gang of hop pickers."

My throat turns dry. Mrs. Thorpe knows something. She knows
I am too late. Lines of verse whirl into my head . . . *Affection's chain
was all too rudely wrench'd in twain . . . blighted hopes, and friendship
fled . . . She is flung neglectedly abroad, where fostering love is not . . .*

Bizarrely, I have a sudden image of my feelings in recipe form:
one pound of fresh despair, three pecks of very firm frustration,
five ounces of pure guilt, a strewing of newly cut regret, and a
few grains of self-pity.

"Are you well?" Mrs. Thorpe is peering curiously at me, her
ringed fingers dabbling at the slender gold crucifix hanging at
her neck—a gesture that informs me of both her matrimony and
her piety.

"I would like to visit Ann."

She draws her eyebrows together. "You don't need my permission for that."

"Yes, but I have no address."

"Did you not record it when you hired her?" She opens her
eyes righteously wide. As if I am more of an imbecile than she
imagined.

"Oh, I am such a novice at these things." I try to remember

what Ann said about her home. Did I ask her anything? When I add up all I know of her, it amounts to very little. To my chagrin.

Mrs. Thorpe purses her lips and appears to think. "Perhaps you should come back when my husband is here, and then we can discuss your poetry too. Although I must tell you that my dear husband is not in favor of scribbling ladies, particularly unmarried scribbling ladies. I am broadly of the same opinion, but you may be able to sway me, Miss Acton."

I am so taken aback that for a second I cannot speak. I want to tell her that no less than thirteen clergymen subscribed to my first book of poetry, that the reverends Cobbold of Ipswich, Fletcher of Woodbridge, Kirby of Suffolk, and Mortimer of Kent all acknowledged receipt with appreciative notes, that one—Reverend Kirby?—wrote gushingly of my sincerity and charm. Then I remember the returned volume, with its terse and disapproving note, from Reverend Bull of Tattingstone Rectory. The hairs on my arms rise up, as if an icy blast of air has swept into the room.

I push away the memory of Reverend Bull's scowling, hostile words and stand, my head held high and my back as straight and unyielding as a butcher's blade. "If you cannot give me Ann Kirby's address, I will find it elsewhere."

Something about my bearing or the tone of my voice makes Mrs. Thorpe change her mind. She sighs and pulls the little silver bell from her skirt. A most ungodly feeling of triumph—I have won!—runs over me, mingled with relief. The housemaid is dispatched to bring paper, pen, and ink, whereupon Mrs. Thorpe writes three lines of directions in her best copperplate.

"I cannot answer for what you will find," she says, passing her folded notepaper to me with obvious reluctance.

I frown, wondering what I am to find at Ann's home. But when I leave the rectory, the sky is so high, blue, scoured clean that I immediately dismiss Mrs. Thorpe's sour words. I walk past the Rose and Crown, past the wine merchant's shop and the bookseller's, past the Mechanics' Institute, past the brick works and the paper mill. Then out beyond the water meadows and through the hop gardens, golden green and blurred with October sun. The air is grainy, thick with chaff, and the land swarms with pickers. Barefoot children, black-haired Gypsies, wizened men, and stooped women with heads wrapped in handkerchiefs, all of them crouching, bending, stretching between the endless rows of hop poles.

I keep an eye out for Ann, but instead I catch sight of a hedgehog shuffling into the undergrowth—an unexpected glimpse for they are shy, nocturnal creatures. Something about his gait, his spines, makes me imagine a sweet dish in his image. A hedgehog pudding . . . How might I make the spikes? Slithers of blanched almonds . . . impaled in a stiff white icing? Browned in a hot oven to re-create his russet color? And beneath his armor of icing and almonds . . . a Madeira sponge? A stiff blancmange? As I ponder how to make the hedgehog's body, I notice an apple tree, its boughs stripped of fruit but for a single split pippin at its apex. An apple hedgehog! A thick puree of apples drained until almost dry . . . with a center of apricot jam flavored with lemons. I imagine Ann at my side as we construct our apple hedgehog— and suddenly I have my skirts in my hands and I am marching, almost running, in the direction of her home.

CHAPTER TWENTY-FOUR
ANN

DAMSON CHEESE

The miller doesn't talk much as we make our way to Barming Heath. I'm glad of this, for it leaves me free to spot blackberries and bullaces, codlings and crab apples, and to fancy the pretty dishes they might make. I wonder if Miss Eliza is making blackberry jelly or damson shrub. And when a pheasant runs squawking from the road, I wonder who is picking the fowl now. Hatty is too squeamish for such things. Miss Eliza must have a new girl. But I don't want to think about Miss Eliza or Hatty because it makes me feel emptied, as if I have nothing inside me.

"The asylum is a new building." The miller speaks with great pride, as if he built it himself. "Designed by the same man as built Maidstone jail." He nods in a satisfied way and points ahead with the willow stick he's been using as a whip on his old nag.

Iron gates loom up, and beyond them a road unrolls. At the end of it I can just make out a building, very big, very gray. All corners and angles and scaffolding. My heart gives a little bound. I am soon to see Mam! And the nurse that cares for her. Maybe even her doctor, her room . . .

"Still building it," adds the miller, with the same proud note in his voice.

As we get closer I see the asylum is very grand, with a fine clock and great squatting columns and long thin chimneys that point to Heaven. Around the building runs an iron railing with spikes on top. On either side of the iron gates are a pair of matching gatehouses, oil lamps flaring from their small square windows.

"Hundreds in there," says the miller. "And all of 'em raving lunatics."

He drops me at the gatehouse and tells me to be ready for collection at four sharp. When the nag clops away, I'm struck by a feeling of loneliness, as if everyone has died of plague and there's just me left. An odd feeling and one I never had at Bordyke House. But then a small hatch opens in the wall and a face is peering at me, red like a steak and riven with pox scars.

"I'm here to see Mrs. Jane Kirby, please, sir," I say, lifting my chin like Miss Eliza did when she was talking to Ma'am.

"We're closed." The hatch is pulled shut. My chin tumbles. Why did no one tell me asylums close? I thought they were like churches, open all hours.

I tap on the hatch with my fingernails. "Please, sir! I'm all the way from Tonbridge to see my mother."

He pulls the hatch back, sharpish. "It ain't visiting day."

"I don't know anything about visiting days," I say, my voice cracking.

He sighs and asks if I have anything for him, his fingers scratching at a scab on the side of his nose.

"I have my wages, sir," I say, relieved I brought all my shillings and pennies. Which I did only to stop Pa spending them on drink.

"How much?" he asks, and has the decency to look away. "Only I must share it with the nurses. To make it worth their while to bring her to you, seeing as it's not a regular visiting day."

"Bring her to me?" I frown but the man looks blank. "I wanted to see where she's living . . . her room."

He laughs as if I have made a very funny joke. "Her *room* . . . ," he says, wiping at his rheumy eyes with a filthy handkerchief.

"I have near enough five shillings," I say. "But I must keep some by for the man who rode me here."

"How about three shillings?"

I nod, wanting to be rid of the grasping greedy man. I push the money—the best part of my earnings—through the hatch. He snatches it up and slides the hatch door closed. While he's gone I look down the long drive and examine the big gray house—the closed windows, the chiming clock tower, the rows of bony yew saplings. All at once, I see a figure at a window up on the third floor. Beating at the glass with their fists. And then gone. Just like Punch at a Punch and Judy show when the puppet master whisks him from the stage. I train my eyes on the window, for the sight has unnerved me. But the window stays blank, so I tell myself it's my mind playing tricks on me.

Eventually the lodge keeper returns, his hand scratching at the fork of his trousers. "Mrs. Jane Kirby don't have no daughter," he says. "She is assured of that."

"I'm her daughter! I swear it . . . she has no memory. That's why she's here." My voice climbs higher and higher. And then I remember: I must make myself agreeable if I'm to stand any chance of seeing Mam—or getting my three shillings back. "Please, sir, I'm her only daughter, come to wish her happy birthday."

"She hasn't mentioned no daughter or birthday," he says, suspicious.

A strange thought comes to me. Perhaps they don't want me to see Mam. I can't think why this might be, but a small voice speaks, soft and cunning, in my head: *They are keeping her from you. Even for three shillings, they are keeping her from you.*

"Four shillings!" I say, desperate now.

But the man shakes his head. "It ain't up to me, missy. They'll have her ready for visiting day. I'll let 'em know Mrs. Jane Kirby is to have a visitor." He returns my three shillings, hot and greasy from his pocket, and shuffles back into the gatehouse.

Oh my Lord, I think. He turned down four shillings . . . what have they done to her? My stomach is turning over like a bottle jack, and there is a cold sweat in the pits of my arms. I rap on the hatch; and when he slides it open, with an irritated expression, I ask, "When is visiting day, please, sir?"

He tells me the next one is a fortnight Saturday, adding, "A little sweetener for the nurses never goes amiss. Shall I tell 'em to expect something?"

"Yes, and there'll be coins for your kindness too, sir." I slip a penny through the hatch and wonder if perhaps he'd like a square of damson cheese. If I could afford just a small bag of Lisbon sugar, if I could collect enough furze for a clear brisk fire . . . I have an hour before I must meet the miller. I will hunt for kindling, I think.

I turn back for a last look of the lunatic asylum. Its empty windows gape at me like hollow eyes that cannot close. From the chimney tops, carrion crows whirl up and flap their wings. And from a small barred window beneath the clock I see a face peeping out. Is it Mam? It's too far away to make out any features, but I wave my hand and smile. Then I blink—and the face is gone.

CHAPTER TWENTY-FIVE
ELIZA

TEAKETTLE BROTH

Mrs. Thorpe's directions are faultless, and within thirty minutes I arrive at the alehouse she described. I hear it before I see it: the sound of scouring throats, hawking, coughing, raised voices. A straggle of navvies, laborers, and truant pickers lounge in the dust, drinking from pots and pewters, and sucking on little black pipes. They doff their caps with feigned obeisance. One spits loudly, another shouts out with the coarsest and most uncouth of words. I quicken my step. But as I pass, something hits me from behind. Something small, hard, round. A crab apple? A stone? Their rough laughter rings in my ears as I hurry around the corner, my petticoats tangling at my legs. I feel a goad of anger at the thriftiness that compelled me to come on foot. I should have taken a wagon and paid the price.

Ahead of me lies a copse of elm trees, and at its mouth a mud and stud hovel no bigger than the scullery at Bordyke House.

Can this really be Ann's home? Although I have seen many such dwellings from a carriage window, to connect this hovel with someone I *have feelings for* is a shock. I expected a cottage, with chickens scratching in a small but well-tended vegetable garden, perhaps a munching goat, a decent window at the very least.

But that is not what I see. The thatched roof is threadbare and fissured, with thin bundles of straw hanging, drunken and disheveled, from the eaves. The little chimney is cracked and tilts perilously to one side. Ivy rampages over the single window that is no more than a hole in the wall stuffed with rags. Paint peels and flakes from the front door, which is open and hanging from its hinges. There are no goats. No chickens. Just a dog with protruding ribs that has been tied to a post and is barking and jumping at me.

I call Ann's name. The dog strains on his rope and barks with greater ferocity.

"Mr. Kirby?" I push the door and my fingers sink into the spongy wood. Inside is a single room: low ceilinged, reeking of stale beer, mildew, the cheapest tallow. A mattress, straw bursting from its corners, lies in a shallow puddle of water that appears to have seeped up from the floor of beaten earth. There is an open fireplace, over which an iron pole hangs, and on the stone hearth sits an iron kettle, a single frying pan, and two tin plates. A square of worn oilcloth acts as a rug on the puddled floor, which bears the marks of bird droppings that have fallen through the ragged thatch.

My eyes adjust to the gloom, and I notice a dented metal chest in the corner. The flour chest? I ease open the rusting lid. Inside are four blemished apples, a covered jug of water, a jar of lard, two small eggs streaked with chicken feces, a dish of blackberries, and a bowl of flour so coarse it better resembles grit from the road. I close the lid, thinking of the larder at Bordyke House and how it spills with meat, fish, butter, cream, sugar . . . I think of Colonel Martin's careless demands for plover's eggs and finnan haddock cooked in cream and fine salt, of how Mrs. Martin left half a roasted pigeon and the best part of a salmon pudding upon her dinner plate, of all the lavish food served and wasted in monied kitchens everywhere.

A queasiness comes over me and a line of poetry tumbles into my head . . . *Few save the poor feel for the poor: The rich know not how hard it is to be of needful food* . . . Why did I allow Mother to dismiss Ann? Why did Colonel Martin leave victorious and Ann in ignominy? For a minute I am lost inside my head. Then I pull myself back to the present and scan the room for any sign of Ann's dead mother. In vain. The clothes hanging from pegs hammered into the wall are those of a man, all of them patched and fraying. There are no shoes laid out, no books, no pictures on the walls, no linen, no lamps, no good china or glassware. The mattress has a single flattened pillow and is wrapped in a balding blanket. There is no washtub—how does she wash the dishes, the clothes, her own body? A throbbing builds behind my eyes.

I pull from my pocket the note I wrote at Bordyke House and leave it under a stone in front of the door. The dog starts barking again, showing his yellow teeth in an angry, stinking snarl.

I look behind the cottage, thinking foolishly that perhaps Ann or Mr. Kirby is tending a vegetable bed. A narrow, roughly dug plot, no longer than a broomstick, has been squeezed between the cottage and a lurching wooden fence. Beyond the fence lies pasture, a vigorous green, grazed by fat, contented bullocks who flick their tails and amble curiously toward me. I wonder who owns this land, who takes rent from Ann's family and gives so little in return.

On my way home, and in spite of the insistent throbbing in my skull, I decide to look in at the alehouse. Perhaps Ann will be there, I think. As soon as it comes into view, the laborers start their catcalls and cussing. They are still squatting in the dust, but I stride past, lowering my head to enter. The room, which is quite unlike any of the inns and taverns my father once owned, has smoke-blackened beams that graze the top of my bonnet. There is a table in the center that carries the remnants of a week's ale and ash, the ash in little heaps as if tapped from many pipes and not yet cleared. The greasy dribblings of a tallow candle run through the ash and ale, like wax tributaries.

The waft of boiling giblets, gizzards, bones, fat—from an iron cauldron suspended on a pothook above a meager fire—adds to the oppressive odor of drink and smoke and unwashed clothing. My eyes begin to smart from the chimney smoke, the tobacco smoke, the thick greasy fug of the place.

A woman appears from the shadows, a pipe between her teeth, and scowls silently at me. I want to ask how she lives and eats, but her expression does not invite questions. I cast around instinctively for the nearest exit. There is only the front door, now blocked with a cluster of filthy, half-naked children who watch me with soup-bowl eyes. From beyond, the laborers—rick burners? cattle thieves? poachers?—begin to sing a bawdy, tuneless song about an old maid. They have noticed I am without a wedding ring.

"Are you wanting summat to drink?" The woman speaks through her pipe, pointing at a wooden pail of scum beneath the table.

"No, thank you," I say, suddenly fearful for my safety. Whatever impelled me to step inside this lair? I move swiftly to the door, but the children block my exit with their stick-thin bodies.

"Teakettle broth then? Boiled with the best mutton bones." The woman wipes her hands up and down an apron stiff with dried blood and dirt. "A ha'penny to you, lady. Unless you want parsnip peelings too?"

A laborer cuffs the head of a child, pushes past, and weaves his way to the table where he dips his tankard into the scummy bucket, a string of oaths flying from his lips. Seeing the sudden breach I throw a shilling upon the table and make a dash for the door. I have seen enough, I think. Indeed, I have seen more of how the poor live in one hour than I have seen in three decades. As I walk away, their lewd song follows me . . . "Was an old maid from Tunbridge Wells, made her bed on old seashells, invited me to join her there, I dropped my breeches without a care, she jumped up and I held her down . . ." On and on it goes, until finally I can hear no more. Only then does it occur to me that perhaps Mr. Kirby was among that crowd of drunken oafs.

Mrs. Thorpe's cryptic, vinegary words float ominously back to me: *I cannot answer for what you will find.* I have no need of an answer, I think. I merely want Ann back. And now I have seen her threadbare, loveless home I am quite determined to get her back.

CHAPTER TWENTY-SIX
ANN

QUINCE JELLY

I am back to Bordyke House today. I rose early, before Pa was awake, feeling as happy as a lark. Even the sun seemed to greet me as it nudged its rays over the hop gardens, the orchards, the pickers stumbling from their canvas tents. I was so happy that when the boys throwing stones at the crows turned a few pebbles on me, I just laughed and threw them back. I sang below my breath all the way to Tonbridge: ballads, lullabies, nursery rhymes. And when my throat was dry from singing, I danced. Jigging and country dancing until I arrived at the quarry on the outskirts of town. Then I made myself grave and sober, fit to be a kitchen maid—yes, a kitchen maid now—for Miss Eliza Acton.

She left the nicest note on our doorstep, kindly asking me to return as a kitchen maid with wages of six shillings a week. And at the bottom of her note, which I swear was perfumed with vanilla essence, she had drawn pictures of a three-tiered cake, a molded jelly, a raised pie, and a boiled pudding on a platter. I smiled for three hours straight. When Pa came home, he was not best pleased about my grinning. But when I said my position was returned to me—and as a kitchen maid—he grinned too. I didn't have the heart to tell him about the asylum. And he didn't ask.

I start work on the range, blacking and polishing 'til it gleams like coal. It's not until I stop humming and rubbing that I hear a sound from the scullery. As if someone is playing with the copper pans. I stiffen, for who could it be? I creep down the passage to the scullery and put my head, very cautious, around the door. A tiny girl with frightened eyes is polishing the coppers. Hares and rabbits and a brace of pheasants swing from the rack above her head.

"I'm Ann," I say, relieved. For this child must be a new scullery maid. "What's your name?"

"Mary, o' course."

I look at her dumbly. "Why of course?"

She stops looking frightened and looks confused instead. "All sculleries are Mary. But my real name is Lizzie."

"I was the scullery maid before you," I say softly. "And I was always Ann. Miss Eliza likes to use our real names."

She grins shyly. "I like Lizzie better than Mary."

"Are you picking those pheasants and skinning those rabbits and hares today?" I ask, wondering what dishes Miss Eliza has in mind.

She nods and I wonder how old she is. Ten? Eleven?

"There is a gentleman boarder coming today," she adds, as if that explains why the scullery is swinging with birds and beasts.

"Have you done much picking and skinning?"

She nods and I notice her hands, which are raw and calloused with no nails to speak of. Her presence makes me feel most peculiar, as if I'm grown in stature. As if I am older and wiser. Only I am not. But there's no time to dwell on this, for in bustles Mrs. Acton, who greets me, very brief, and says Miss Eliza has gone for a haunch of venison and I must get a good brisk fire going and then pare and quarter four pounds of quinces from the larder.

I can tell she's in a state of some excitement, because her fingers are constantly at her ring, at her cuffs, at her neckline. As if she cannot still them. She flaps around the kitchen as I lay the fire, opening and closing the window, moving things on the dresser, running a finger over the salvers and the soup tureen, squinting at the sherry glasses, looking for fingerprints and dust.

I go to the larder for the quinces and stop in amazement. For the larder is brimming over with food. Baskets of field mushrooms. Trugs of green apples and yellow pears. A metal bath containing two pink crabs. Slabs of newly churned butter as bright as a dandelion flower. Wheels of pale yellow cheese the size of my head. An earthenware bowl of cobnuts. A ham soaking in a pail of water. Who is to eat all this food? And why has Miss Eliza gone for a haunch of venison when we have supplies to feed a king?

"How many boarders have we this week, Ma'am?" I know it isn't my place to ask questions like this, but I'm too curious to hold back.

"Mr. Arnott arrives this afternoon," she says, and her fingers fly to her neckline, arranging it for the umpteenth time. "He's from London and only eats the finest food. Do not disappoint me, Ann Kirby." She looks over my shoulder at the quinces and I wish she would leave me be. I cannot peel these knobbled monsters with her breathing down my neck.

"Has that knife been properly scoured?" she asks. "Mr. Arnott has been in France and French gentlemen greatly object to the flavor of the knife. Indeed, Mr. Arnott has been everywhere. He is exceptionally well traveled and we must not appear provincial."

I want to ask what *provincial* means. Instead I ask, "How is Miss Eliza to serve the quinces, Ma'am?"

But she does not answer me, for she sees something from the corner of her eye that makes her fly into a fit. She swoops her arm behind a serving dish on the dresser—the china one wreathed with oak leaves and acorns—and pulls out a book that is so prettily bound in crimson watered silk my eyes are on stalks. Ribbons are threaded through the cover, in pink and white—it's the most elegant and fashionable book I have ever seen. Mrs. Acton flings the book onto the table, then starts moving all the china on the dresser, looking behind the platters and tureens, then opening the drawers and rummaging among the linen. I try to concentrate on peeling the quinces, but it's impossible with the elegant silken book in front of me, and Mrs. Acton breathing like a bullock behind me.

After a few minutes she cries out, victorious, "Aha!" and pulls a huge book from the drawer in which Miss Eliza stores the boxed cutlery with the bone handles. I get a glimpse of the book and it is so beautiful I long to open it and see inside. The cover is of green leather tooled and gilded with twining flowers and fat cherubs. Even I know these aren't Miss Eliza's cookery books, which are all of dull brown calfskin. Mrs. Acton sweeps up both albums beneath her arm and flounces out. I am so surprised I gape into space, until little Lizzie creeps into the kitchen, her eyes shooting in all directions.

"Do you need help?" I ask

"No," she says, in such a small hoarse voice I wonder if she hasn't got something wrong with her throat. "Miss Eliza showed me everything last week."

"You've been here a week?"

"Yes. All the talk has been of the gentleman boarder who comes today." She tiptoes back to the scullery, leaving me to wrestle with the quinces so as they don't carry any *flavor of the knife*. But I can't stop thinking of Mrs. Acton's queer behavior . . . *confiscating* Miss Eliza's special books.

I'm so deep in thought, I don't notice Miss Eliza until she's sailed in, her cheeks glowing, her eyes shining. "How marvelous to have you back, Ann!"

I wonder if she will take me in her arms, like she did before. Although circumstances were quite different then. She doesn't, but I know she's pleased because her smile is stretched very large across her beautiful face. "Yes, Miss Eliza, it's good to be back. Thank you." I bob my head to show how grateful I am.

"We have a busy day ahead of us," she says. "Mother has doubled our food budget for the duration of Mr. Arnott's stay. No expense is to be spared for our gentleman boarder."

"What is it to be tonight?" I ask.

"Hare soup, hot crab served in its own shell, then roast haunch of venison with gravy, and the sweet dish will be a meringue of pears. I have been practicing all week!"

I feel my face flush scarlet, for I suddenly remember Miss Eliza has seen my home. And the image of it beside her fine food fills me with shame. All at once I feel unworthy. Of her, of Bordyke House, of the food we must prepare.

"Ma'am asked me to peel these quinces," I say, to cover my hot shame.

"Oh, they are for a quince cheese. They must go through the jelly bag overnight."

Then she leans in very close and says, "My mother wishes to impress Mr. Arnott, so everything must be as perfect as we can make it." She arches her brows, then rolls her eyes in a manner that flummoxes me. Why all the effort, all the mountains of food, for a single boarder?

"When you have poached the quinces," says Miss Eliza, "I have some books I wish to share with you. Indeed, I shall lend them to you." Her eyes are shining like new pennies.

A tingle runs up my arms, for there is nothing I like better than to look at Miss Eliza's new books, to picture the puddings and preserves, the sauces and gravies, the sweets and ices. To fancy myself as a good plain cook, slicing and stirring, tasting and seasoning.

But Miss Eliza is not reaching for the shelf where she keeps her recipe books. Instead, she's at the dresser, opening and closing the drawers and looking behind the serving platters and the salvers.

"How very peculiar," she murmurs.

"Ma'am took them." I stare hard at the paring knife in my hand.

She wheels around. "This is becoming intolerable! At moments like this I wish to God I was my own mistress."

"They were beautiful books." I put the quinces in a pot and scrape some sugar from the loaf. *But they were not recipe books.*

"Two can play at her game," mutters Miss Eliza. I don't understand her words and must concentrate on the sugarloaf that is as hard as a rock.

"As it happens, I have memorized one for you. Should you like to hear it?" She starts reciting, one hand at her breast:

> *"My heart's in the kitchen, my heart is not here,*
> *My heart's in the kitchen, though following the dear,*
> *Thinking on the roast meat, and musing on the fry,*
> *My heart's in the kitchen whatever I spy."*

She claps her hands and laughs. "It's a parody of a verse by Mr. Burns," she says, seeing my blank look.

I have no idea who Mr. Burns is or what the word *parody* means, but I smile because I'm so happy to be back.

"I am quite determined to teach you the art of poetry, Ann," she says. "We shall do it as we cook. But perhaps not until Mr. Arnott has left and we no longer have to produce five-course banquets for a single gentleman."

An image of Mrs. Thorpe shouting at her girl, Florence, floats before me; and it seems that every inch of me grows, expands, bursts with joy. And then I hear a voice in my head, struggling, swelling, muscling Mrs. Thorpe aside. It's Mam. I reach for her words: *Sound on, thou dark unslumbering sea! . . . Thou sea-bird on the billow's crest . . .* Is she reciting to me? Reading to me? The words seem familiar but I cannot place them.

"Poetry has been the greatest solace to me." Miss Eliza avoids my eye and I know she's thinking of my home, my *hovel*.

She pushes the slate and chalk toward me. "I want you to record weights, measures, and timings today."

We spend the next few hours preparing dinner, which Mr. Arnott has asked to be served at five o'clock. It turns out Miss Eliza has cooked all these dishes several times over—with the help of Hatty and little Lizzie—and is now adjusting the cooking times, seasonings, and quantities. She writes everything down in her notebook, and for two hours I hear only the scratch of her nib. Finally, as I am emptying the cooled quinces into a jelly bag, she lifts her head and says, "When you write down your timings and measurements, I would be grateful if you could add any other observations."

I frown. "Observations?"

"For instance, when I stewed quinces last week the juice was almost scarlet, but your juice is dripping through in a glorious golden hue. So your blancmange will be prettier than mine. Why might that be?"

I blush. "Your instructions were to simmer them for an hour, but they were soft at a half hour. So I took them from the fire early. I beg your pardon, Miss Eliza."

"Marvelous!" she says. "That is exactly the sort of observation I wish to include in our cookery book."

Our cookery book? *Our?* I am so flooded with feeling I cannot speak. And then I realize she means Mrs. Acton, of course. What a dunce I am! It is to be the cookery book of a mother and daughter. I can see the frontispiece now: Mrs. and Miss Acton in their best clothes, drawn in pen and ink, with the best Dresden china behind them and pheasants and hares dropping from the ceiling. Like the frontispieces of other recipe books Miss Eliza has.

There is a wrench in my heart. *Mam.* All of a sudden I am seven years of age again. Mam is lifting quince pips with a tin skimmer. She chops the flesh and gives me the cores that I may suck at the golden clinging fruit, which is melting soft, sweet, perfumed, and slips down my throat like cream.

"My mother always left the quinces in their liquor overnight," I say tentatively. "With the pips and cores. She said it set firmer and faster like that."

Miss Eliza gives me a long, unblinking look. After a while, she tells me to add *that sort of detail* to the slate. I hope my spelling is good enough for *observations*, I think, glad of all the nights I crept to bed with a cookery book in my apron. And when her back is turned, I press my hands together and murmur, "Please make my spelling good enough, dear Lord."

Chapter Twenty-Seven
ELIZA

PEAR MERINGUE WITH BON CHRÉTIEN PEARS

I am changed into my velvet dress with the silk bodice and pearl fasteners when Mr. Arnott arrives. I've scrubbed the onion and garlic from my fingers, rinsed my hair in lavender water, daubed my wrists and throat with rose oil. Mother has instructed me to play the hostess, saying I am to take credit for the fine food but without admitting that I cooked it and without showing too much enthusiasm that might *reveal my appetites*. She has also forbidden me from saying anything about poetry, except to admit that I read and appreciate it. And the cookery book? Not a word to be breathed, she hissed, adding that no man wishes to marry a woman who *worships at the shrine of ambition*.

"So how exactly are we to converse?" I replied, my voice edged with sarcasm.

"Express an interest in his business," she said. "It should not be too difficult."

"And what is his business?"

"I have told you several times, Eliza!" she said, most exasperated with me. "You have had your ears closed all week. He is a spice merchant, importing spices from all over the world. He is an exceptionally well-traveled gentleman."

"A spice merchant?" I repeated. That was the exact moment I began to think of Mr. Arnott as, possibly, the key to my freedom. A gentleman who is frequently abroad, who can discuss flavor and food . . . I heard again that little, tempting voice of hope: *a chance for liberty, respect, motherhood?*

Mother's words burst into my thoughts. "Yes, an *elderly* spice merchant. But not too elderly to beget children, my dear. Exactly like you."

I peer through the back window, for he has arrived by carriage and the yard is full of sleek prancing horses and men in tight frock coats. Half of me watches his footman lifting traveling trunks, while the other half of me frets over what is happening in the kitchen. Ann will have to manage, I think, for I cannot be both cook *and* demure discoursing lady. I sniff at my cuff for any residual odor of roasting marrow bones or chopped onion. There is only the faintest smell of washing lye and the rose oil Mother insisted upon. No doubt to mask any exposing taint of the kitchen.

To my surprise, Mr. Arnott alights nimbly from his carriage. He has a full head of hair, silver but thick. And when he turns I see that his skin is the color of a hazelnut, his figure is trim, and his clothes are of the latest fashion—a dark tailcoat; a cravat of twilled silk; narrow, fly-fronted trousers that strap beneath his gleaming shoes. He is not what I expected. My fingers race to my hair, pushing the loose strands from my face, then quickly pinching at my cheeks.

Mother scuttles out to welcome him. My instructions are to await him in the drawing room, where he is to be offered tea, my freshly baked almond macaroons—and conversation. I half expect him to desist, for surely he will be fatigued after his journey. But no, I hear him and Mother approaching, the door opening— and behold!

As soon as he is seated, I study him. His face is closely shaved and handsome, although he cannot be less than sixty. His tailcoat is of Irish tweed and when he moves there is a flash of gold from the heavy watch chain beneath. Every time he lifts his hands, the diamond studs at his cuffs wink encouragingly at me. Of course we must discuss his journey and the weather and the virtues of Tunbridge Wells and its waters. And then we must talk of the old days when he and my father were acquainted.

Hatty brings a tray of tea. Mr. Arnott takes a macaroon and bites into it. "Exceptionally good," he says. "I believe Jordan almonds have been used."

"Indeed," I say, regarding him with interest.

"Your cook is accomplished," he adds. "If I'm not mistaken, the almonds have been browned first in a slow oven, for this macaroon has a pleasantly toasted flavor."

Mother leaps in. "We are fortunate to have a good plain cook, but she works entirely to the orders of my daughter. Eliza is the brains behind everything you shall eat here. She would be delighted to dine with you, should you want company. She can talk you through the menu at the same time."

I look at her, askance. How am I to produce a five-course feast if I am sitting at Mr. Arnott's table for hours?

"I should enjoy both the company and the instruction," he says, appraising me with a keen and narrowed eye.

My smile fixes stiffly upon my face and a panicked tightness comes to my throat.

As soon as Mother takes him to his rooms I dash to the kitchen, all decorum forgotten. Ann is calmly making mayonnaise in the manner I have shown her, whisking oil into egg yolks, drop by drop. Her serenity fades once she knows she must prepare and garnish every dish and that I will not be in attendance for a single second. Her eyes fill with dread and her hands begin to shake so that the oil falls too fast into the yolks.

"We can manage," I say. "The crab can go to the table cold instead of warm—so we can prepare and arrange it together. The hare soup is simmering and all you must do is season it with salt and cayenne, then send it to table very hot. The venison is on the spit but you will have to carve it and prepare the gravy." I stop for a moment and take a long calming breath. "Let us cook the potatoes very plain in the Lancashire way. The pear meringue we shall do now."

"I c-cannot carve," Ann stammers, laying down the whisk.

"I shall teach you, exactly as my father taught me," I reply, keeping my tone steady to conceal the racing of my pulse. "Carving with propriety and self-possession is a skill every woman should possess."

Two hours later and Ann is calmer. But I am so fretful I have to clasp my hands beneath the dining table to stop them fidgeting—

even as Mr. Arnott regales me with amusing anecdotes about his recent trip to Amsterdam. I feel as if only a slender fraction of myself sits at table while the larger part of me is in the kitchen.

When the soup tureen comes, I run my finger quickly around its rim. Clever Ann has remembered to warm it on the hearth. Mr. Arnott, who seems not to have noticed how distracted I am, takes a spoonful of soup. I do the same, letting it run around my mouth. The temperature is perfect. And every drop of fat has been properly skimmed, so the broth is clean and meaty and leaves no greasy residue upon the tongue.

"Excellent soup," says Mr. Arnott, his lips making an appreciative smacking sound.

"Thank you," I say, greatly relieved. "It is my own recipe. Do you think the herbs strike the right note?" The question leaps from me, as if of its own accord. Immediately I regret it: Will he think my question suggestive of *appetites*? I'm about to smooth away my hasty question with something more appropriate, when Mr. Arnott nods vigorously and asks a question that surprises and delights me.

"What spices have you used?"

"Mace and cayenne, of course." I laugh, with relief and gratitude.

"I am resolved to broaden your cook's use of spices," he says. "May I have a delivery sent directly to you?" He proceeds to tell me about blends of curry powders, the benefits of fresh spices, the tamarinds he is now importing in the shell. I am so absorbed I forget the kitchen—and my unfeminine blunders—entirely. He describes the smoky flavor of cumin, the black bitterness of fenugreek seeds, the sweet richness of fresh coconut flesh, the fierce blast of fresh gingerroot.

Hatty clears the soup bowls while Mr. Arnott tells me of his favorite curries. I try to commit his words to memory, repeating everything after him. "Grate and simmer the flesh of two coconuts, you say?"

"They must be fresh—a rancid coconut is not a thing of beauty. You seem uncommonly interested in my trade, Miss Acton." He eyes me over his glass of port, and for a minute I wonder if he's assessing my *appetites*. But his eyes are so frank and bright and honest I resolve to stop any pretense of being appetiteless.

"I am," I reply. "Your knowledge of spices and curries and oriental food has impressed me greatly."

When the crab arrives, I realize I've barely given any thought to Ann and her ministrations. To my surprise she has added a few finishing touches of her own. The crab sits snugly in its pink shell, beside a neat mound of delicately green mayonnaise. How has she colored it green?

"This could be made into a curry," pronounces Mr. Arnott. "In Madras, curried sea oysters are considered the pinnacle of fine food. Anything can be curried . . . fish, fowl, even eggs."

"Eggs?" Again, he has intrigued me.

"Indeed eggs," he says. "Hard-boiled and placed in a hot curried gravy, they are quite delicious."

I taste the mayonnaise, trying to fathom how Ann has greened it. Simultaneously I try to commit Mr. Arnott's recipe for curried eggs to memory, while also checking the seasoning in the crab.

"Do you think the crab would benefit from a little more lemon juice?" I ask. "Or perhaps chili vinegar should have been used."

"It is certainly fresh." He slowly savors the crab upon his tongue. "It tastes of the sea." Then he turns quite suddenly and fixes his eyes upon me. "I have never met a lady so fascinated by food. So curious . . . so knowledgeable. It is most refreshing."

I feel myself swell beneath his admiring eye. And when Hatty clears the plates, I hardly notice her. My moment of conceit passes as I anticipate the venison that is to come, and everything that can go wrong with a spit-roast haunch. Even when served with plain boiled potatoes and a simple gravy of beef stock and port. But Mr. Arnott distracts me yet again by describing his favorite soup, a curried dish he calls mullagatawny, cooked with marrows, cucumbers, apples, and a curry powder of his own blending. He pronounces it to be the most delicious soup ever, excluding my hare soup, of course. I half suspect him of flirting with me, for he keeps looking piercingly into my eyes. And I wrest my gaze away with the greatest reluctance.

The venison follows, thick moist slabs of it. The potatoes swim in melted butter, and the gravy has been expertly sweetened with a little red currant jelly. Ann has forgotten nothing, I think, until I feel the dinner platter and it is stone cold.

Our conversation turns to Hastings, where Mr. Arnott first befriended my father. It is such a relief to talk of my father without having to pretend he is dead that I am quite overcome for a moment. "In Tonbridge we must maintain the pretense that my mother is a widow," I explain haltingly. "Just while we establish ourselves. It has been a testing time."

"Yes, I can see that." He reaches over and touches my arm, and something about this little avuncular gesture makes me feel deeply content.

The venison is taken away, replaced by the pear meringue, which we eat with long-handled spoons. The grainy sweetness of the pears bursts and melts in my mouth, adding to my deep sense of contentment.

"What variety of pears are these?" he asks.

"They are bon chrétien pears," I reply. "I make a point of always knowing the variety of fruit I'm using and cooking only with the ripest."

He raises his eyebrows and I know instantly that I have revealed myself. A slow scarlet heat crawls up my throat and over my cheeks.

"It is delectable," he says after a long pause. I look at the bronzed peaks of meringue and feel his brain turning over and over, as if he is trying to comprehend me.

Hatty appears with the coffee tray, Mother close behind her. As we sip our coffee, she questions Mr. Arnott on the size of his business, the location of his London house, his servants, the professions of his two children, his health, and how he likes to spend his leisure time—a full interrogation that she conducts without a shred of shame. As he patiently answers her litany of questions, a white spark turns, flashes, skims across the table. His diamond studs. Yes, I think, perhaps marriage to a man like Mr. Arnott might suit me. Perhaps, just perhaps, my heart is mended—and I am ready.

TURNIPS IN BUTTER

Mr. Arnott is spending the weekend with relatives, so Miss Eliza gives me a day's leave. I think she'd like me to visit Jack in London because she keeps asking about Monsieur Soyer. But today is visiting day at the Kent County Lunatic Asylum and that's where I'm headed.

I'm bone-tired, for while *she* has been dining with Mr. Arnott, I have been cook *and* kitchen maid. My arms ache from kneading and whisking and beating. My wrists are sore from chopping and cutting and grating. My legs throb from standing for hour upon hour. And my hands are riven and blistered with cuts and burns. In fairness, Miss Eliza has also worked to the bone. Most mornings I have come down at five upon the hour, and she is already in the kitchen, poring over her books. I have done the same whenever time permits—even by moonlight after Hatty has fallen asleep and I can barely keep my eyes open. No matter how

tired I am, the recipes jump from their pages in a great swarm of
smells and tastes: possets and syllabubs, stews and soups, boiled
puddings and baked puddings, potted meats and pies, jellies and
jams. Already I have surprised Miss Eliza with my own touches
to her dishes. On these occasions she comes to me, in very good
humor, and asks, "What did you slip so expertly into that dish,
Ann?" And my heart turns right over in a somersault.

Now that Mr. Arnott is enticing her from the kitchen with his
wily ways I'm more determined than ever to please her. Hatty
says they have eyes only for each other and that it's only a matter of time before he asks for her hand. She says they barely notice the food I've slaved over. But when Miss Eliza appears, she
showers praise upon me, looking at me all the while with such
fondness that when I think on it later, tears stand in my eyes.

Recently Miss Eliza has not been quite herself. This morning I came down and she was not at her books but staring at
the dresser, where the everyday china hangs. I waited for her to
make a comment about greasy fingerprints on the soup bowls.
Instead she said, "'It is a dreadful thing for woman's lip to swear
the heart away . . .'" She sounded so wistful I was emboldened to
ask her meaning. "I am quoting from poetry, Ann," she replied.
"You know what a solace it is to me."

I wondered if she needed *solace* because of what I'd overheard the previous day. All I'd wanted was some instruction on
how best to truss a corncrake, for they are small skinny birds.
But when I sought her out in the drawing room, the door was
closed—which is not usual. And I could hear high angry voices.

Miss Eliza and Ma'am were shouting, quite out of turn. I knew it was private and I should turn away, but I listened at the door instead. Miss Eliza was demanding to know the whereabouts of her poetry books and manuscripts. And Ma'am was saying nothing, until Miss Eliza raised her voice very loud and cried, "If you will not return them, I will not keep quiet about certain other things that you find infinitely more disgraceful than my writing of verse." There was a very long silence, so I crept back to the kitchen and trussed the corncrake as best I could.

What did she mean? Why is Ma'am so quick to hide Miss Eliza's books and poems? There is still this itch in me to read her verse, but it's dawning on me that there is something amiss in those poems, something Ma'am wants none of us to know. And the more this notion settles in my mind, the more curious I become. It makes my head hurt, thinking over and over, and then it strikes me that perhaps Ma'am has sold the book of verse. Or buried it. Or . . . A memory of Mam and Pa creeps, unwanted, into my head. He is tearing the pages from a book, twisting each one to make a paper spill, pushing it into the little fire, shouting that we will freeze and starve, while she sobs with her head in her hands, her scrawny hands that are red and blue with cold. A chill runs over me, so I push the memory away and think what a pleasant bright day it is, how fortunate I am to have a day's leave, how pleased Mam—in her big warm house brimming with food— will be to see me.

The asylum is ahead of me now, rearing up from the flat fields, its circle of iron railings glinting in the low autumn sun. I have a few shillings saved for the lodge keeper and the nurses, and for Mam I have Mr. Arnott's leftover dinner (a slice of pink roast beef, potted mushrooms, cold buttered turnips, and a scoop of brandy trifle). The lodge keeper slides back his hatch, scowling.

"Mrs. Jane Kirby please, sir." I slip him a shilling that he grabs most zealously.

Then I must wait for a long time, while word is sent that Mam has a visitor. Eventually the lodge keeper returns and says Mam will meet me in the grounds. He points at a staked yew tree and says she will be out in a minute.

I thank him and say, by way of conversation, "It's awful quiet for visiting day."

"No quieter than normal," he replies. "The lunatics don't much like visitors. And visitors don't much care for the lunatics either."

His words strike me as heartless and cruel, but I hold my tongue and stare at the yew saplings blowing in the wind. When three people appear from behind the building, he unlocks the gate and lets me through. I run toward them, one hand curled tightly around the coins for the nurses and the other around the little basket holding Mam's lunch. I want to run to her, but something stops me. She has a nurse on either side of her, both of them wearing bibbed aprons and with their sleeves rolled up to show their brawny arms. They appear to be guiding her toward me, cajoling and wheedling.

"Mam?" I say. "It's me, Ann."

She looks blank at me. Her eyes have a strange lifeless quality, like a dead river trout.

"She is settling in very nice," says one of the nurses. "Very nice indeed."

"Her memory is gone," says the other nurse. "She don't recognize anyone." She raises her voice to a holler, adding, "Not even her favorite nurses, do you, Jane?" And she leans around and pinches Mam's cheek, as if Mam's a pet child who is short of hearing.

"Mam, it's me," I say again and I reach out to stroke her cheek where the nurse has left a scarlet thumb mark. Then I remember my sweetener for the nurses and give them each a shilling. The cheek-pinching nurse bites the coin between her teeth and then slips it inside her dress. The other nurse holds her coin to the light, then rubs it on her apron and grins.

"You brought her up nice, Jane," bellows Cheek-Pincher and gives Mam a little shake. "Have you something to say, Jane?"

Mam looks confused, then a dull light comes into her eyes. "I am very happy here," she says in a single breath. And when the whispered words are out, the light disappears from her eyes as quick as it came.

The nurses nod in a satisfied way, their arms still upon her. "Oh yes, she is happy all right. Will you be coming every visiting day?"

"Yes," I say, very definite. "And if she's well, there'll always be something for your kindness." I know these are rash words and that much of my wages will go to these women. But there is something about them and this place that unsettles me. And I must see Mam right in the only way I can.

"Good, good," says the cheek-pinching nurse in a low, sooth-ing voice. "We shall take special care of your mam, won't we, Fran?"

The other nurse nods and leers. "Our special lunatic," she agrees.

"Can I hug her?"

The two nurses share a look I can't decipher, and then Cheek-Pincher says, "You can hug her while we hold her. Only she might harm herself if we let go."

"Or try and escape." Fran cackles. "Ain't that why she's 'ere?"

"We treats her like one of our own daughters, don't we, Fran?"

"Better than we treat our own daughters." Fran nods, her square head wobbling on her thick shoulders.

I put my arms around Mam's little waist, all skin and bone she is. The reek of the nurses' breath is everywhere. A reek I know only too well: ale. I feel Mam flinch beneath my touch, so I offer up my basket. "I have roast beef for you, Mam," I say. "And tur-nips in butter. And brandy trifle with Kent cherries. Shall I feed you like I used to? With an egg spoon . . ."

"Oh no, no, no," says Cheek-Pincher, her tongue clicking an-gry against the top of her mouth. "Those fancy victuals is too rich to eat now. But if we feed it to her at the regular hour, it will do very nicely." She turns to Mam and shouts in her ear, "You will enjoy this later, won't you, Jane?"

Fran drops Mam's arm and snatches the basket from me, her greedy hands pulling out the roast beef wrapped in waxed paper, the pot of mushrooms, the jar of trifle, the tin box of buttered turnips. She opens each container and sniffs loudly at it. Then she unwraps the beef and smells that too. "Oh, Jane will enjoy this fine fancy food, won't you, Jane?"

While Fran examines the food, I glance at Mam's dangling arm. The sleeve is pulled down as far as it will go, but I can just see her wrist, hanging loose. The inside is a strange yellow color. Cheek-Pincher follows my gaze and says, very sudden, "Your mam is in fine fettle. We treats her like a princess, you can be sure of that. Now, how did you come by this fancy grub?" And she winks at me.

"I work in a kitchen," I say, for I know by that wink she has me as a thief.

"Of course you do," she says, nodding and smirking. "We believe you, don't we, Fran?"

Fran nods and hooks the basket onto her wrist. "We'll give your basket back when you comes next. Your mam will be waiting on tenterhooks, won't you, Jane?"

Mam nods, like a docile child. Her empty eyes blink. Then she opens her mouth and whispers, "I am very happy here."

Fran pats her on the back and says, "So you are, Jane. So you are."

"We have to take her back now," says Cheek-Pincher. "Time for her daily visit with the doctor." She turns to Mam and bellows, "You like the doctor, don't you, Jane?"

"She sees the doctor every day?" I ask, relieved.

"Every day." Cheek-Pincher nods. "As regular as rain. And if she's late, we get a flea in our ear, don't we, Fran? And your mam don't like that. Your mam likes us happy, don't you, Jane?"

Mam looks at me, confused. Her nose twitches. Her eyes roll. For a second I think she's about to speak to me. "Mam?" I say again.

But she shakes her head, very fast, frantic. So that her cap falls askew, tilting to one side and covering an eye.

"Quick, Fran. She don't want to miss her appointment with the doctor. I can feel her getting agitated." And the two nurses turn and march her back to the asylum. I wonder if she will look back at me, acknowledge me with her eyes. But she doesn't. She doesn't look back once.

As I watch them go, I notice something peculiar. It's the back of her head. Where her cap has risen. Is there hair missing? A bald patch? I fix my eyes upon the spot, but the nurses are hurrying and Mam's head has become a blur.

I walk the fifteen miles home in a stupor, not knowing what to think. Her dress was clean, her hands and nails were scrubbed. She had proper shoes on, with good strong soles. She has two nurses all to herself and a doctor that visits daily. She lives in a grand house with walls as thick as my arm and real glass in the windows and its own clock tower. And yet my heart is heavy. For Mam was a ghost of herself. But she isn't running around half naked and she's safe, says my voice of reason. She has a fine thick roof over her head and food when she's hungry and no one throttling her when she wets herself by mistake.

Too thin, too yellow on the wrists, too subdued, says my other voice. After a while I can bear the two battling voices no more and I make myself think about Bordyke House. What is Miss Eliza doing? What are Hatty and Lizzie doing? What dishes will be in the larder when I get back? As I left, Miss Eliza had just taken delivery of a basket of new-laid pullets' eggs, still warm from the nesting box. Yes, she will be making custard, I bet. Flavoring it with nutmeg, or perhaps with finely rasped chocolate or lemon grate. Or maybe with honeyed liquor or a sweet German wine. I quicken my step, keen to get home. Home.

Chapter Twenty-Nine
ELIZA

INDIAN CURRIED FISH

For three consecutive days I dine with Mr. Arnott. He entertains me with his travel tales, interspersed with accounts of how spices grow and dollops of culinary information that I suck up with an unladylike enthusiasm. He teaches me how to avoid cayenne pepper that has been thinned with brick powder or mahogany sawdust. He explains how to cook Patna rice the Indian way so that it never clots. He tells me of dishes so ferociously hot they would make an English lady swoon. And afterward I rush to the kitchen and make notes lest I forget.

Then he goes to visit family in Hastings. On his return, three days later, he does not request my company at dinner. This is a grave disappointment to Mother, who is convinced he's heard gossip about me. But, at the very point she is most deeply in despair, he sends a request, via his footman, for my company. I confess: my heart danced. Rather to my surprise.

Mother leapt from her bed and hugged me. "I knew it, my dear! You have charmed him with your wit and seduced him with your menus! If you can lure him to a proposal, we can bring your father home from Calais and Catherine and Anna can be released from their governess positions."

Her words sent a shiver down my spine, for I saw then the full extent of her machinations. And I felt the weight of responsibility, like huge logs upon my shoulders: I am to rescue the Acton family from ignominy. I took the chance to pounce.

"Well, may I have my poetry books returned?"

She brushed at the air with her hands, in that irritating way of hers. As if I am a tetchy, spitting cat that must be mollified. "All in good time, my dear. But with his footman and manservant snooping around, we cannot take any risks."

I did not press my point, for our recent squabbles have robbed me of all energy. And today I need my full wits about me, if I am to be cook, hostess, and prospective wife, all rolled into one.

The mood in the kitchen is calm and unrushed. Ann is inspecting a delivery of carp using the methods I have taught her. She suggests, in her shy and tentative manner, a cucumber sauce.

"The season for cucumbers is over," I say, but she tells me there is a fresh firm cucumber in the larder, delivered only yesterday. I cannot help smiling. Since her return, she has blossomed into a competent plain cook, making herself wholly indispensable to me.

She begins scraping at the carp's scales, then pauses and gestures at the larder. "There's been a delivery of spices for you, miss. From London."

I clap my hands with delight. Mr. Arnott is certainly a man of his word, and prompt to boot. "Dare we attempt one of Mr. Arnott's favorite dishes?"

"May I ask if you are to be in the kitchen or in the dining room tonight, Miss Eliza?" She looks up and I see her eyes are ringed with dark shadows, like purple bruises.

"I must dine with Mr. Arnott tonight," I reply. Her face falls. "But don't fret—curries are best prepared in advance. I think we'll attempt a curried fish recipe he has described in glowing terms."

The spice delivery has been unwrapped from its chest. Black enameled tins, tiny glass jars, little hessian bags, each labeled by hand, are laid out for me to examine: cloves, turmeric, cayenne, blades of mace, whole nutmegs, powdered ginger, dried red chilies, a jar of pickled capsicum, woody scrolls of cinnamon bound with twine, black peppercorns, green peppercorns in brine, and various spice blends that Mr. Arnott has composed himself. I pick out a small tin, labeled "Arnott's Bengal Currie Powder."

"We shall use this," I say, placing the tin upon the kitchen table. "If it's successful, the recipe can sit in the Foreign and Jewish section of our book." Unless Mother forbids it, I think. But then I am reminded of a new future . . . in which I am Mrs. Arnott and need take no notice of Mother's imperious ways and antiquated thinking. A future in which the countless petty slights I've endured as an *old maid* have been whisked away—forever. I hold up my left hand and imagine it with a ring upon my wedding finger. For a second I feel the old void, the emptiness in the crook of my arm, but then Ann asks in a quavering voice, "Will you be the first of your sisters to marry, Miss Eliza?"

The question startles me, reminding me once again of the uncommonly frank relationship we have. We are more like cook and kitchen maid than mistress and servant, I think. Which is as it should be, for am I not more cook than mistress at Bordyke House? And is she not of unusual intelligence for a servant? But then Ann blushes and apologizes and lets slip that the kitchen gossip is all of me and Mr. Arnott. I like this in her—so candid and guileless and yet shy and humble at the same time.

"No need to apologize." I ease open the tin of Bengal Currie Powder. A dust of heat and spice rises, pungent and dry, into the air. "I have a younger sister who is married. She is a doctor's wife." I offer Ann the tin. "Mr. Arnott has composed this blend himself. I think it may be rather fiery for the English palate."

"How about I start with a salt spoon, and then taste as I go?"

I nod and give her bony hand a little squeeze. "You are the perfect pupil," I say, and her fingers push back briefly against mine.

We spend the day preparing dinner, working together as smoothly as the wheels of a clock. Only Lizzie's hoarse and toneless humming from the scullery perturbs me, but I push it aside, telling myself it is Lizzie's presence that has allowed Ann to bloom as a cook. And it is Ann's blooming that has enabled me to turn my charms to Mr. Arnott. As Ann chops, slices, fries, stirs, scrubs, and keeps the fire at the right briskness, my mind lingers on Mr. Arnott and what he might expect of a wife. I have conditions, of course. Delicate conditions that must be raised very carefully. Conditions I have not discussed with Mother. I am unsure how to raise them, but raise them I must. My thoughts flip to and fro as I note down Ann's cooking times and the weights and measures she uses, as I taste from her proffered spoon, as I advise on seasoning and flavor, as I dwell on Mr. Arnott.

Later, at dinner, Mr. Arnott beams at me. The waters of Tunbridge Wells are working, he says. He has never felt in such fine form. Then he looks straight into my eyes and says, "Miss Acton, there is another reason I am of such a genial disposition at the moment."

I look demurely at my bowl of apple soup, which has been artfully flavored with his gift of ground ginger. "I am pleased for you, sir." Oh, how I dislike all this pretense! Why can't I look directly into his eyes and tell him I am a published poet, with a checkered past and a commission to write a cookery book? But no, I must maintain my silence, as I've promised Mother. For the sake of the disgraced Acton family.

"It is you, Eliza," he says. "May I call you Eliza?"

I nod, concentrating hard on all he has to offer. Money. Freedom. Respect. A family of my own. Possibly. Am I too old to bear a healthy child? My left hand stumbles unbidden to my womb and clutches it beneath the table.

"My wife—God bless her soul—died in India, three years ago. Since then I have buried myself in my business, to the detriment of my health. Hence I am here."

I meet his gaze, for I cannot stare at my soup any longer. Not after seeing a thin trail of oil snaking over its surface. Soup should always be thoroughly strained of fat, I think, with mild irritation.

"And now I feel my spirits lifting, my health improving." He pauses and tugs the napkin from his collar, tossing it onto the table as if to signify his renewed vigor. "I think I may be ready for matrimonial life again."

The grease in my soup moves, slithers, twists into a shining tendril. A blush slides across my cheeks. Hatty comes to clear the table and I know full well she will scurry back to the kitchen with talk of Mr. Arnott's dramatically discarded napkin and my burning face.

"With you, Miss Acton," he adds, as soon as Hatty is out of earshot. "If you will have me . . ."

The bluntness of his proposal deprives me of breath for a moment. But if we are to continue in this straight-talking vein, there is something I must tell him without further ado. "I have no dowry," I murmur.

"Not a penny?"

"My father lost everything," I say. "This house is rented."

"I assumed there would have been something hidden away, but no matter. I have more than enough." He coughs, as if to cover his embarrassment. I wonder if he will see me in a different light, now he knows I'm a penniless old maid.

"Let us speak honestly, Eliza," he says, seizing up his napkin and dabbing at the corners of his mouth. "I need a wife that can run a household, deal with servants, oversee a kitchen, entertain the wives of my business associates, stimulate me when I return from work. You know . . ." He waves his hand carelessly across the table.

"And what else do you expect of your wife? I mean, what freedoms will she have?" My questions—stripped of any finesse—blurt from me and hang, like soup steam, in the air between us.

"She may do as she pleases," he says, frowning. "Unless, of course, it affects the good name of the Arnott Spice Company."

Hatty returns with a platter of Indian curried fish and a bowl of pilaw rice. She arranges them, very slowly, on the table, then makes a lengthy show of repositioning the glasses and the cruets and polishing the serving spoons.

I glare and she leaves. All this talk of matrimony—which appears no more than a slightly distasteful transaction—has made me long to lose myself in the food. I taste the fish and feel a jolt of pleasure. The buttery sauce is unctuous and rich, its flavors unveiling themselves in layers: garlic, white ginger, bruised coriander seeds, lemon juice, the subtlest hint of turmeric. The flakes of fish are meltingly soft but still with bite. For a few seconds I can think of nothing but the sauce upon my tongue. Mr. Arnott, however, is still talking.

"I believe I am an easy man to live with. My wife made no complaints. She was an ideal companion and you have many of her traits, so I do not see why we shouldn't live a long and contented life together, Eliza." He tastes the curried fish, his mouth working enthusiastically. "Excellent. As good as my own cook's. You will enjoy overseeing him, although he has become used to working without any supervision."

"Him?" I ask. And now it is my turn to be surprised, for only the grandest households have male cooks.

"Yes, his name is Louis. He likes to be called a chef, but I prefer the English word, cook." He puts his knife and fork down and gazes upon me again, but I am too flustered to meet his eye. I have a sudden wish to be alone. So that I can concentrate on my palate, on the way in which the spices are unfolding upon my tongue. Would it be improved with more garlic, less butter, a different type of fish, chili vinegar instead of lemon juice? But my mind is darting here and there . . . a French chef who has not been supervised for three years . . . the chance to have a child . . . marital love . . . my dishonesty . . . reclaiming Father from Calais . . . My mental turmoil comes to a sudden end when I hear the whine of floorboards from beyond the door. Mother is listening.

"Would you care to be the next Mrs. Arnott?" he asks, at length. The hall floorboards creak again. Mother clearly cannot contain her excitement.

"Sir, I like your proposal," I say. And suddenly it occurs to me that I like his proposal very much indeed. And I am tired of Mother and I am tired of poverty and I am tired of the relentless indignities of being old and unmarried and poor, of having to pander to the likes of Colonel and Mrs. Martin, of being answerable to my mother at the age of thirty-six, of having to put up with slighting letters from Mr. Longman—who has sent me yet another dictionary. As if I cannot spell! I am so weary of it all.

"Would a short engagement suit you?" He reaches over and takes my hand, covering it in both of his. I am briefly conscious of how it must feel, my scabbed *cook's* hand. But he holds it very lightly as if he understands the tenderness it carries—and does not mind.

"I shall tell you in the morning," I say. But I leave my hand in his. And it feels good.

CHAPTER THIRTY
ANN

MAURITIAN CHUTNEY

Everything at Bordyke House is at sixes and sevens. Miss Eliza is to be Mrs. Arnott and Ma'am is like a woman possessed. Hatty can talk of nothing but the wedding; and even little Lizzie is excited, although I cannot think why, for she will have to wash scores of pots and pans for days on end. Reverend Thorpe has been summoned for discussions and Mrs. Thorpe is offering advice on everything from wedding gowns to the dressing of the church.

Only Miss Eliza seems subdued. One morning I find her in the kitchen, in the ladder-backed chair she sits in when writing her *Observations*. Only she's not writing. She's staring at her hands. I wonder if she's fretting over the burns and cuts and how they will look now she is to wear a ring. Over the weeks her hands, which were so pale and beautiful, have become a bit like mine. Not red and calloused, but bearing a few scars of the knife and a burn on her thumb that is shiny and bright pink.

"Good morning, Miss Eliza!" I say. And to cheer her, I add, "Shall we be testing that Indian breakfast recipe this morning? I kept a nice piece of cold turbot for it."

"How thoughtful of you," she says. "I think Mr. Arnott would like that indeed, for he leaves us this morning, as you know." She gives such a wan smile, I think my eyes are playing up in the poor light. For isn't a newly engaged lady the happiest in the land? But then— fool that I am—I realize it's his departure that's making her sad.

I go to the larder and find the turbot, the Patna rice he likes, butter, cayenne, and two freckled eggs, which I know to be his favorites. When I return to the kitchen, she's still sitting there, staring at her hands. I start raking the cinders from the stove, but she doesn't move. Eventually I ask if she's unwell.

"I am quite well," she says. "I have been thinking of a verse I wrote. Would you like to hear it?"

I nod and she starts reciting in her soft voice, and it's like a melody, like the wind soughing in the trees:

> *"Pause!—'ere thy choice hath clasp'd the chain*
> *Which may not be unloos'd again;*
> *For though of gold the links may be*
> *They will not press less painfully."*

"That's beautiful, miss," I say, hoping she will carry on reciting, for the sound makes me feel like I do when she touches me. Less alone, I think. That I am not by myself.

But then she frowns and looks at me, worried. "In all the excitement I have not given you your wages, have I?"

"No," I say. "I didn't like to ask with all the—the excitement." I don't tell her it has been heavy on my mind, for I must give the nurses their gift when I next visit Mam and I need coins for Pa, who still owes the carpenter that made his new crutches.

"That was remiss of me," she says, quite vexed. "Most remiss and I apologize." She gets up and goes to the dresser drawer where she keeps her money tin. But as she rises, something falls to the floor. I assume it's a cookery book and she's been planning menus. She doesn't notice and is busy sorting shillings and pennies from her tin, pressing an extra sixpence piece upon me in a most apologetic way, then locking the tin with her curly key.

"May I take my wages to my room now, miss?" I cannot risk losing even a ha'penny, I think, hurrying to the attic where my purse is safe beneath my mattress.

When I get back to the kitchen, little Lizzie has arrived and is tying on her apron. But Miss Eliza has gone. My eye falls on the dark shape of her book, still lying beneath the table. How distracted she must be, I think. For Miss Eliza is a most organized and tidy lady and would never leave a cookery book on the floor. The sorting of my wages must have taken her mind off things.

I stoop and pick up the book and that's when my heart misses a beat. It's not a recipe collection. It's a book of poems. Her poems. The poems I've longed to read since first I came here. What happens next is not worthy of me. But I cannot help myself. Instead of placing the poems where Miss Eliza will find them, I slip them under my apron and scurry to the attic. Hatty is at the washstand, splashing cold water on her face. I slide the book under my mattress and go back to the kitchen, heart beating like the wing of a bird.

By the time I finish cleaning and laying the stove, my fingers are iced with cold and black with coal dust. I refill the scuttle and light the fire, prodding and blowing at it until the flames are good and fierce. I'm about to flake the cold turbot onto a plate when Miss Eliza returns and starts looking around the kitchen, most anxious.

"Ann, have you seen a small book? Bound in blue silk?" She circles the table, her hands wiping at her skirts, her eyes darting here and there.

Now is my chance to be honest and truthful. My tongue flaps, bewildered, and my brain blurs. And when the words shoot from my mouth, it's as if someone else is speaking. "No, Miss Eliza."

"Have you been here the entire time?"

"I nipped to my room to hide my wages, miss." My face feels scalding hot and I am thankful for the dimness of the kitchen, which is always gloomy and short of light.

"Oh yes, so you did." She starts opening and closing the dresser drawers. "Perhaps Mrs. Acton has been in here." She goes to the scullery and asks Lizzie if Ma'am has been in the kitchen. Or Mr. Arnott's footman . . . or Mr. Arnott's manservant. I hear Lizzie saying she's been in the scullery and not seen a soul.

"I am going quite mad," she says to me. "I must have moved it myself and forgotten, in all the excitement."

"Moved what, Miss Eliza?" Oh, how I hate myself as these words spring from my wicked lips. Every part of me cringes in self-loathing. But it's too late. I'm a thief and I cannot confess my crime now. Only last month a man was sentenced to transportation for life, just for taking a bushel of apples. Stealing a book is far worse. Men have swung from the gallows for less.

"I was reading some verse before you came down," she says, her brow creased, her hands still clenching at her skirts. "I must have placed it somewhere safe and forgotten where."

I nod, unable to speak. I have such an urge to confess, to fall at her feet and beg forgiveness. But I cannot risk being sent to Botany Bay or to the gallows. And the thought of her disappointment in me is horrible. That decides me: I'll return her poems secretly. I'll run to my room, pull it from under the mattress, then place it behind a serving platter—or some such place—for her to find. Something tells me she's fretting it might fall into the wrong hands and that the *wrong hands* are Mr. Arnott's. Although why this should be so, I can't think. Wouldn't any man be proud to have a writer for a wife?

"No doubt it will turn up. There is too much on my mind." She gives a nervous laugh. How jittery she is this morning, I think. And now I've made her more so with my nosy prying, lying ways. Dear Lord, I say in my head, please forgive me my sins.

"We must finish preparing the kedgeree. Mr. Arnott wishes to breakfast with me early today."

I reach for the slate so that I can chalk up my *observations*, but she throws up her hands and says, "Don't bother with your observations, Ann. They won't be necessary."

Confusion sweeps over me, blotting out my guilty spirit and my heavy heart. And then it comes to me in a flash of understanding. *There is to be no cookery book.* I feel my insides turn to liquid, as if all the substance of me has been sucked clean away.

"Oh, Miss Eliza," I gasp. "Is there to be no cookery book now you are to be Mrs. Arnott?"

She sighs, such a big sigh the room echoes with it, like a wind from the chimney that has no escape. Then a silence falls across the kitchen. I notice my fingers are shaking as they tear the turbot apart.

"I hope you will come with me, Ann. But the truth is Mr. Arnott has his own French chef who will not want my interference."

All at once I see my future dwindle to nothing. My throat goes dry and a gulping, choking noise bursts from my mouth. For if I am not cooking with Miss Eliza, what am I to do? I want only to cook . . .

"Oh, Ann," she cries. But then her voice goes very firm. "All will be well," she says. "Let us not become histrionic."

I don't know what *hiss-tree-on-ic* means, so I blink away my tears and escape to the larder to pull myself together. When I return, Miss Eliza is her old self, beating up the eggs with a brisk hand and asking me to find the Mauritian chutney we made the other week. We finish our cooking in silence, each of us absorbed in our own melancholy thoughts. Then she passes me a clean wooden spoon and asks me to taste the kedgeree.

I put a spoonful to my lips and instantly my mind calms. The turbot is warm, almost silky, on my tongue. The grains of rice are coated in a buttery smoothness. The heat and spice plunge me into another world—of foreign shores and exotic lands, of man-eating tigers, snake charmers, camels and elephants, rajas in jeweled turbans, hot dusty plains. All the oriental things Jack has heard talk of in London float into my head as the kedgeree slips down my throat.

"More salt? More cayenne?" Miss Eliza's questions bring me directly back to earth. "Mr. Arnott has a predilection for heat, as we know."

I pause and think. "A touch more cayenne . . . a salt spoon's worth, I reckon."

"Good!" She claps her hands together, her spirits fully restored. "I must go and prepare myself for Mr. Arnott. Put the chutney in the silver sauceboat and remember he likes plenty of leaves in his tea."

I nod, my mind swooping back to the book I've stolen. I must return it to the kitchen. Before Hatty finds it stuffed beneath my mattress. Before God can punish me. Before I'm caught red-handed and must swing from the gallows.

CHAPTER THIRTY-ONE
ELIZA

KEDGEREE

Mr. Arnott (whom I am now to call Edwin) has received some bad news. He is not in his usual jocular spirits, but admires the kedgeree all the same. I am not myself either. I have mislaid the only copy of my verse, after going to great lengths to retrieve it from Mother's hiding place. She thinks I know nothing of her *hiding places*, or where she keeps her *secret* keys. But I know of both. My poetry books have been taken and hidden for my own benefit (she insists), but last night I had such a yearning to remember who I was, who I am, only a look at my own verse would suffice.

I found my book, reread my paltry puny efforts, relived that terrible time when only the writing of poetry kept me from insanity. Mother says Edwin—Mr. Arnott—must never know. But what sort of a marriage is that? He may not love me and I may not love him, but surely we must have trust? And honesty? I have this odd feeling that all that I am—my tenacity, my courage, my pluck—is being stolen from me, wiped away. I no longer know who or what I am. And into this blank space creeps a vast chilling shame.

Mother is entirely pragmatic, insisting I owe it to my family and reminding me that with marriage comes money and respect and dignity and protection from loneliness. When she said the word *loneliness*, her voice faltered and a tear came to her eye. "Father will return from Calais," I said to comfort her. But then she pounced, reminding me we're still at the mercy of his later creditors, the Ipswich brewer and the butcher who missed the proceeds of that horrid public sale where our worldly goods sat for all and sundry to pick over, like carrion crows. "Only marriage and money bring freedom, Eliza," she said, dabbing at her pink eye. "Without them, you will grow old and lonely and bitter, a hated old maid who must serve others for a pittance." When she said this I heard again those coarse vile voices that followed me from the alehouse, taunting and jeering . . . *"There was an old maid from Tunbridge Wells . . ."*

"Eliza, my love." Edwin places his hand over mine. Such a large warm hand. A tingle skims up and down my spine and I long to lean my head against his chest, to feel the steady beat of his heart, to hold him to me. I imagine him, fleetingly, as a recipe: take one wealthy widower with two substantial houses and three thriving businesses, add one thirty-six-year-old failed poetess with a bankrupt discredited father. Add one practical deceiving mother. Scatter with three secrets. Press him to you. Stir . . .

"Yes, Edwin, dearest?"

"I would like to open an account for you with a London seamstress. You will need a new wardrobe as Mrs. Arnott."

I look down at my dress and see it through his eyes. Tired. Shabby. Unfashionable. The dress of an old maid.

"And jewelry. I noticed you have none. Mrs. Arnott must drip with pearls and diamonds. Whatever takes your fancy."

How do I tell him that I *chose* to sell my jewels and keep, instead, my poetry books? How do I tell him of the joy I feel slipping on my bibbed calico apron and inspecting a brace of rabbits or a delivery of fresh perch? I must tell him. I must be honest . . .

"Would I have your permission to undertake some charitable works, Edwin? If I'm not to help Mother with boarders, I will need something to keep me occupied."

"Which is exactly why I mention jewelry and dresses." He pats my hand, then pronounces himself "full to the gills," pushing half his kedgeree to the side of his plate. Something about the carelessness of this, the brief harsh scraping of the knife on his platter, makes me feel an unexpected twinge of anger. A fine turbot died and was carefully gutted, cleaned, scaled, poached, and flaked that you might eat, I think petulantly. I recall Ann's face as she tasted this dish an hour previous, the look almost of rapture, of beatification. Her first taste of turbot, no doubt.

I retrieve my hand from beneath Mr. Arnott's—Edwin's— and begin to eat. The kedgeree is perfectly spiced, rich, buttery, moist. My mind drifts off and I begin wondering where best to place kedgeree in my book: Foreign Cookery or Fish? Or should I include a Breakfast section? And then I remember—I am not to be Eliza Acton, writer of a comprehensive cookery book. I am to be Mrs. Edwin Arnott.

"But after I have a full wardrobe," I persist, "might I do some charitable work?"

"I fear you will be infinitely busier than you anticipate, dearest Eliza. I have many servants, many business associates who must be flattered and cajoled. Your feminine charms will be put to full effect as Mrs. Arnott." He chuckles quietly, as if he knows things that I do not. "I have been remiss since my wife died, entertaining only at my club which has none of the intimacy of a home." He pauses, wipes at the corners of his mouth with his napkin. "I fear my business rivals have stolen a march upon me, for at the club I cannot host wives. I know, for a fact, that my most significant rival has a wife who is assiduous in her efforts. Luncheon parties for ladies, dinners at home that are widely talked of . . ."

In an instant, I see myself not as Mrs. Arnott at the seamstress and milliner but as Mrs. Arnott, hostess. I see myself in my new garb of the latest fashion and the highest quality, presiding over a table of Edwin's most important associates and their embellished wives. I see the table . . . etched Bohemian glassware, twisted silver candlesticks that shout their price, bone china dinner plates, and cutlery polished until it gleams like gold. Is this not the life I have always longed for? The life I was made and educated for?

"My houses are kept fastidiously clean," he continues. "But they lack . . . character, a woman's touch, those little things of whimsy that make a home. I need you, dearest Eliza, to do all that for me." He takes my fingers in his. "You may do anything you wish to my houses. Change the drapes on the beds, order new swags at the windows, purchase some Turkey carpets or a new pianoforte."

"That is generous indeed," I murmur. "And will your French chef have no objections to me supervising him?"

"Oh he is a little indisposed at times, because he is French," Mr. Arnott says, with a stoic smile. "But you can humor him, speak to him in his native tongue. Preparing ladies' luncheons and lavish dinners will allow him to parade his French genius."

"And the servants?" My voice is tentative. "May I change them if I wish?" I am thinking, naturally, of Ann. But his talk of the French "genius" chef has left me with a sense of disquiet. I would rather hire a good plain cook . . . as Ann is turning out to be. A good plain cook happy to have me—with all my quirks and demands—as her mistress.

"You may change any of the servants that do not please you." He gives my fingers a final squeeze, then pushes away his coffee cup and tugs his napkin from his neck. "Any except Louis."

"Thank you," I say, smoothing at the small frown on my forehead. I want to ask Mr. Arnott a final question. I want to ask if I may write poetry. But why do I need his permission? Why should I not pen my verse when he is working and I am neither choosing clothes nor entertaining the wives of his associates nor adding whimsical decorative touches to his houses? Isn't this why I am marrying . . . to have freedom?

"Oh, dear Eliza," Mr. Arnott gazes upon me. "I am so pleased to have found you, lurking here in Tonbridge. What an asset you shall be to the Arnott Spice Company!"

And the thought of spice cheers me. At least—as Mrs. Arnott—I will always have the purest and freshest of spices.

CHAPTER THIRTY-TWO
ANN

LEEKS WITH WOODLICE

While Miss Eliza has her last breakfast with Mr. Arnott, I dash to the attic bedroom, which Hatty has left in her usual state of disorder. Her bed unmade, her nightgown on the floor, water splashed from the ewer, the rag rug rucked up, the chamber pot unemptied and reeking. No time to dwell on Hatty's messiness, I think, heaving up the mattress, and reaching beneath for Miss Eliza's book of verse.

My plan is to return it to the kitchen and tell Miss Eliza I found it on the dresser, behind the fish platter, and hope she's so bewildered she doesn't remember *not* putting it there. I know this to be devious, but I cannot think what else to do. The book gawps from my hand in an accusing sort of way. As if it sees what I'm doing and would speak out if only it could. It's bound in blue silk, the color of a cornflower. Fancy gold lettering on the cover: *Poems by Eliza Acton.*

I don't want Hatty bursting in upon me, so I lean my back against the door. Very slowly, I turn the cover. The first page declares the printer to be Mr. Richard Deck of Ipswich. The next page has the title and her name again, in an elegant script that is all lines and sharp corners. I know I should stop immediately, that I should ask Miss Eliza's permission, that I am behaving like a common thief. But something is tugging me on, as if I am borne upon the current of a mighty river. I run my fingers over the lettering and my heart lurches, although whether from fear or penitence or excitement I can't tell.

I come to the first poem, run my finger below each word as I read, feel my lips move. It takes a few seconds for the meaning of the words to strike me. And when they do, I close the book, startled and confused.

Then I open it and read on.

A moment later I sink to the floor. The anguish in her verse is terrible to read. Shocking and terrible! Poems that speak of wanting to die, of having to *go forth to the cold bleak world again*, of being *vile dishonor's slave*, of *remorse . . . wretchedness . . . shame . . . scorn . . . servile guilt*. And I am flummoxed. For Miss Eliza has everything one could want. Has she ever felt the grinding gnaw of hunger? Has she ever been so cold she cannot sleep for shivering? Has she had a mad, naked mother strapped to her waist for days on end? And yet it seems she has been sadder than I've ever been.

I do not know her, I think. I have never known one tiny bit of her. All the days we spend side by side in the kitchen. Me thinking of her as *my friend* . . . All at once I feel very small and very far away, as if I have been lifted to Heaven and am looking down on everything, tiny and squeezed together.

I close the book, sharp. My curiosity has fled. I'm ashamed of looking, uninvited, into her soul, for her verses seem more written in blood than in cold black ink.

And fused with my shame is confusion. As if I am standing upon shifting sands. As if all I thought was certain in life has gone.

I hold the book beneath my apron and hurry down the back stairs to the kitchen. Mrs. Dolby has arrived to take the laundry and is tying everything in sheets. Hatty is carrying a tray of dirty breakfast china to the scullery for little Lizzie to wash.

"Some nice leeks for you to clean, Ann," she says, jerking her head at the table where the muddiest leeks I have ever seen sit in clods of sticky earth, with woodlice crawling all over them. It will take an hour to have them washed proper, by which time my hands will be raw from the cold water. But today I'm glad of it. Glad of the distraction. I feel a sudden—and peculiar—friendliness toward the leeks, toward Hatty and little Lizzie and Mrs. Dolby with her red meaty arms.

I slip the book of poems behind the fish platter. When Miss Eliza comes in I say, as innocent as pie, "I think I found the book you were looking for."

She is so relieved, her face lights up like a candle. "Oh, Ann, wherever was it?"

"Behind the fish platter," I say, staring hard at the leeks and making a show of brushing the woodlice into a bowl. I feel wretched and despicable and hot in the face.

"How odd!" Miss Eliza says. "But what a relief—it's my only copy." She goes to the dresser, peers behind the fish platter, and pulls out her book.

"Have we new boarders coming, now that Mr. Arnott is gone?" I ask, wanting to change the subject as quick as possible.

"All going well, we won't be needing boarders for much longer." She gives me one of her tender smiles that usually melts the corners of my heart. But today it only makes me feel wicked. "Mrs. Acton thinks we should stop taking boarders now, so that we may concentrate all our attentions on Mr. Arnott. But I—I am not so sure."

I say nothing, for she seems to be talking more to herself than to me. Instead I take the leeks to the scullery and start stripping them of their outer leaves and the lumps of mud that cling to them and the worms burrowing around in them. "Oh, Lord, forgive me, forgive me," I say beneath my breath. "And make her happy. Please make her happy."

CHAPTER THIRTY-THREE
ELIZA

ORANGE-FLOWER MACAROONS

Today is *her* birthday. As we have no boarders, I was able to sit up in bed and attempt some verse. I began by writing a poem for her. But every word I wrote was thin and inept. My first stanza was so stale and clumsy, so blundering, I tore it into tiny pieces. I can't help but wonder if all that grief—once so savage, so keenly felt—has been pushed too deep inside me, squeezed into a narrow crevice between my heart and my ribs. So that I can barely feel it now. Except as a dull ache. Not enough for a poem. Or perhaps I am no longer a poet?

These questions vex me, but I feel much improved once dressed and in the kitchen. Recently I've noticed how the creation of verse mirrors the creations of the kitchen—the sense of being truly alive, the utter concentration so that one exists solely in the moment of exertion. These apply equally when I prepare a dish or when I write a recipe and must use the perfect prose. Before, I gave the gift of my poetry and now I give the gift of my food. So if I cannot write a good verse, then I shall bake a cake in her name. I get straight to work, testing a recipe for a good soda cake.

"I need fresh butter, sifted sugar, currants that have been cleaned of grit and stalks, and three well-whisked eggs," I say to Ann.

The girl is quieter than usual and keeps her head bowed very low over the currants as she sorts and cleans them.

"We're testing a recipe for a good soda cake," I explain. "I will also need grated nutmeg, fresh lemon peel, and fine dry flour free of weevils."

"Is it . . . is it . . . for the cookery book?" she asks, frowning into the currant jar.

"Yes," I say staunchly. "A soda cake resembles a pound cake but is much less expensive and far more wholesome."

I comb through recipes from Mr. Henderson, Mrs. Glasse, and Dr. Kitchiner, and make some notes on quantities. I am just re-calculating the weights of flour, when the front doorbell chimes, long and deliberate. A minute later Hatty appears, in her usual breathless swirl of excitement.

"Ma'am requests you in the drawing room. Reverend Thorpe and Mrs. Thorpe are come. Shall I do a tray of hot chocolate and buttered toast?"

I throw up my hands in irritation. "I am just about to test a soda cake! Why are they here now?"

Hatty stares at me, flustered, then ventures, "To talk about your wedding, Miss Eliza?"

I shake my head as way of an apology. "I did not mean to snap at you, Hatty. Ann, you'll have to proceed as best you can." I untie my apron and fling it on the table, then add, "No hot chocolate or buttered toast, please. That will merely prolong their visit."

In the drawing room, the scene is not as I expect. Reverend Thorpe is pacing, his hands gripped behind his back. Mrs. Thorpe perches primly on the couch, prattling away. She stops when I enter, a thin sculpted smile frozen upon her face. The room is briefly silent and I have a sudden presentiment that they are not come to discuss my wedding.

"Eliza, my dear, the reverend wishes to talk to us of Ann Kirby."

My body stiffens, as if bracing itself. Mother gestures to me to sit down and as she does so, the iron keys at her waist rattle.

Mr. Thorpe gives a flash of well-picked teeth, then strokes at his mustache. "Ann Kirby's father has been accused of poaching. He was caught snaring rabbits by Mr. Mugridge's gamekeeper."

I smile sweetly at him. "And what is that to do with Ann?"

Mrs. Thorpe coughs into a lace handkerchief. "My dear husband, who has done so much for the Kirby family, forgets to mention that Mr. Kirby was also drunk when he was caught. We think it might be better if Ann returns home to keep him out of trouble and away from the ale. We all know the duties of an unmarried daughter."

"I have no intention of releasing Ann. When I leave this parish, as Mrs. Arnott, Ann Kirby will be coming with me." My words—with their flair and finality—ring boldly in my ears. *As Mrs. Arnott . . . no longer burdened by the duties of an unmarried daughter.*

Mother rises from her chair, flustered. "Nothing has been decided, my dear. And if Ann Kirby has inherited bad blood, we might not want to subject her to all the temptations of Mr. Arnott's accumulated wealth and London's . . . depravity."

I stare at her, struck by the arrogance of their comfortable allegiances, the singular lack of kindness or compassion. When I am Mrs. Arnott, I think, I will be free of people like this. Cruel, small-minded people . . .

"Mother, when I'm married I shall be making my own decisions," I say. "Mr. Arnott has already said I may choose my own servants and dismiss his, should I wish."

"Even the French chef?" She cocks an eyebrow, and I know full well she has listened at every dinner Mr. Arnott and I have shared.

Mr. Thorpe flexes his fingers so that his knuckles crack. "Forgive our intrusion, ladies. Mrs. Thorpe and I are particularly proud of the sobriety of our parish and would like to keep it that way."

"Of course," says Mother. "My daughter can be most contrary but she does not mean all that she says."

I wince. Knot my fingers together. Bide my tongue.

Mrs. Thorpe smirks and says, "You have lost a husband and Miss Acton has lost a father. It cannot be easy."

I make my face suitably somber behind my clenched jaw and my tight eyes. All these lies . . . But Mother looks appropriately sorrowful and gestures at a framed sampler on the wall bearing the words "In God We Trust." I wait for her to say "God rest his soul" or some such thing, but to my relief even she is not brazen enough for that.

"What is to happen to Mr. Kirby?" I ask.

"He will be punished at Mr. Mugridge's discretion." Reverend Thorpe flexes his fingers again, each cracking knuckle like gunshot. "Lesser crimes have meant the hulks and transportation for life."

"I believe he lives in considerable poverty." I keep my voice soft and placatory. "No doubt he trapped the rabbit as food."

"He stole the rabbit, Miss Acton. Stealing is a crime." Mrs. Thorpe rises from the couch and adjusts her peaked bonnet, as if she's had enough of this conversation and wishes to depart.

"But surely Mr. Mugridge has hundreds of wild rabbits," I protest. "And what if Ann does not wish to look after her father?"

"You sound like a French revolutionary, my dear." Mother gives a nervous laugh.

I ignore her and look squarely at Mr. Thorpe, who is still pulling on his fingers. "And the mother who taught Ann to read and write? Was she also a felon?"

He says nothing but gives a violent tug at the knuckle of his index finger, then bows to Mother.

When Mother returns, she is shaking with fury. "Why must you be so argumentative and contrary, Eliza? You know exactly the predicament we're in. You know full well that we cannot afford to make a single enemy among the local gentry and clergy."

"Do you think I care about our *predicament* today?" I say coldly. "Have you forgotten what day it is?"

Her expression changes rapidly and a glimmer of kindness and understanding seems to flash across her face. But then it shifts again, hardening into something cold and immutable. "We agreed *that* would not be mentioned. Ever." She looks away.

"I want to speak of it to Mr. Arnott," I say. "How can I marry him if he does not know?"

"It has been discussed and agreed, many years ago. And if Mr. Arnott hears anything, rest assured he will call off the marriage. And then what of us? And your father? And your sisters who are slaving as governesses up and down the country?" She moves toward me and puts a hand on the small of my back. "We must be sensible, my dear. And once you are married, with a ring upon your finger and perhaps with child, you may decide to mention your past. But until then . . ."

I shake her hand off my back. "Very well, but I am baking a cake in honor of the day. In *her* honor."

Her voice goes very quiet. "The servants must not hear anything of this." The iron keys at her waist clank furiously as she sweeps out.

In the sudden silence, some past words of mine tick into my head:

> Let not the cares which round me cling,
> Obscure one moment's bliss for thee.

And in their wake I think of orange blossom, newly gath-ered, picked from the stem and snipped swiftly into fresh Lis-bon sugar, then whisked with the whites of several freshly laid eggs until the whole resembles snowbound mountains. Orange-flower macaroons, I think. A soda cake is far too dull. I should have made her orange-flower macaroons.

CHAPTER THIRTY-FOUR
ANN

A GOOD SODA CAKE

I take the soda cake from the baking oven. The kitchen fills with the smell of nutmeg and sweetness, folding soft around me like a wool blanket. Or like Mam's arms when I was little and the air was hard and tight with frost. As I ease the cake from the tin with the blade of a knife, Hatty runs in, flushed and wide-eyed.

"They are talking about you, Ann Kirby. Nothing to do with the wedding!"

"Me?" I think instantly of Pa and his drinking, then Mam and her lunacy. Then I think of Miss Eliza's poem book. And my skin goes cold. Was I seen putting it under my mattress? Did God see me and report me to Reverend Thorpe? Oh Lord, surely I will burn in Hell!

"Yes, you, Ann. Have you missed church?"

I shake my head. My mouth is as dry as autumn leaves.

"You must have done summat. Why else would they come here to talk of you?" Her eyes narrow to little slits. "Did you take a bit of dripping or some candle wax?"

I cannot speak. Because I *did* take something.

"Ain't we friends?" Hatty stares at me through her slitty eyes. "You can tell me, Ann."

I shrug. "I haven't taken anything." *That I haven't given back . . .*

"Likely your name just cropped up." Hatty grins, as if her suspicions have faded clean away. "They found you this position, ain't that right?"

I nod.

"It don't matter where you work, they always think you've stolen something from 'em. First place they'll search is our room, so if you've put the family silver there, best move it now." She laughs, as if she's said something very funny. Then she squeezes my arm, straightens her apron, and goes out to pump a pail of water.

I wait for Miss Eliza to return, unable to settle. I sieve a pail of cinders, then scrape last night's wax from the pewter candelabra, then I shave sugar from the sugarloaf so the cake can be strewn with it. I dust the day's soot from the dresser and the open shelves, shake more coal into the range, and lay out the silver tea service for polishing—the teaspoons and the sugar bowl and the little curly milk jug.

When Miss Eliza comes back to the kitchen, she is most queer in her manner. And her face is glum, with pinkish eyes and a red mottle all over her neck. After a few minutes, in which

Miss Eliza sniffs and scribbles in her notebook, she says, "Ann, put a candle on the cake."

"A candle?" I say, startled. "On the cake?"

"Yes, a good beeswax one. And a full candle, not a stub."

Her instruction distracts me. Candles are expensive and why she wants one on a cake makes no sense. Surely the cake will be spoiled by dribbling wax? I wonder if I've misheard her, but she reads my mind and says, "It's a Continental custom I came across on my travels. You'll need to make a small well in the cake's surface to keep the candle stable." Then she goes to the dresser, unlocks her little money tin, and gets out five shillings that she pushes across the kitchen table. "Your father needs money," she says. "This is for him."

A huge wave of relief washes over me. So there was no talk of his drinking or Mam's lunacy. Or—praise be—of me stealing Miss Eliza's poem book. But then my mind goes into a foggy muddle. Why is she giving me money for Pa? Why is she looking so downcast?

She reads my mind again. "Your father is in trouble for poaching. Five shillings should buy his freedom."

"Did you hear of it from Reverend Thorpe?" I dare not look her in the face. I know poaching is a heinous crime, that Pa must have been half-starved or else too drunk to know what he was at. I slide the shillings into my apron pocket, my cheeks burning with shame, and my skin cold with worry.

"Yes," she says. "The Thorpes want me to send you home, to keep your father from crime and drink."

I gulp, then take a deep breath. How do I say I love my pa but that I cannot go back to my old life, that I cannot leave our book of recipes? "We would have no money but for what Jack sends home. Pa cannot work the fields like other men, for he has just the one leg."

"He started drinking after your mother . . . died?"

"Yes," I say, very low and soft. And I hate myself for the lie. And for denying Mam, for murdering her . . . which is how it feels. And I hate myself for not wanting to go home, for feeling only shame of my pa.

"I thought as much." Miss Eliza walks around the table and places her hand upon my arm. And I cannot bear it. Every little bit of me wants to shrivel up. I am desperate for comfort, but I am overflowing with disgust. At Pa. At Mrs. Thorpe who made me promise never to tell of Mam's lunacy. At the whole world with its cock and bull. But mostly at myself.

"I will find that candle, Miss Eliza," I say. And I disappear as quick as my feet will take me.

The larder is gloamy, for there is only one small window, very high and covered with mesh. A thin light trickles through, wobbling over the flagstones. Enough light for me to see my reflection in a silver tray. I hate what I see. My lying, filching, selfish face.

When I get back to the kitchen with a good wax candle, Miss Eliza is standing very straight reading a letter.

"We are to go to Mr. Arnott's London house, Ann," she says. Her beautiful face is glowing at this news, her eyes as bright as a bird's. She has such a broad smile it near stretches from one ear to the other. "Is this not the good news we deserved today?"

"Yes, Miss Eliza," I say, thinking *we* means her and Ma'am and that soon I am to be discarded, returned to my poaching drunken father and his wretched hovel. Doubtless Mr. Arnott has many servants already. London girls without the foolish notions of poor country girls like me. London girls with respectable fathers who can hold their ale and have no need of stealing.

"We shall meet his French chef," she says. "And view his house so that I can suggest changes to the decoration. He is a generous man indeed! He has invited you too, Ann. He knows how highly I think of you."

I gape at her. Me? To London? "Am I to come with you, miss?"

She nods and goes back to her letter, while I stand with a huge stupid grin plastered over my face. Pa stumbles into my head—who will look after him while I'm gone?—but then he vanishes and I think only of London. At last I am to see London!

"We shall leave next week," she says after a few seconds. "Perhaps you can visit your brother?" She puts the letter down and smiles. And then she does something I've never seen her do before. She lifts her skirts and jigs around the kitchen. I feel like jigging too, but I can only stare. When she sees me staring at her, she stops, brushes down her skirts, pats at her hair, and tells me to put the cake upon the cut glass stand and take it, with the candle, to the drawing room. And so I do, keeping my hands as steady as I can, for the thought of seeing Jack in London has made my heart race, even as Pa creeps back into my head. Making my skin go clammy all over again.

CHAPTER THIRTY-FIVE
ELIZA

ORTOLANS GARNISHED WITH COCKS' COMBS

Mr. Arnott's house is in Albemarle Street and from the very second I step down from the coach, I am enchanted. The steps are scrubbed white, the shutters are newly painted, the brass door knocker gleams. The entire façade is neat and well tended. Even the pavement has been swept clean of the chewed bones, clods of dung, moldering rodents, and rotten vegetables that litter most of London's streets.

Mr. Arnott, in an embroidered waistcoat bulging with shiny buttons, comes bounding down the steps. I feel a rush of joy. This is to be my home! This is the house where I shall—at last—be mistress!

"Welcome! Welcome," he cries, bowing low to Mother and me. While Ann and the footmen unload our luggage, we are ushered inside, where a line of uniformed servants shuffle and stare: housekeeper, butler, and six maids. They bob and bow although Mr. Arnott seems not to recall their full names so that the housekeeper must jump in and make the introductions in a dialect—Scottish?—I can barely understand. Behind them ticks a longcase clock with a painted face of cherubs. A mahogany table groans beneath a gold-rimmed vase of hothouse flowers. Pictures of men on horseback, in fat gilded frames, adorn the walls. Hundreds of candles glow from sconces and two glittering chandeliers, so that the maids, the furniture, the flowers, rugs, and paintings seem to ebb and flow, one minute in shadow and the next illuminated in rippling light. I look sideways at Mother. I can tell she is calculating the value of each item and every good wax candle, for her fingers move one by one against her skirts.

Our tour begins in the dining room, its floor buffed to a shine, its walls thick with mirrors and portraits. Twelve dining chairs covered in maroon leather are arranged around a long table with a mahogany buffet server on brass casters at each end, and a sil-ver candelabra, surrounded by small pineapples, as its centerpiece. The fireplace has beside it a substantial plate-warming box painted with Chinese ladies lurking seductively behind ornate fans.

"I thought you didn't entertain," I say, with just the smallest hint of flirtation. Mother nods approvingly.

"Everything is as it was when my wife lived here. You may change anything you do not like." He indicates the room with a grand flourish of his hand. "There is little of fashion here."

"Chintz curtains would be an improvement on the shutters, which are very plain," says Mother.

"Do not change anything," I say. "I cannot abide waste in any shape or form." Mother glares at me.

From the dining room we go to the morning room, then the drawing room, then the library, where the meager collection of books causes me to raise my eyebrows. As we leave, Mr. Arnott says, "I cannot very well show you my bedchamber and you will see your own chamber later, so I suppose the tour must end here. Now, how about some tea, ladies?"

I muster my courage, cough, twist my hands together. "I would like to see the kitchen, dear Edwin. May I?"

Mother glares again, then interjects, in her most imperious voice, "My dear Eliza, the kitchen is for servants. Fashionable London mistresses never see their own kitchens. Is that not so, Mr. Arnott?"

"I believe that is the case," smiles Mr. Arnott. "But if you would like to see it, you may. I dare say you will never want to see it again."

We trail down the stairs, Mother breathing furiously through her nose. At the rear of the building we come to a flight of dark narrow stone steps, whereupon she says, "I won't descend any farther, thank you, Mr. Arnott."

Edwin looks uncomfortable, as if he is not sure what to do. "Perhaps we should stay abovestairs," he says. "Louis dislikes my presence anywhere near the kitchen. I have keys for the wine room and the silver room, but I do not poke my nose elsewhere."

"You stay with Mother and I will take a quick glimpse," I say, hurrying down the steps to the kitchen corridor, which is low ceilinged and stained with damp. Beyond the storerooms I can sense the kitchen, feel its heat spilling over, smell the scum of a simmering stockpot, frying onions, mutton fat. And struggling beneath this odorous skirmish, the wooded scent of chopped rosemary.

The kitchen is painted blue, but its walls and ceiling are blackened with smoke. From its narrow rafters hang strings of onions, cured hams, long bunches of dried sage and bay leaves, dangling threads of red chilies. One wall is lined with barrels and tins; and against the other is a vast dresser crammed with pots, copper jelly molds, platters in all shapes and sizes, dish covers, dripping pans, graters, sugar nippers, spice tins, biscuit presses, strainers, hair sieves. On the table are stacks of wooden boards, knives, pastry trays, several rolling pins, and a bolt of tammy cloth.

A thread of evening light falls from a high window, through which I can see the boots and shoes of passersby on the pavement outside. It is quite unlike the kitchen at Bordyke House, which is lofty and airy and where the smells of food sit comfortably side by side. Here, in this dark constrained space, they brawl and scrap. And although my kitchen also has a single north-facing window, I keep it open at all times to allow for a wholesome circulation of fresh air. Here, the glassless window is grilled and barred and no bigger than a fish kettle. The walls run with steam, so the whole room is like a miniature furnace—hot, damp, airless, noxious.

"Who is in my kitchen?" I hear the clear twang of a French accent and in walks the man I suppose to be Louis the chef, followed by a girl carrying a box of sea coal. He is not a tall man, and the kitchen is gloomy, but in spite of this he casts a long shadow.

"I am Miss Acton," I say, assuming he will know my name.

For surely he has been briefed as thoroughly as the rest of the household staff that stood in line to welcome us on arrival?

He looks me up and down as if he cannot tell whether I have entered via the tradesman's door or the front door. And then he pushes his hand roughly through his thick black hair and says, "*Mais oui*, Miss Acton." It is the first time I have heard French in several years and I falter for a second, but then I notice his apron is filthy, stained with blood and grease. And I think it odd he has not deigned to change into a fresh apron.

"You need more air in your kitchen. The maids will asphyxiate in here, as will you," I say, holding his insolent gaze. "I will look at the larders now, if you have no objection."

"I do," he says most impertinently. The girl looks up from the stove, where she has been shoveling coal, and titters.

I straighten and lift my chin a fraction. "Very well, Louis. But I must inform you that I plan to take a considerable interest in the kitchen when I become Mrs. Arnott."

"The master calls me 'Chef,'" he says. "I would ask the same of you, please." The girl titters again, then burps and slips out.

I nod, shocked at their impudence. Are all London kitchens like this?

"The last Madame Arnott never comes 'ere." Louis glides his hand through his hair again. His nails are rimed with dirt and his fingertips stained a grayish maroon, as if he has been handling red cabbage. I have an overwhelming urge to point out how unhygienic his *hair fiddling* is, but I decide not to. When I am married, I think.

"I intend to run things differently." I dab discreetly at the perspiration building on my face, trickling from my temples. Whether it's from the heat of the stove or from his impudence I know not.

"Englishwomen cannot cook," he announces. "You ladies learn to paint a pretty picture or play a tune or you learn to speak my language, but you do not learn to cook."

I know I should turn and leave, but for some reason I remain rooted to the spot.

"English food is very bad," he continues, in his heavy, accented drawl. "Why do you think London gentlemen eat at taverns and dining halls and chophouses? The only good food is from French chefs. We are artists. Artists!"

I finally find my tongue. "I cannot agree with you. I shall take a very close interest in Mr. Arnott's meals once I am mistress here." For the first time I feel no thrill, no ripple of satisfaction as I say the word *mistress*.

"You English have no . . . taste. No palate. Always vinegar and cayenne. Always to disguise that you cannot cook, that you can only poison." He puts his greasy hands to his throat and mimes the act of strangulation, then laughs.

"I must return to Mr. Arnott," I say, desperately in need of air and shaking with fury beneath my new dress, new hat, new mantle, new gloves.

He bows. "Au revoir, Mademoiselle Acton."

I turn and walk, trembling, up the two flights of stairs to where Mr. Arnott and Mother are discussing whether brocade curtains would be a welcome addition to the morning room.

"What I would like," Mr. Arnott is saying, "is to have the

ceiling painted with golden cherubs perching on the spreading branches of an English oak tree." He motions at the ceiling rose, then notices me standing at the door.

"I have met . . . the chef," I say, adjusting my cuffs to conceal my disquiet.

"Yes—insufferable is he not? I have nothing to do with him, neither did the late Mrs. Arnott. But his cooking is remarkable, as you will see this evening."

"Does he cook only French dishes?" I ask, thinking of my future husband's predilection for curry and spice.

"I insist on a weekly curry, which he prepares with great reluctance, and then he sulks for days." Mr. Arnott laughs and Mother joins him, catching my eye to indicate that I should laugh too. But I'm still inwardly trembling at the chef's insolence.

"And can I ask what you pay him?"

Mother's laughter stops abruptly. She glowers at me and then opens her mouth to speak, but Mr. Arnott is too quick. "Sixty pounds per annum, my dear Eliza. But he is quite indispensable to me. Besides, he would get the same wage at any good London house. Indeed, I'm told Lord Melrose pays sixty-five pounds per annum for his French chef."

His answer renders me speechless. A good female cook is paid just ten pounds per annum. I could make a saving of fifty pounds if only I can persuade Mr. Arnott to dismiss the loathsome *chef*.

"Think of the lavish and enviable dinners you can host, Eliza," says Mother in a coaxing voice that belies the cold anger in her eyes. "Think of how you can help Mr. Arnott's business."

I want to cry out, *But think how many more I can help with my cookery book or my poems!* Instead I close my mouth and face, hard and tight.

"That is the beauty of Louis," agrees Mr. Arnott, nodding affably. "We need never venture to the basement!"

Later, we prepare for bed in Mr. Arnott's guest chamber and Mother berates me for my *unseemly interest in the kitchen* and for my *unforgivable question regarding the chef's wages.*

"But if I am to be mistress of this house, surely I must know these things?"

"You do not even have a ring on your finger yet, Eliza. Why must you be so impatient, so contrary, so willful?" She pushes her hair into her nightcap with angry prodding fingers. "Fashionable London ladies do not bother themselves with the filth belowstairs. They are charming, amusing, and clever. That is how you will maintain Mr. Arnott's place in society."

I pull the quilt over me, turn away from her, and snuff out the candle. She continues, snapping into the darkness, "And you saw the magnificence of the chef's creations . . . sippets shaped as swans, ortolans garnished with cocks' combs, a meringue pyramid shaped as a woman's head . . . that dinner was in *our* honor, Eliza."

"I know, Mother." Louis's dinner had been magnificent and extravagant, six courses that had my tongue so tied I could barely make conversation.

"I saw you prodding obstinately at the soup," she adds. "And examining the sippets, like a—like a medical man! Why can you not eat like a lady?"

"There was too much food. Half of it went to waste," I mutter

into my pillow. The truth is Louis's food is still upon my tongue
and I know I shall spend all night chewing over its intrica-
cies and complexities, or else I shall find it in my dreams. The
scorched sweetness of his roasted viands; the fish—brill?—that
appeared to float upon a tepid cloud of rising steam; the delicate
herbs—chervil?—strewn across the peas and suffused in every
sauce; our names inscribed in spun sugar over a meringue as
light as pollen. And yet who can afford to make or cook food
like this?

"And why would a bit of waste matter? Really, Eliza! Your
thrifty ways have no place here. And nor do your . . . appetites."

I sigh into my pillow and remind myself that one day this will
be my home and I will be a wife, not a daughter. And the future
I once envisaged—pushing a petulant mother around in a cheap
shoddy bath chair—is whisked away. Gone!

CHAPTER THIRTY-SIX
Ann

ORANGE CRUMPETS LEFT BY GENTLEMEN

London is all pitched roofs, rearing up, tall and black, for mile upon mile. The roads are one great jostle and shove: wagons and barrows, donkeys heaving water carts, hackney carriages, little traps they call hansom cabs that duck and dive, ragged boys that dash beneath their wheels to grab at tossed apple cores or fallen farthings. The noise is deafening: hundreds of ironclad wheels clattering over the cobbles, the cries of the drivers and the lashes of their whips, the ceaseless hollering of the costermongers, the wailing of the beggars. I hear it all—even in Mr. Arnott's underground kitchen, even in the back scullery where I sleep upon a pallet of straw with four snoring housemaids and hundreds of scuttling cockroaches.

London, I decide, is also the dirtiest, most reeking place I've ever been. Excrement and dung and rotting fish and decaying cabbages, then waves of roasting chestnuts and pea soup and baking apples, which make me by turn hungry and queasy. In Kent, the stench comes and goes, depending on where you're passing or the direction of the wind. Here it is constant, so that by our second day I am quite accustomed to it.

Two days after we arrive Miss Eliza says I can visit Jack. She draws me a tiny street map and says I am to speak to no one except to ask directions. I leave the next morning, while Ma'am and Miss Eliza are still in their chamber. I'm glad to leave Mr. Arnott's home—for the houseboys are always grabbing at my skirts and the footmen keep pressing against me in the narrow halls and the butler has put his greedy hand inside my bodice three times already.

But from the minute I appear alone on the pavement, blinking like a rabbit out of its burrow, the costermongers are at me. Would I like to buy . . . sheep's trotters, rat poison, hot eels, oysters in their shells, baked potatoes hot from the brazier, kidney puddings and penny pies, shoe polish, turnips, hair tonic made from tree bark, milk that has already curdled, scabbed apples, wooden pegs, leaflets, scrubbed beach shells? Until I'm so dizzy I must walk with my head down, looking neither to right nor left and stopping only to examine my little map. And only when not a single eye is upon me.

By the time I reach Pall Mall, my mouth and nose are coated in soot and my head throbs from the din. But all of this I forget the minute I see the Reform Club. My courage is forgotten too, for it's a huge building, very grand and clean. Gentlemen with top hats and bursting with golden buttons and rattling watch chains sally in and out of the entrance, swooshing their canes as they go.

I find the tradesmen's entrance and say I have come to see my brother, Jack Kirby. And then Jack appears, startled, and so spotless white I think he must be an angel. He hugs me hard enough to crush the breath from me, then steps back so he may see me better. I tell him my business in London, that I am soon to be living here, and he grins from ear to ear—the two of us standing and grinning like a pair of clowns.

"I've missed you, little sister," he says, and passes me a long white apron, stiff with starch. "Put this on, and I'll slip you in." He takes me to a door where I get a quick peek at the kitchen. It's like a great white ballroom, only full of cooks and servants, all in white. All so clean, so orderly. There is a strange smell I cannot place, but even that is cleanish, not like rotting meat or milk that has curdled.

"That's him, the great chef, Monsieur Soyer." Jack points at a man all in white but for a red velvet beret that sits aslant on his head. The man is moving around on the balls of his feet, dipping a ringed finger in and out of pans. "But he must not see you, for he will know you are an imposter."

"I'm a visitor," I say, indignant.

"He will know you as an imposter because you are plain and he only hires pretty girls," says Jack, tugging at my arm. But I cannot tear myself away. I want to stand and watch the cooks forever. They have such grace and purpose. One chops herbs on a board, then passes it to another who adds something from

a spice tin and pounds it in a huge mortar. Then it is passed to
another who scrapes it from the mortar and stirs it into a vast
stewpan. Then Monsieur Soyer is called. He tastes and grinds
in a little pepper, then he calls to another who comes with a
straining spoon and skims the surface. "It is like . . . a dance," I
whisper.

"A dance?" Jack rolls his eyes and gives my elbow another tug.
"Since when did you see a dance?"

"My notion of a dance," I say. "Where everyone must move
together to create a story."

"I wish you could see the dishes that go to the dining room.
You wouldn't believe them, Ann. They would feed the whole of
Kent for a month. Come—I'll sneak you into the meat room."

"Why isn't it boiling hot in here?" I ask, realizing of a sudden
that I haven't smelled smoke or tasted soot upon my tongue or
wiped boluses of sweat from my brow. Like I do in Mr. Arnott's
kitchen.

"Gas," Jack murmurs in my ear. "There ain't no charcoal used
here now. All the lighting is gas too. Can't you smell it?"

I sniff at the strange-smelling air and nod. "Will you be poisoned?"

"Likely I will." He steers me toward a room where the air
is so heavy with frost and ice, I shiver and pull my shawl tight
around my shoulders. The carcasses of sheep, bullocks, and roe
deer hang from hooks along one wall; and from another hang
hundreds of birds, their claws tied with twine: tiny larks, plovers, quails, woodcocks, snipes, wild ducks, pheasants, pigeons,

partridges, capons, and geese. So that the whole wall is a mass of
feathers, beaks, scaly claws. At the far end is a wide marble shelf
on which lie rabbits and hares, stretched out as if in sleep.

"So much meat," I whisper, thinking of Pa poaching a single
rabbit, on his own, with his one leg and his wooden crutches.
And his punishment not yet decided, even though he has the
good word of Reverend Thorpe and Miss Eliza's five shillings as
a sweetener.

"That's my work for today. I must skin fifty rabbits and pluck
all those fowl. And then I must gut five-and-twenty carp we keep
in iced drawers." Jack's hand is on my elbow again, maneuvering
me toward the door. "Is Pa still working the graveyard?"

"Yes," I lie. For I cannot bring myself to tell him the truth.
And lying seems to come so easy to me now.

"Oh!" Jack hits his palm against his brow. "Wait there." He
disappears into a long white corridor; and I think how beautiful it is to have everything white, just how I fancy Heaven to
be. Not that I will ever see Heaven now, not with all my lies.
While Jack's gone, I slip back to the huge white kitchen and look
through the gap where the door hinges are. Monsieur Soyer is
laughing, his red beret bouncing up and down. The cooks stand
at the long table, cutting, slicing, mixing, rolling. Others are at
the huge smokeless stove, stirring, shaking pans, tasting from
long wooden spoons. I fancy myself one of them, all dressed up
in a crisp white uniform, coming every day to this calm white
place that has more food than I can dream of.

Jack returns with a hessian sack that smells of old blood. "For

Pa. Some catsup and pickles, and some orange crumpets that the gentlemen diners left this morning."

I try to find words to say how proud I am to have a brother working in this heavenly palace—where the master wears a red velvet beret and where fish is kept in *iced drawers*—but they don't come. Instead a gulp rises up my throat. Pride. Envy. Sorrow. Awe. All trapped in my chest so I can't speak.

"You've put some flesh on your bones," says Jack. Then he looks down and adds, "I can't send money for a bit, Ann. My rent is doubled and there's nothing spare, but I'll send some as soon as I find cheaper lodgings."

As he says this I have a strange feeling of being rolled very flat, like pastry. The air knocked from me. Winter is coming and fancying myself a chef isn't helping anyone. Nor is imagining myself in Mr. Arnott's grand house, a million miles from where I should be. Because Pa is all down to me now.

Chapter Thirty-Seven
Eliza

Saddle of Mutton with Gravy

All night I toss and turn while Mother snores soundly beside me. My discourse—if it can be called that—with Mr. Arnott's *chef* repeats and fragments in my mind, spinning me down such a multitude of avenues I become quite giddy. *Englishwomen cannot cook . . . we have no palate . . . all vinegar and cayenne . . . taught to paint pretty pictures but not to eat . . .* And his face, louring and yet familiar, swims in and out of my restive brain. Eventually I fall into a fitful slumber and dream I have returned to France and that he, the *chef*, is making love to me beneath a market stall groaning under a vast weight of Smyrna figs. I wake, hot and full of self-reproach. Mother is still sleeping; but light rushes, rosy and golden, over the skyline, so I know it's after my habitual time of rising.

I dress quickly, splash some water on my face from the porcelain ewer on the washstand, and make my way down the creaking wooden stairs. It was my intention to work in Mr. Arnott's library, to compose a private verse, a poem to give him at our engagement dinner. For wouldn't such a gesture smooth the way for a frank discussion of my poetic aspirations?

But my feet acquire a life of their own and take me past the library door, down the next flight of stairs. And then on until I am descending the narrow stone steps to the kitchen corridor. Not one sound breaks the spell in which I walk. Not the whinge of the water pump nor the rattle of coal. Not the slam of a door or the clinking of glass. Instead my feet move on, past the coal cellar, the wine cellar, the silver room. Past the washroom, the side pantries, the scullery. All of them draped in a chill dark gloom.

And that's when I hear him, faintly sneering, curious.

"Mademoiselle Acton, eh?" He leans on the frame of the kitchen door, arms folded, watching me.

The spell is broken. What am I doing here? Why am I not in the library? I turn to leave, fumbling for any words that might explain my presence in the kitchen at this hour. But he finds the words before I do.

"You wish to see how I prepare the master's breakfast?"

I nod. "And I wanted to see Ann, my servant girl."

"Oh, Ann," he says. "She is already gone to find her brother." His eyes roll over me, up and down my body in such a slow and insolent way, I know I must assert myself. As his mistress to be. Before it is too late.

"Very well." I look at the floor, willing myself to turn away, ascend the stairs, find the library. But his voice is like a strange narcotic to me. All those memories of France, of love, of ungovernable passion. All of it rushing back, as he speaks with his soft, loose lips. As his dark eyes rove so candidly across my breasts.

"I am sorry, Mademoiselle Acton." His eyes lift to my face. "I was too rude about the English."

"You were right, in part." I force myself to meet and hold his gaze. "We are not taught to cook, only to amuse gentlemen with our singing and piano playing. I ran a school for many years, for private ladies of means. I sorely regret that I did not teach them to cook."

His heavy-lidded eyes open a little wider. Then he jabs a finger at me. "You English had the best food, the best dishes, in the world. A long time before the French. And then . . ." He shrugs. "Your bread is full of poison now. Your coffee is an abomination."

"I was in France many years ago," I say, speaking in a voice clipped tight to smother any wistfulness. "The food was very good and I learned much about your use of herbs, your appreciation of delicate flavors, how you use olive oil and lemons."

His face is suddenly alight in the dimness, as if a candle has been placed inside his skull. "If I had known, I would not have been so rude to you. Most English ladies . . ." He throws up his hands, but his eyes have acquired a new luster.

"They all want you to cook saddle of mutton with gravy?"

"*Vraiment!* Always saddle of mutton, always with gravy, always with cayenne. And so I come here." He points at the ceiling and smiles. "And the master says I can make any dish I want, but one day a week I must cook curry." He gives another expansive shrug.

"You do not favor curry or food from the Orient?"

"It kills the tongue. How can you enjoy an elegant flavor—
like chervil or bay—if you eat curry?"

"You may be right," I say, thinking how peculiar it is that talking to Louis is so much more enjoyable than talking to Mother
or Mrs. Thorpe. Snatches of my dream come back to me . . . the
sweet sticky scent of splitting figs . . . Louis . . . I swallow quickly,
as if to swallow down the self-disgust that accompanies such a
perverted dream.

"There exist very old books on English cuisine," he continues.
"Gone now, but my last master had some. Written by English
ladies. Ladies who would rather cook than paint a silly picture or
play badly a tune upon the pianoforte."

"And if I am more like these ladies, will you permit me to
come into your kitchen?"

He pauses, his full lips pouting as he thinks. "London ladies
do not do this," he says at length. "But if you will watch me, I
will teach you."

"Very well," I say, thinking of the dinner he cooked the previous evening, the sauces of cream and wine—each suffused with
a different herb: thyme, sorrel, parsley, tarragon. Each sauce had
opened like a flower upon my tongue, one flavor floating into
another. Until Mother kicked me beneath the table, forcing me
to swallow my food expeditiously and with none of the con-
templation or reverence it deserved. Of course the dinner was
excessive, each dish flaunting its own convoluted brilliance. And
yet, those flavors unrolling in my mouth . . . the soup, like green

velvet . . . the sippets, golden and with perfect crunch . . . the milky-white sweetness of a mousse as light as suds. Hardly surprising I could not sleep!

"And if the master does not wish it?" He raises one black eyebrow.

"Mr. Arnott knows of my culinary interests," I reply, and my voice seems to flounce coquettishly, so that I barely recognize it as my own. "What time should I return?"

"I will show you potage bonne femme." He wipes his hands on his apron in a gesture of exuberance, as if he would like to begin my lesson this very minute. "No one makes soup like a Frenchman. Come at midday. I will be waiting."

Only as I climb the stairs to the library, do I realize how foolish I have been. I shove the thought away. Just one lesson, I tell myself. All the better to understand the workings of my future kitchen and the temperament of my future chef. My own words convince me; and when Edwin asks, over a fashionably late breakfast, if Mother and I would care to take a carriage through Hyde Park, I ask if I may have a half hour to watch the chef prepare a French soup . . . *in order to better understand the workings of his kitchen that I may manage it to my very best abilities.*

His brow furrows very briefly, then he nods and says, "If you think that would be beneficial, my dear, although it is rather hot and dirty down there." Mother protests, her knuckles white upon her knife and fork, until Edwin says, "My daughter and her husband are dining here this evening, Mrs. Acton, so Louis is unlikely to want dear Eliza in his kitchen for more than a few minutes. Just long enough for her to feel at ease—as mistress here." He raises his voice on the word *mistress* and Mother puffs pink with pride and stops her scowling protestations.

When midday comes, and Edwin and Mother have left for their carriage tour, I find Louis in the kitchen, inspecting a delivery of carrots and parsnips. He throws a clean apron at me and, without a single word of welcome, begins his instruction.

"The stock must never boil. Only simmer. You English are boiling everything."

I nod curtly and say a little snappishly, "Yes, yes, but tell me how you made those sauces last night."

He looks up, surprised. "A fine dish can stop time, eh?"

A small sigh escapes from me, and he seems to understand it, for he frowns and asks, "You were not able to—to concentrate on my flavors? You were not able to groan with the bliss of the moment? To enjoy the tingle and joy on your tongue?"

I laugh. "They were exceptionally good sauces."

He shakes his head so vigorously drops of sweat fly from his hair. "No, no! Not *good*. They were divine. They had rhythm, balance. Like music. Like the very greatest music."

I think of how the flavors had unfolded, one after another, how each one had brought to mind a scene, an image, a memory, as if in that one moment I had traveled to and fro through my own past. Until the toe of Mother's slipper had prodded angrily at my calf.

"When you eat my sauces, you feel as if you are sucking the very bones of life, eh?" His eyes flare in the gloom of the kitchen. "But you feel also the joy of being an animal, eh?"

I want to say there was too much food, that we left stuffed to suffocation. But the passion of him mesmerizes me and I can only nod.

"You English have only one sauce. Butter. Always butter. But I have many. And each one will stop time so that, for one minute, you live truly in your body and soul." He pauses and knocks his fist on his chest. "That is my art. To give joy and life, even as Death snaps his jaws."

He leans over and, before I have time to move away, his thumb brushes my cheek. The sensation is like lightning. As if his thumb has sent a shower of scarlet sparks through my body.

"Kitchen dirt," he explains simply. "Now, the soup. The secret to a potage bonne femme is fresh sorrel leaves, with a little sugar to balance the sharpness. And parsley root, plenty of it, added to the stock. Egg yolks and cream, beaten in at the very end. And you must use only a silver spoon."

I try to focus on his words, his *lesson*, but my body is still trembling from his touch, the lightning heat of it. From somewhere I hear the sharp clang of a pan lid dropping upon the flagstones. My eyes widen and blink, like those of someone jettisoned from a trance. What am I doing down here? What on earth was I thinking? Dazed, I turn and mumble an excuse. I quicken my pace, hurry up the steps, ascend two flights of stairs, find myself a chair in Mr. Arnott's library. My body shakes and my mouth is as dry as sawdust. In my craven mind's eye, Louis leaps before me. Disrobed. His loins as smooth and brown as the shell of a hazelnut. I shake my head with all the force I can muster. No, no, no! It must not be. It cannot be. I look frantically around the room, seeking out something. But what? A key, I think. I want the key to lock tight this Pandora's box.

"Eliza, whatever are you doing?" Mother is at the door, removing her bonnet and frowning at me.

"Bonne femme," I croak. "Potage bonne femme." I put my head in my hands and start to weep.

CHAPTER THIRTY-EIGHT
Ann

LITTLE WHITE LIES

We returned to Bordyke House earlier than expected. Miss Eliza was feeling unwell, showing all the signs of a fever, and Ma'am was most anxious to get her home.

As I lie in our little attic room, I tell Hatty of my London adventures. She is only interested in wedding talk, but I want to tell her of Jack's master and his place of work, how white and shining clean it was. And of all the filth and vermin of the London streets and of how the footmen flirted with me and how I felt nothing for them, although the kitchen maids said any footman would be a fine catch. All this I say, but she can only ask, "Has she a ring?" and "Did a London seamstress visit for the making of a wedding dress?"

Finally, the talk peters out and I turn over to go to sleep. That is when she springs a most peculiar question upon me.

"Why does Miss Eliza favor you so, Ann?"

"She doesn't," I say, surprised. "I am her only servant, that's all."

"No," says Hatty. "'Tis more than that. Talking to you of poems, making you from scullery maid to kitchen maid so quick, buying you new boots with leather soles."

"I had no boots," I say softly. I do not say that my appearance shamed Miss Eliza, that it reflected poorly on Bordyke House.

Hatty ignores me and carries on. "And Reverend Thorpe coming to discuss you. And you going to Mr. Arnott's London house rather than me who has been two years with Ma'am who is mistress here."

"I suppose it's because I may be going to London too," I say, keeping my voice gentle so as not to hurt Hatty's feelings.

"No, something else is at play," she says, decisive. "I seen how she looks at you. It's not normal."

I feel a strange thing when she says this. Confusion and pleasure—rolled up like a hedgehog, soft and prickly at the same time.

"How do you mean?" I regret the question as soon as it's out. For Miss Eliza is mine and I do not want her tarnished by Hatty's jealous words.

"It just ain't normal that a lady would favor someone like you. And so soon, so quick."

I know nothing of how ladies treat their servants, so cannot reply. But part of me is overjoyed—*I am special to her! And Hatty has seen it too!* I hug my knees to my chest beneath the thin sheet, my lips curling into a smile.

"It ain't normal," repeats Hatty.

"Maybe," I say, very tentative, very quiet, "it's because she has no little ones of her own."

Hatty snorts into the darkness.

"Or maybe she feels sorry for me," I say. "For having a father with one leg and no—no mother."

"I think it's strange, that's all." Hatty rolls over, very heavy, so that the frame of her bed grunts and groans. And then all goes quiet. And I listen to my untruth about Mam echo in my wicked ears. A lie begets a lie, I think to myself. But then that other voice—the wicked one—pops into my head telling me it's not a bad lie, just a lie of convenience.

I close my eyes and listen to the wind stirring in the trees outside. A lie of convenience . . . Mam had a word for lies like that. Little white lies, she called them. Lies that never hurt anyone. I screw my eyes up very tight and a picture moves across my inner eye: Mam, sleeves rolled up, arms plunging in and out of the stream as she washes Pa's clothes. I'm sitting beside her, perched on an eel trap, scraping mud off dirty clothes with a sharp-edged flint while sunlight scatters all around us. "Little white lies, my dearest one, are always forgiven by God," she says. And her smile catches me and holds me like a bag of softest silk. "If they make life more bearable for others, they are white lies and nothing more."

My eyes snap open. Hatty is breathing from the back of her throat and shifting on her mattress. Outside a barn owl screeches. Mam and all the ghost lands of my past go as quick as they came. But her words cling on. Whose life is made more bearable when I pretend Mam is dead? The little attic room sours around me. I drag back Hatty's talk of how Miss Eliza favors me. But it's too late. The words that cheered me a few minutes ago have lost their shine—for I have seen and felt my own wickedness.

I push my hands together, press them hard against my chest, and close my eyes. "Dear God, forgive my untruths and have mercy on me. Make Miss Eliza better and take away her fever. Make her the happiest woman that ever lived. Make Mam better too and take Pa from the ale so that I may stay with Miss Eliza . . . Make it so I have no need of lying, Lord. Amen."

CHAPTER THIRTY-NINE
ELIZA

SWAN'S EGG EN SALADE

I soon grow tired of feigning fever—my disposition is by nature a restless one—so when Mother flounces into my room, announcing jubilantly that Father has written from Calais and intends to do everything possible to attend my wedding, I know the time for honesty is upon me.

I draw breath and smooth at the eiderdown, inviting her to sit beside me. "Mother, there is something you must know."

She sweeps past and tugs the curtains back, so that buttery light falls in a neat square upon the floorboards. "Your dear father has it all planned. He shall slip aboard a ship he knows, where no questions will be asked. We must be very careful that none of his creditors hear." She pauses and inspects my face in the light. "Why, you look much better, my dear. It was the London air and the foul city water, I'm quite sure. You never were a strong child. Perhaps I shall buy him a hat with an especially broad brim. What d'you think, my dear?"

"Mother, there is to be no wedding. I have broken off my engagement with Mr. Arnott." Silence falls over the room. I stare at my hands twisting white in my lap. Exactly as they had when I broke the news to Edwin in his drawing room. The words had blurted from me then, just as now: *Edwin, I cannot marry you.* He had asked—in a voice flat with stoic disappointment—for an explanation. As he had every right to. And I had given him one. For didn't he deserve to know? He had shown me nothing but kindness and he deserved to see my willful, contrary self, to hear its brag, to know its restive spirit.

"I cannot marry Mr. Arnott." My hands knot and unknot. Mother stares at me, astonished. Then she frowns and says, "You still have fever, Eliza. I will send Hatty for Dr. Collins immediately." She moves toward the door, her tongue clicking with irritation.

"I have told Mr. Arnott. That is why we left his house with such urgency; the illness was a ruse that suited both of us. I'm sorry."

She stops and turns, the lids of her eyes blinking very fast, her face pleated in confusion. "Not because of . . . ?"

I wait for her to say Susannah's name. But she doesn't. Instead she reaches for the bedpost, a soft whimper gurgling from her throat.

I get out of bed and go to her, but she backs away, her face hardening, her mouth a pout of willful intent. "Explain yourself," she says, her hand gripping harder at the bedpost so that it resembles the claw of an old hen.

I take a long breath, then climb back into bed and pull the eiderdown up to my chin. I have a sudden need to be swaddled, to feel the muffle and warmth of my bed linen. "Yes, in part because of her. Of course I didn't tell him that. But there are other reasons. More pressing reasons." Mother visibly relaxes, then knots her face again and waits.

"I could not be the Mrs. Arnott he wanted. I have inside me . . ." I pause and try to recall the words I used with Edwin. He had seemed to understand, had nodded with an aura of sympathy. As if he too were familiar with the throbbing sense of purpose that afflicts me. But Mother . . . she will never understand.

"And what exactly do you have inside you?" she prompts, her eyebrows shooting into her hairline. "What can be so important your family must suffer for it?"

"No one is suffering. Catherine and Anna have excellent positions in good families and Edgar is making his fortune in Mauritius. And Mary is content and well married. My marrying Mr. Arnott would never have saved Father from his creditors."

"And what of me? Serving boarders with my spinster daughter lurking in the kitchen like a miscreant!"

I sigh and push away the eiderdown. Now is not the time to hide behind its quilted floral panels. Now is the time for honesty. "I realized, in Mr. Arnott's kitchen, that there are things I must do. Things I need to do. That I cannot do as Mrs. Arnott, but can do as—as Eliza Acton."

Mother snorts and pouts. I ignore her and continue, like a cook that must butcher a hog however hard, however unwieldy. "England is losing its ability to cook, to understand good food. Not the fancy French food of London kitchens and clubs, but the food we've eaten for centuries. Bread, properly baked. Pies, properly raised. You heard Mr. Arnott's daughter . . . she has never set foot in her own kitchen. Imagine a generation from now. We shall be at the mercy of overpriced Frenchmen and the foul contaminated food of the street."

"Don't preach at me, Eliza. Where is your feminine humility?" Her hand loosens on the bedpost, as if her body wilts beneath the weight of my words.

"I feel as if my book of recipes has never been more needed than it is now."

"And so you chose your foolish book over marriage to Mr. Arnott." She shakes her head in disbelieving fury.

"It is not a foolish book. It is an important book that I have slaved over for months, that I love almost like a husband. Why should I give it up to spend time being measured for dresses and hats? What good is that?"

"Very well, Eliza. But your sisters shall hear of this. I shall tell them how you refused to stoop to marriage. That one day, there will be a kitchen book bearing your—our—name in circulation and that this book is the reason they are governesses and not the ladies they were bred to be." She sniffs and draws herself up. "And I will tell Mary too."

I stiffen. "Let me write to Mary. I can explain it myself."

"Oh no, no, no." She prods the air with an angry finger. "I

see no reason why our little agreement with Mary should be breached. I will write to Mary. And if she chooses to write one day to you, then so be it."

I close my eyes and hear the sharp clack of the latch. Mother's footsteps disappear in the direction of her own chamber. My pulse is racing, so I lie very still and listen to the crows collecting on the chimney pots, the whinny of a horse, the cry of a barrow boy, the slow chime of the church bells. Mother's fury, her disappointment, is as I expected. And now it's spent, my mind calms and my pulse slows. I think of my book—*our* book, for it is no less Ann's than mine—and imagine how it will be, how it will feel in my hands. In my mind's eye I see it in kitchens, smeared with butter and flour, sticky with sugar and fruit, fingerprinted and stained and ringed with oil, blood, the cracked sheen of egg white. I see it in bookshops and bedrooms, in drawing rooms and parlors. Why not? I hear it discussed at table, over breakfast, over luncheon. I hear it talked of in butcher's shops and fishmongers, in the gilded kitchens of gentlemen's clubs and in public houses. Why not?

A sudden sense of urgency whips through me. Time is running out. We have barely touched on soufflés and omelets. And what of baked puddings? Or milk puddings? And syrups, vinegars, liqueurs? And so much more to do on forcemeats, entremets, shellfish, potted meats. And swans' eggs! We haven't a single decent recipe for swans' eggs. I must write to everyone I know, request their favorite recipes, attempt them in my own kitchen. My thoughts swerve back to swans' eggs. Such splendid things—their whites are purer, more translucent than those of any other egg. Perhaps their boiled yolks might be mixed with firm fresh butter, essence of anchovies, minced herbs, even a chopped shallot. And then returned to their hardboiled whites in softly beaten mounds. A swan's egg en salade, I think, smiling.

I had such a dish in France, all those years ago. Louis reminded me of those times too, of memories best kept locked away. Of feelings best kept locked away. I did not tell Edwin any of that, naturally. And nor do I want to think of it now. I want to think only of how I might re-create—and improve upon—a swan's egg en salade. What herbs might taste well? Tarragon? And perhaps a dash of cucumber vinegar . . . And to follow? Something good and plain—and English! A pot of tender cutlets swimming in a sticky, meaty gravy, richly flavored with life and death . . . and everything that falls between . . .

I throw back the covers and leap from my bed. Outside the crows flap and shriek. Get up! Get up! Get up!

Yes, I reply. Work to do! Work to do! Work to do!

CHAPTER FORTY
ANN

A GOOD PLAIN IRISH STEW

I am in the scullery, helping little Lizzie scour the pans with sand, when I hear Miss Eliza in the kitchen, humming to herself. I poke my head around the door and she smiles at me.

"Ann," she says, "we have a busy day. Can you pump plenty of water and make a good bright fire, please."

I do as she asks, lugging in pail after pail of water and heaping the stove with coal 'til my arms ache. She sits in her ladder-back chair, poring over her books. But books I do not recognize. "Have you new books, Miss Eliza?"

"Yes, Ann," she says, looking up with such a cheery expression I figure she must have had good news already. Perhaps her betrothal ring is coming today. But then she points at the books and says, "These came from Mr. Longman while we were in London. They are no longer printed and I do not know how he came by them, for they are a hundred years old, but"—she pauses with a little triumphant smile—"they are by ladies."

I tie on a clean apron and wonder why cookery books by ladies make her so cheery, particularly as she is soon to be mistress of a house where she won't need to go within a mile of the kitchen. As always she seems to read my small mind.

"What did you think of Mr. Arnott's chef, Ann?"

"I thought he was a fine cook," I say, not wanting to mention how oft he placed his stinking garlic hand upon my arse.

"Yes, indeed. But too fanciful for most households." She taps at the cover of her notebook with a knuckle. "Today I shall compile a list of all the people I know who might like to contribute a recipe to our book."

"Oh?" I cannot hide my surprise, for how is she to complete her book in Mr. Arnott's house? Is she to dismiss the loathsome Louis?

"And prepare yourself for new boarders, Ann. I shall be placing an advertisement today."

"New boarders?" I echo, confused.

"I shall not be marrying Mr. Arnott," she says, very flat, so I cannot tell if she is sad or happy. "Mother has taken to her bed, but my mind is made up."

I stare at her, shocked. Why would she not want to marry a man as rich as Mr. Arnott? Why would she not want servants and footmen at her beck and call?

"We have an important job to do, Ann. Our book must be completed and it will not be completed in Mr. Arnott's house."

"Can't you finish it now, and then be wed in the spring?" I ask, although I know it's not my place to ask such questions.

She shakes her head, most vigorous. "No, no. Such a book as this will take ten years to test and write. It must be done properly. And by then I will be too old to wed."

I am so flabbergasted I cannot reply. Ten years! She would rather spend ten years writing a book and be an old maid than be married with a fine London house and possibly a babby of her own? For a second it crosses my mind that *she* should be in the Kent County Lunatic Asylum. For surely she has gone quite mad!

And then she says something even more peculiar. "Mr. Arnott's chef has renewed my sense of purpose." She lifts her eyes to the narrow window and adds, "In so many ways."

That odious, arse-groping Frenchman? How can that be . . . ? I frown so deeply she sees how bewildered and troubled I am. I wait for her to say *Close your mouth, Ann Kirby, and mind your own business*. But she doesn't. She says something most unexpected.

"As you know, I spent some time in France. It was a difficult time for me. The happiest and the saddest time of my life. Talking to Louis reminded me of . . . of certain things that I cannot speak about . . . but he helped me see how ill prepared I am for marriage." She pauses, her eyes stuck above my head so that I cannot tell if she is speaking to me or to the copper pans hanging from the ceiling. I think of her poems, the man who broke her heart. God forbid that her heart still isn't mended after all these years . . .

And then she starts talking again and I can sense she is in a chatty mood. "Mr. Arnott's chef thinks English ladies have lost all interest in the kitchen. He is right and nowhere is this more apparent than in London. They have been turned into silly little dolls.

Mr. Arnott's married daughter was a grave disappointment . . .
She could talk only of her new lace collar, the flock wallpaper
she selected for her drawing room, and other such fripperies. I
do believe she has never set foot in her own kitchen!"

"But she did sing beautiful," I say, for I had overheard her singing the very evening she and her plump red husband came to
dine.

"She was out of tune, toneless, and without any expression,"
says Miss Eliza, sharpish. "But no one had the wit to tell her."

"Oh," I say, wondering if I should point out how pretty Mr. Arnott's daughter was with her golden ringlets and her rouged
cheeks. For it seems to me that Miss Eliza is being quite harsh
on the poor lady.

"Mr. Arnott's chef told me that London gentlemen prefer to
eat out at private clubs and he intimated that his last mistresses
have been entirely disinterested in his menus. Do you not see
where this takes us, Ann?"

"No, not wholly . . ." In truth I have no notion where this talk
is going, for Miss Eliza is rarely so direct. It strikes me I should
feel more disappointed than I do, for there will be no wedding.
And I won't live in London, near Jack. But I feel more pleased
than disappointed. I would have been sore pressed to look after
Mam and Pa from London. And all those footmen and cooks
handling my arse like it was a bag of turnips . . . No thank you!

"The kitchen is a place where ladies used to reign as queens."
She gestures at her new-old books in their scrappy bindings. "We
have relinquished that and now we are at the mercy of French

chefs or scoundrels who ply their poisonous pies from the streets. I trust you didn't eat from the street in London, Ann?"

"Only a pickled herring, miss," I reply, thinking of the chewy soused fish that had me gagging with its bones and vinegar.

"In London I heard of new foods being invented so that people no longer need to cook. Apparently there are factories along the banks of the Thames making powdered sauces and custards." She pulls a face, like she's bitten into a rotten egg, but then her face lightens. "It is our mission, Ann, to change this. Nothing is as nutritious or wholesome as proper food cooked in the kitchen."

I nod, but in a blank, not-understanding way. Why does she always include Ma'am when she talks of her book? Even today, when Ma'am has taken to her bed, she speaks of *our*. Yet even I can see that Ma'am is not best pleased by *the book*.

"You and Ma'am will print a fine book." I pick up the water buckets and am just leaving the kitchen, when Miss Eliza calls out, "My mother has nothing to do with it."

She's talking to herself again, I think, continuing toward the scullery where Lizzie's wooden pattens are clacking up and down on the stone.

Her voice follows me, higher and louder now. "When I say *our*, I mean you and me, Ann. Not my mother."

I stop in my tracks, frowning. *Our* mission? *Our* book? She means *me*? The stiff iced air of the scullery is like a blast to my senses. I must move to keep warm, so I start pushing and pulling at the water pump, but all the while my heart is dancing.

And when I return, my shoulders hunched forward from the

weight of the water buckets, I ask, "What recipe are we to try today?" My voice bursts from me so loud and strong Miss Eliza blinks in surprise.

"My sense of purpose must be contagious." She laughs.

And I laugh too, for I feel as if I've swallowed a bushel of happiness and it is flooding out of me, out of every pore in my skin. "Oh, it is, Miss Eliza, it is!"

"Well, let us perfect an Irish stew, shall we?" She motions at the dresser. "Bring down the brown Nottingham jar from the top shelf and then you must run to market for some mutton cutlets. We shall show everyone how to make a good plain family dinner."

As I reach for the jar, the ache in my arms and shoulders vanishes and I feel as light as a lark. I am to be with Miss Eliza for ten years, working on *our* book!

"And swans' eggs," she adds. "See if they have swans' eggs today."

"Yes, miss!" And my smile is so broad my cheeks smart from it.

CHAPTER FORTY-ONE
ELIZA

JEWISH ALMOND PUDDING

For two weeks the house is calm and undisturbed. Every day Ann takes our tested recipes on a tray to Mother's room. Hatty collects them, the soup bowls and platters invariably as clean as a whistle. Mother's *shattered nerves* have clearly had little effect on her appetite.

Eventually she appears, pale and tight-lipped. She comes to the kitchen, her head held very high and her eyes refusing to meet mine. "I need a little broth for dinner, but nothing more," she says.

"We have a new boarder arriving on Monday." I brace myself for a histrionic display of nerves at this pertinent reminder of our future.

She pauses, then sniffs. "Who?"

"A Jewish lady, come to take the waters."

"I am sure you can manage without me." She sniffs again, as if to remind me that her nervous frailty is all my fault.

"You might enjoy her company. Her name is Lady Montefiore and I believe her to be very well connected."

Mother's head tilts and her eyes brighten for a second. Like a bird that has spotted the writhing end of a worm. "Very well. If I must."

"She's written to tell us what she can and cannot eat. I shall need more money to buy oil, bitter almonds, and orange-flower water."

"There is no more money, as you well know." She shoots me a look of such bitterness I turn swiftly back to Lady Montefiore's letter—thick watermarked paper, expensive ink from an expensive nib, perfect copperplate.

"We will be reimbursed." I pick up the letter and read out the opening lines: "'We Jews are forbidden to mingle butter or other preparations of milk or cream with meat at any meal, so oil is much used in our cookery of fish, meat, and vegetables. Although these restrictions are not rigidly observed by many Jews in this country, I follow them. I will gladly reimburse you and I shall bring my own Jewish almond pudding which will suffice as a sweet dish while I am boarding with you.'"

"She is bringing her own pudding?" Mother splutters.

"Nor can she eat pork, shellfish, hare, rabbit, or swan," I add, my eyes scanning the remainder of her letter.

Mother gives another haughty sniff, then leaves, closing the door with unnecessary force so that it shakes in its frame. I glance at Ann and think how it might have been if she didn't know her place so well, how we might have shared a rebellious and irreverent chuckle at Mother's expense. As sisters might. As friends might. But Ann is too dutiful, too submissive, to overstep herself like that. A shame, I think. For there are times now when my melancholy rears up and I am sorely in need of a friend. A life with Mr. Arnott would have put paid to loneliness. Isn't that what marriage is for? A chance to be rid of loneliness? Have I made a terrible blunder?

As I'm pondering these thoughts, Mother returns, her chin wobbling.

"Your father educated you to be a lady, a wife to someone exactly like Mr. Arnott." A sob breaks in her throat. "And now I must write to John and tell him it is not to be, that he must stay in those vile lodgings in Calais, that we must continue taking in boarders, that your sisters must remain as glorified servants. How could you do this, Eliza? After all he spent on your schooling . . ."

I busy myself chopping sage leaves. *Thy heart, thy heart is cold as stone, and feels but for itself alone . . .* Old words of mine rise up, are borne away, replaced . . . *giant-clouds of shame, in dark'ning masses, clust'ring came . . .* Until my head reels and I must lay down the chopper before I draw my own blood.

"How could you?" she repeats. "After all I've been through. I have only risen from my bed because today is the anniversary of Lucy's death."

Every organ inside me shrinks and cringes with guilt. How callous I am! I have been so bound up in myself, my *mission*, I have given no thought to Mother's pain. I put my hand upon her arm, but she shakes me off.

Briefly my mind flits back, more than twenty years. That terrible piercing shriek that I mistook for the keen of a squabbling gull. Mother running down the stairs shaking Lucy as if she were a rag doll. Lucy's head lolling. The two dark recesses of her eyes. Her tiny arms hanging limply at her sides. The nursemaid running behind, whimpering with fear, her feet slipping on the painted stairs. Then me running like a hound to fetch Papa from the brewery, even as a stitch split my rib cage asunder. We were too late. When we returned, Mother had Lucy so tightly pressed to her we couldn't tell if the baby breathed or not. And as Mother's tears ran over the baby's head, the nursemaid stood and stared, yellow trails of vomit on her apron, her cap, the sleeves and cuffs of her dress.

"You could have saved Lucy," gulps Mother. "You were with her. You could have stopped the nursemaid from feeding her enough laudanum to sink a ship."

"No, Mother," I say softly. "I was twelve. It was a horrid accident, a mistake. Let's not dwell on it now." The memory has returned so vividly it seems as though my baby sister's vomit lingers in the air.

Mother's upper lip trembles, her chin shakes. I take her hand, veined and wrinkled now, and feel a sudden sympathy for her. This was not the life my father promised. An image of our Ipswich home swims into my head: the huge library of books, the prints and gilt-framed looking glasses, the velvet curtains, the silver service and candelabra, the mahogany furniture inlaid with mother-of-pearl, the Turkey rugs. All gracing the homes of other more fortunate people now. I had the chance to return Mother to that life. And I turned it down.

Her face sags. "How can we live together like this, if I cannot forgive you?"

"You must. And you must have faith in my book. It will be our salvation, I promise."

"Oh, your wretched books!"

"He would not have married me anyway, Mother. The truth of my situation would have come out."

"Everyone else manages it. You are stubborn and belligerent, Eliza." She puts her handkerchief to the corner of her eye. "Perhaps I will go and live with your brother in Mauritius."

I know she says this to punish me, so I say nothing. I steer her to her bedchamber and give the bolster a good pounding, but she insists on sitting at her dressing table, where she demands paper, pen, and inkpot. I beg that *I* may write to Papa and explain my reasons for remaining unmarried. But she insists on writing in her own hand.

All my recent cheer fades as I watch her struggling to pull the cork from the inkpot. She seems so small, withered almost, the skin on her face hanging in leathery folds, her fingers gnarling at the joints. I have aged her, I think. I have pushed her to the brink of her own grave.

"You may as well have your books of verse back. No need to hide them now you are to remain a spinster."

"Thank you. Where are they?" I know full well where they are—hidden in her wardrobe, behind her good winter coat with the fur collar. I pile the albums, annuals, and books into my arms and feel as if a limb has been mysteriously returned to me.

As I descend the stairs to the kitchen, my thoughts turn to Lady Montefiore and the Jewish almond pudding she will bring. We shall need other puddings, of course. Sweet dishes made without cream or butter or milk. Perhaps made with rich amber syrups instead. And perhaps I can make an almond cream to substitute for milk in soufflés, custards, blancmanges. Blanched almonds, pounded and mixed with boiling water, then wrung through a tammy cloth. I can hear Ann in the kitchen—the comforting chop, chop, chop of a blade on a wooden board as she hews herbs. Their green fragrance reaches me like a balm. My spirits lift, my step quickens. And I can think of nowhere I would rather be than in my own kitchen with its endlessly altering perfumes, its familiar sounds that are as music to my ears, its warmth and daily rhythms that mark the rising and setting of the sun and the turning of the seasons.

Take one capacious kitchen, I think to myself, add a brisk fire and ten well-lined copper pans, throw in five molds, seven wooden spoons, a good set of steel blades, and one competent and devoted assistant. Strew over a variety of gravy strainers, dredgers, sieves, strainers, nippers, rolling pins, chopping boards, and paste brushes . . .

CHAPTER FORTY-TWO
ANN

DRIPPING

The house keeps on quiet, with Hatty creeping around and Ma'am in her bed and little Lizzie looking at us with her big frightened eyes. Knowing there's to be no wedding has been a grave disappointment to everyone, except me and Miss Eliza. Even Reverend Thorpe and Mrs. Thorpe came visiting with their condolences, their sharp noses twitching like dogs after a scent. There was no one home to see them, but Hatty took the message and said she near burst into tears on the doorstep. Afterward she came to the kitchen, wiping her eyes on the corner of her apron and asking why there was to be no wedding. I didn't answer, just shook my head. It's not my place to share Miss Eliza's confidences. Not even with Hatty.

One afternoon I slip out and deliver Jack's little bag of preserves to Pa. I thought to find him in the alehouse, but to my surprise he's at the cottage, planting out seedlings. Nor is there any stink of beer upon him. Just the smell of autumn smoke from all the brushwood being burned along the fields. I'm even more taken aback when I push open the door and see how spick-and-span the cottage is. The mattress has been sewn up where the straw was leaking out, and a line of moleskins is pegged across the floor, so I know he's been skinning the creatures for a few coins. Septimus bounds up from the hearth, rubbing his wet snuffling snout into my skirts.

I tell Pa there won't be money coming from Jack for a bit. He sits upon the turned earth, tamping the last seedling into the ground, and says, very solemn: "I'm giving up the drink, Ann. I'll ask Reverend Thorpe for another chance."

"I don't think he'll want you," I say, glum.

"I've given up the poaching too." He gives a little indignant pout. "Mugridge said he'll let me off this time, but if he catches me again, he'll shoot me with his own hand."

An idea comes to me, like a clap of thunder. I crouch down beside him and take his muddy hand in mine.

"I could bring you the candle stumps and the bones and the meat dripping we don't use. Miss Eliza is most frugal, but there's always leftovers; and I learned in London that most cooks sell these bits and bobs and pocket the money for themselves."

"How would it work?" He looks at me, all curious.

"I bring them here, you melt down the stumps for new candles, and pick the dripping clean for potting. Then they're sold at market."

"Have you the time?"

I shrug. "We can try it. And I'll have a few pennies from my wages, although the rest is for Mam's nurses."

He opens Jack's little sack and brings out a jar of pickled onions, a bottle of mushroom catsup, three orange crumpets now hard and stiff as tree bark, and the broken remains of a spun sugar flower. "A feast," he says, rubbing his muddy hands together.

"Miss Eliza likes me," I say, feeling a flush of pride. "Even the other housemaid has noticed that I am . . . special to her."

"Rich people don't ever care for their servants—they care only for themselves and their money." He puts a strand of spun sugar into his whiskery mouth and sucks it. "She may think you can chop a nice onion, but she won't be thinking you're *special*. And nor will she be *liking* you."

"But she talks of *our* book and *us* working *together* for ten years."

"She treats you well because you're a good hard worker, not because you're special to her. If a better worker came along wanting less money, she'd drop you like a hot cinder and take the new lass." He leans toward me and smacks a beardy kiss upon my cheek. But I pull away, hurt.

A new thought pops into my head. "She's not like other rich folks. She just turned down marriage to a man as rich as a king." I'm determined not to be infected by Pa's doubt.

There's a silence and I hear the mice scratching and scurrying in the thatch.

"Likely he wasn't so kind, or so rich."

"What I think is that she wants to live like a man."

"Like a man?"

"She wants her own money, not a gentleman's money. She doesn't want people telling her what to do." I pause and look up at the sky, huge and white today, with a single crow beating and cutting above us. "She's been teaching me about poems," I add, hugging my knees to my chest as her fine words flow through my head . . . *There is no joy on earth to me, where thou art not* . . . "You see, Pa. She's not like other ladies." And she doesn't treat me like a servant either, I think to myself.

"Well I never." Pa rubs at his wiry beard in a thoughtful way, as if he doesn't know what to make of Miss Eliza. "Sometimes I wonder if all women ain't a bit daft in the head. All, excepting you, Ann."

She is what I want to be, I think. She is strong and true. She has courage and honesty. I stand up, brush the earth from my skirts and offer Pa my hand. He has perfected a means of raising himself from a seated position to a standing position, without using anything to support him. He shows me this with such pride, my heart swells up.

All the way back to Bordyke House I think about how I can help Pa. Winter is coming. I can feel its edge on the wind, its snap in the broken branches beneath my feet. Will melting down candle stumps and gouging the marrow from old bones be enough? Can he turn a living from a few moleskins? At least Mam will be warm and dry and well fed in her big fancy asylum. And for that I gratefully offer God a few words of thanks, my palms pushed hard together and my eyes skewed to heaven.

CHAPTER FORTY-THREE
ELIZA

MINCEMEAT PUDDING

As I put my notes and recipes in order I feel my book flutter into life. It is a most peculiar sensation, as if there were something at the heart of it, a pulse or a soul.

With life comes responsibility: I must lay out plans for my book as a parent plans for the arrival of a child. I put a clean sheet upon the table, dip my pen into the inkpot, and write *People to Whom I Shall Send My Book*. I place a ruler beneath the title and underline it not once but twice, all the while thinking, It must go to those with influence. I start my list with a single name: Charles Dickens. He writes regularly in the *Evening Chronicle* and I sense that he and I share a feeling of compassion for the less fortunate. He shall be the first to receive a signed copy.

Recipes now come in the post regularly, for I have spent several days writing to both acquaintances and strangers, requesting their most favored dishes. I lay out the newest donations: a

potage of pearl sago, veal stock, eggs, and cream from Sweden;
an apple cake and custard sauce from Germany; an Arabic recipe
for pilaw rice in which the fowl is boiled almost to rags. Oh, and
an unsolicited recipe from my little married sister, Mary, that I
have quite overlooked. Her cramped lettering is all angles and
points, and she has had the audacity to name her own dish the
Good Daughter's Mincemeat Pudding. Laughter of the unkind
and sarcastic sort bubbles up in me. Clearly Mother has been
writing to her, bemoaning my *bad daughter* traits. Compared to
me, Mary is a veritable angel.

   Although I have not seen Mary for more than a decade, I can
recall clearly her pink complexion, her brown hair peeled calmly
back from her face, her serene haughty manner. Of course she
may be gray haired and flustered now, with a face full of broken
veins. But still, she is married and living an irreproachable life
of compliance. While I am unwed and have published *divulging*
poems under my own name, and now keep myself buried in a
kitchen with servants. And worse, far worse, I have rejected the
hand of a man who could have plucked me (and the entire Acton
family) from the ignominy in which I live as a scribbling *cook*.

   I run my eye over Mary's recipe. It is a simple wholesome one,
thick layers of bread and mincemeat baked in a creamy custard.
I am just about to file the page with my other donated dishes,
when I notice my sister has written something on the back. I
turn it over and see her spider-leg writing amid ink blots and
smears. To my surprise it is a note, hurriedly written I suppose
from its inky messiness.

My dear Eliza,

Now that a great many years have passed and I have a fine brood
of children, I think we should renew our sisterly relations. I know
my insistence on discretion lies counter to your belief in honesty,
but I think the time has come for us to meet halfway, in a com-
promise of sorts. This is all the more pertinent now that you have
chosen to remain unwed. Of course, Mother may disagree or dis-
approve. But without Papa her opinion carries less significance.
And so I would like to invite you to Suffolk. Does the latter half of
November suit you?

I trust you will not take umbrage at my title for the mincemeat
pudding recipe . . . it is meant only to amuse. So change the title
as you will.

Your sister,
Mary

I read her letter a second time and then a third. For I know
Mary's earnest ways, and this decision will not have been made
lightly. She is pitying my unmarried plight, I think, knowing I
will never experience maternal joy or familial bliss, that I will
be—forever—only half a woman. Or less. The mere ghost of a
woman.

But buried in her words is an olive branch, as if she reaches
to me, begs my forgiveness. An odd feeling of sadness and regret rushes over me. For all that has passed and gone and can

never be returned. And then I taste something else—at the very back of my throat. Anticipation. Yearning. I write back and accept her invitation and then I force it from my mind, for Lady Judith Montefiore is due tomorrow and I have dishes to plan and ingredients to buy.

In the kitchen Ann is making quince marmalade, stirring ceaselessly at the pan. Perfumed steam hangs in the kitchen, collecting on the glass panes of the window, trickling down the cold northern wall. A fly buzzes over the sugarloaf, where Ann has been scraping and rolling fresh sugar crystals.

"Tonight we shall serve a roast beef heart stuffed with a veal forcemeat," I say. "You'll need to pound the veal until perfectly smooth. It must be quite smooth, you understand."

I wait for Ann's assent, but all I hear is the scrape of the spoon on the bottom of the pan and the soft bubbling of the quinces.

"If you can find some mild, finely grained turnips at the market, we shall serve them alongside the heart. But be sure they're not woody or tunneled by root maggots."

Still she does not speak. Nor nod. Nor give any indication she has heard me. "Is something amiss, Ann?"

"In London, the cooks are given the candle stumps and the fat from the dripping pans, and the old bones and pelts too," she blurts. "And I would like the same."

I am so startled at her outburst, I take a long breath. "You know full well that we make broth from our bones and dripping from the old fat. You may take the feathers, hides, and pelts, if you must."

"And the candle stumps?" she asks in a most determined way.

"Whatever for?"

"My father will work them into new and sell them. My brother can't give money any more, for his lodgings has increased."

I run a few calculations in my head. I know that Ann spends no money on herself, not even for a little lace collar or a few ribbons when the peddlers come to the back door. "Where do all your wages go?" I ask gently.

She does not reply for several seconds. Then she says, all in a rush, "My father needs new crutches."

I unlock the metal money box and take out two florins, which leaves me a mere eleven shillings to feed Lady Montefiore. A little elegant economy will be required. Perhaps we should replace the veal forcemeat with a plain sage and onion . . . or one of mushrooms. The field mushrooms are plentiful and flavorsome at the moment, mixed with a few wild ceps they could rival a veal forcemeat.

I pass her the florins.

She blushes scarlet. "I'll pay you back, Miss Eliza."

"From candle stumps and bone marrow? I doubt it." My words come out more sharply than I intend and she flinches, as if I have raised my hand to her. But Reverend Thorpe's words are repeating in my head . . . and I cannot fathom where her wages are going. On her father's drink habit?

"We shall be tested to our culinary limits, but fortunately Lady Montefiore brings her own pudding. And it will do us no harm to cook to a budget," I say, but Ann's face is crimson and she merely nods.

Lady Montefiore arrives in a rustling, clattering swirl of silk and jewels, and is swept to her rooms by Mother, who introduces me very swiftly as "my unmarried daughter, Eliza." Previously, I was her "dear daughter, Eliza." But it seems I have been demoted. I put my apron back on, disappointed but determined not to care.

Later that evening Lady Montefiore sends word that she would like to see the cook. My heart jumps a beat. Her plates were returned quite clean, so we can't have broken any Jewish rules. But evidently she is unhappy. Did she notice the frugality of the ingredients? Is she to quiz me on the recipes? Perhaps she will demand we reimburse her.

She looks surprised when I appear in the dining room. "Surely you are not the cook, Miss Acton?" Her thick black eyebrows rise up her forehead, as voluminously extravagant as a pair of darkly exotic caterpillars.

"I am, Lady Montefiore. Was the meal to your taste?"

"It was splendid. So light and fresh. English food is usually too heavy, all that meat soaked in gravy with liberal lashings of cayenne. But the apple and ginger soup was delicious, although it did not need a rice accompaniment in my opinion." She gestures at the empty chair. "Please sit and talk with me, Miss Acton."

I take the chair with such a sense of relief I feel almost lightheaded. She leans forward and looks at me closely, her head at an angle. "Do you always cook?"

"Yes, although we do not speak of it. My mother prefers our boarders to think there is a professional chef in the kitchen."

"Nonsense! There is no shame in cooking or eating. Indeed,

they are two of life's greatest pleasures." She dabs neatly at her lips with the napkin, then scrutinizes me again, as if I were a fascinating specimen of some rare breed. "Can you hold a secret, Miss Acton?"

I nod, startled at this turn of the conversation.

She lowers her voice. "My dream is to write a cookery book of Jewish dishes. I have started collating them, but it is slow and delicate work."

"I too!" I say, enthralled at meeting someone with the same impudent ambition as me.

Her eyebrows shoot up her pale forehead again and lie there, beneath her tightly drawn hair that is blue-black like a mussel shell. "Is that so? Well, we must share recipes. You served my pudding in a very clever manner. The puddle of black currant syrup was well done. Did you taste my pudding?"

I flush and confess that a small crumb passed my lips.

"The important thing is that all the ingredients must be intimately blended, and the sugar must be thickly sifted over the entire pudding. I can write down the recipe if you would like?"

For the next twenty minutes, Lady Montefiore and I exchange recipes and cooking tips and talk keenly of the need for freshness and how best to maintain delicate flavors. Jewish food uses much fine olive oil, she tells me, and does not drown in butter or lard. The oil can be reused, she says, promising to give me directions to her London oil merchant where I am assured of finding the greenest-goldest olive oil. We compare how best to cook fresh salmon so that its delicacy is preserved and we agree that salmon—which she tells me is often served cold in Jewish circles—is perhaps the finest of freshwater fish. We are so absorbed in conversation we do not hear Mother enter the room.

She coughs loudly and says, "Was everything to your satisfaction, Lady Montefiore?"

"Your daughter and I are becoming the firmest of friends." Lady Montefiore flashes such a dazzling smile Mother is quite disarmed.

When I return to the kitchen I feel as though I am gliding, like a swan but on a vast meringue cushion of air. I grab my notebook and inkpot and jot down all Lady M. has told me. She has promised to share her favorite dish—Jewish smoked beef. I feel a tingle of excitement in my fingertips, but then I remember how little money we have left. Enough for a thick flank of beef? I doubt it. Perhaps I shall fry rosy cubes of salmon in olive oil and serve it cooled . . . I cannot help thinking that a Mauritian chutney would make the perfect accompaniment to cold fried fish . . . And then I remember my sister's invitation, her olive branch. It has been the perfect day, I think, making no attempt to suppress the smile upon my face.

JUMBLES

Miss Eliza is in such good spirits and so pleased with Lady Montefiore, I take the chance to ask if I may have an extra hour's leave today. She lifts her head from her notebook, where she is always writing now, and says I may, but only if Lady Montefiore's meals are all prepared in advance.

"I've made a quart of almond milk," I reply. "And there is oxtail in the larder, ready for the gridiron. And poached quinces too." I don't tell her of my sly addition to the poaching syrup: the hard black seeds of a cardamom pod, crushed and then strained so the eye will never know.

She blots at a gout of ink. "I'm away for a few days at the end of the month, so Mother will need you here, even on your afternoon off."

"Are you taking some holiday?" I ask, curious, for Miss Eliza never takes a day of leave.

"I'm going to my sister's." Her eyes fall back to her notebook and her quill jabs, impatient, at the inkpot.

"Oh, to one of the governesses," I say, for I know she has sisters who are governesses in grand houses.

"No," she says, "To stay with my sister Mary."

Mary? I've heard no mention of a *Mary*. I know of Catherine and Anna, both governesses. I've heard her speak of her brother, Edgar, who is in Mauritius. But no Mary.

"Does she live very far?" At the back of my mind I recall Miss Eliza mentioning, very curt, a married sister. A doctor's wife . . . Is she Mary?

"My sister lives in Suffolk," she says, which is a surprise to me because Suffolk isn't far at all. "Why don't you take the jumble biscuits for your father? They're too brown at the edges for Lady Montefiore."

So I pack the jumbles in a tin box, with some windfall pears, and start walking to the asylum, hoping I might get a ride along the way. The apple orchards and hop gardens are quiet now—the trees stripped bare and the hops cut to the ground. But the lanes are busy with laborers cutting the hedges with bills and slash hooks and clearing the ditches of old wains and rotten harrows and the rubbish left by the pickers and hoppers.

After much walking and two wagon rides I reach the gatehouse of the asylum. I give a shilling to the lodge keeper and tell him I have more for Mam's nurses. He looks a little mournful as if I haven't given him enough, so I offer him a jumble which he takes and puts whole into his mouth. I can hear his molars crunching into it as he shuffles off.

When he returns, he has a nurse in tow. But she is neither Fran nor Cheek-Pincher. And there's no sign of Mam. He goes back into the gatehouse, leaving me with Mam's new nurse who has a coarse face and a forehead full of scars. She wears a dress of thick gray worsted, with a chain of iron keys attached at the waistband, and stout thick-soled boots. I smile, polite, and tell her I'm here to see my mam, Mrs. Kirby. And perhaps I can see Mam's doctor too. But the nurse doesn't return my smile. Her face is grim and pinched and she has her arms crossed tight over her chest. Quickly I offer her a jumble.

She takes the jumble and slips it in her apron pocket. "Your mam ain't well," she says.

"Not well?" I repeat, like a fool.

"She had a fall, 'tis all. But she can't very well get down the stairs. So 'tis best you come in January."

As she says this, a queer shiver runs down my spine even though the day is mild and I'm wearing an old India shawl of Miss Eliza's that's good and warm.

"Can I see her?" I lift up my basket and point to the apples and pears that sit aside the tin of jumbles.

The nurse shakes her head. "No one is permitted to go inside. But I can take the basket to her and you can collect it in January."

I look over her shoulder at the big grand building with its iron-framed windows. The afternoon sun falls, dappled, on its walls and windows. I think of Mam in there, all cozy, being looked after by a proper doctor. She is better there than in Pa's cottage where the winter draughts bite like teeth and the frozen rain rises up through the ground and turns the bottom of the mattress to ice.

"Is she hurt very bad?" I ask.

"Don't you fret, she'll be fine in January." The nurse takes my basket and peers inside, as if she's appraising the contents. "She'll like these morsels." Her tongue creeps out of her mouth and I see it's coated with a yellow crust. But then my attention is torn away by the sound of screaming, coming on the wind from the big grand building.

"Last night's full moon has sent some of the lunatics into a near frenzy . . . ," she explains, her eyes lighting up. She turns, all eager to get back, but I have more questions and I've come fifteen miles. So I thrust a shilling at her and say, "Please take this for your troubles, Nurse." And when she takes it, which she does with great speed, I ask how Mam came by her fall.

"She was gardening." The nurse waves into the grounds where several elm saplings have been newly planted. "Tripped over a shovel, poor thing." She stops and rubs my shilling on her sleeve. The screaming has stopped, as sudden as it started, and there's only the soughing in the trees now.

"So she's broken a bone? And the doctor has set it?"

"Exactly!" She sounds as pleased as punch at my reply.

"Can she write?"

"Don't be daft! None of 'em can write."

"My mam can write," I say. "Can you ask her to write me a letter?"

She slips the shilling into her apron and winks at me, as if we're sharing a joke. "A letter! Leave it with me, dearie."

Only as I walk home do I understand the nurse's wink. She doesn't believe Mam can write and she thinks the lunacy has been passed to me, that I have Mam's madness. I make a note in my head to send Mam a book. Why have I not thought of this before? I've been too wrapped up in my own affairs, I think. Too fond of Miss Eliza. Too eager to progress at work. Too busy stealing poetry books . . . At least I have a shilling left over for Pa. I curl my fingers around the shilling and hold it so tight it cuts, sharp, into my palms.

CHAPTER FORTY-FIVE
Eliza

GREEN PEAS WITH CREAM

My friendship with Lady Montefiore blooms day by day until I am quite disheartened at the prospect of her departure.

After every meal Lady Montefiore invites me to sit with her and discuss the dishes I've cooked, their flavorings and seasonings, where I purchased the ingredients, how I prepared them. I've never met a more curious woman. She wishes to know everything: Do I weigh by eye or with scales? Do I prefer the flavor of an onion or an eschalot? Do I use an earthen pan or a tin pan? Do I cure my beef with bay salt or common salt? Do I prefer a brick oven or an iron oven? And when she is quite satisfied, her talk turns to Jewish food—the dishes she has taken in Palestine and Jerusalem, the Passover recipes she favors, the very thin matzos biscuits she likes to send as gifts. She speaks with such animation, her fan snapping open and closed, that I am utterly absorbed.

It's invariably at this point that Mother enters, pushing her way into the conversation like some sort of battering ram. After which our discourse turns to more mundane subjects. As if Lady M. is as uncomfortable as I am talking of the kitchen in Mother's presence. As if she too is aware of its implied shame. The kitchen, with its labor, heat, and reek, is humiliating enough. But our interest in food carries a taint and shame of its own. *The hint of profligacy, of appetites, carefully concealed in weights and measures and instructions. But there nonetheless* . . . Louis the chef's words swim into my head: *the joy of being an animal.* Sometimes, as Mother laments the inclement weather or the price of lace, Lady M. glances at me over the top of her ivory fan. Her black eyes smile and her eyebrows rise, infinitesimally. As if we are conspirators occupying a secret world.

On Lady M.'s last evening at Bordyke House, Mother goes out to dine with Mr. and Mrs. Thorpe, leaving me with Lady M. all to myself. As soon as her pudding plate has been cleared, I dismiss Hatty and take the tray of coffee myself. Lady M. gestures at the empty chair beside her, her jet drop earrings swinging from her lobes, her dark eyes flickering in the candlelight. I pour her coffee and she compliments me on the stuffed baked ox cheek, telling me I *simply must* visit her London butcher.

"He's at Thirty-Four Duke Street in Aldgate," she says. "He's Jewish, so you'll find the beef far superior. Jewish butchers aren't permitted to sell animals with a single spot or blemish."

"I had no idea," I say, thinking of some of the animals I have seen at the cattle market, their hooves crusted with fungus and their hides balding and speckled with disease. I am about to quiz her on Jewish butchery, when she abruptly changes the subject with such speed butchery is immediately forgotten.

She leans toward me, her eyes as bright as a sparrow's and a gleam upon her lower lip. "I have an idea for something you should write." She opens her fan, then shuts it so quickly the candles in the candelabra gutter and shadows shoot across the table, rippling over the silver coffeepot, sugar bowl, cream jug. For a second the table seems almost alive, as if quaking streams of quicksilver have replaced the linen cloth.

"Can you guess what I'm thinking?" she asks.

I shake my head.

"You mentioned a book of poems." She pauses, lays her fan upon the table, and observes me shrewdly. "I would love to see it."

"It's out of print," I say, unsure whether I wish to show her or not. Those poems are no longer me, no longer mine, I think. And I want Lady M. to see me only as I am *now*.

"No matter." She waves her hand. "It is not poetry I was thinking of."

"Oh?" I feel something flare inside me. A peculiar sensation that begins in the lower reaches of my stomach and seems to spread through me, warm and vaguely disquieting.

"I have a friend," she continues, nodding softly into the candlelight. "She's a brave, bold woman called Miss Kelly."

I say nothing, for I have no knowledge of a Miss Kelly. Is she a poet? A writer of recipes?

Lady Montefiore leans more ardently toward me, so that I am inches from her luxuriant arched eyebrows, her pinked cheeks, her perfectly preserved skin. "Miss Kelly is an actress . . . from a theatrical background. Like you, she talks freely and forcibly."

My eyes open a little wider. Lady M.'s fingers twine impatiently through the pearls at her neck, as if she is waiting for me to speak.

"An actress?" I echo. I've heard talk of London theaters, of actresses. Lewd and scurrilous talk.

"She is about to open a theater and dramatic school in the West End of London where girls can be trained in the dramatic arts. She's looking for new plays." She stops, picks up her fan from the table, bats at her throat with it, snaps it shut. "It is quite respectable; her patron is the Duke of Devonshire." She pauses as if for effect, and her eyes seem to grip mine. "Have you thought of writing a play?"

"I have years' more work to do on my cookery book. And when it's done, I have a vague idea for a second book," I say slowly. "Very vague at present . . . A cookery book for invalids, for those with delicate health." I've told no one of this idea, not Ann nor Mother nor Mr. Longman. But as I say the words, a sense of regret comes over me. And I seem to feel her disappointment, as though she has some inborn understanding of my predicament. I look down into my coffee cup, at the dark oily sediment, and wish I had the gall to show her my poems.

"Wholesome food for the sick is certainly important, but so is the need to determine oneself, to speak out on the subjects that flame inside one. I sense you have a strong flame, like my friend Miss Kelly."

"I do," I say. And as I speak I realize that Lady Montefiore is the first person who has noticed this, who has seen inside my soul, observed the flickering flame—and dared to speak approvingly of it. Dared to encourage it.

"The recipes you've copied out for me are so much *more* than recipes," she continues. "They are small works of art. And why should they not be so?"

"Oh no," I say, with a self-deprecating laugh. "Recipes cannot be compared to poems."

"Why ever not? Yours are beautifully written, perfectly composed. I read your recipe for green peas with cream and it was as if I was reading poetry . . . 'Boil a quart of young peas, perfectly tender in salt and water, and drain them as dry as possible' . . . See I have committed the first line to memory."

"You are most kind," I say. "But a play is . . ." My voice peters out, lost in the tumult of my thoughts. Why shouldn't I try my hand at playwriting? A play about the subjects that I care most about . . . An image of Ann comes into my head, her scant and spartan cottage, her crippled father and dead mother. How I would enjoy revealing her impoverishment to all those Londoners who think only of their next carriage or whether to have brocade or chintz curtains . . . and who believe country people dwell in quaint cottages with roses around the door.

"You have an innate sense of drama—I've seen it in the way you bring dishes to table. And you have an organized mind, a fine turn of phrase, and . . ." She pauses, as if searching for the appropriate words. "And I sense you have a yearning romantic soul beneath that tidy exterior. Am I right?"

"There *is* something striving within me, although I'm not sure precisely what it is," I mumble, suddenly embarrassed at the personal turn our discourse has taken. But Lady Montefiore is not the tiniest bit embarrassed. She plucks a small square of writing paper from her cleavage and passes it to me.

"My friend's address," she says. "Mention my name and send her something."

"I very much like the sound of Miss Kelly." I take the paper, warm from her breast, and slip it into my neckline.

"She is the boldest of my friends." Lady M. lowers her chin and puts her hand over her mouth as if to quieten her voice. "She has a daughter out of wedlock who lives with her, quite openly."

I lean away, startled at this news.

"Yes, shocking indeed. One must admire her audacity though." Lady M. stops and tilts her head. In the silence we hear the grating of a key in the lock, the squeak and scrape of the front door, Mother's step in the hall.

Lady M. puts her finger to her lips and whispers, "Enough talk of boldness. I fear the waters have exhausted me as ever, Miss Acton. I must bid you good night."

She leaves the room just as Mother sweeps in. I pick up the two coffee cups, thinking I can escape to the kitchen before Mother inflicts a lengthy account of her evening upon me. But her voice stops me in my tracks.

"Have you heard the news of your poetess, Miss L. E. Landon? Mrs. Thorpe was quite full of it and could talk of nothing else. I would have informed Lady Montefiore if she had not left for her room in such haste."

My throat tightens. "What has happened to Miss Landon?" I whisper. Already my head is swarming with lines of her verse. But they do not swarm loudly enough to blot out Mother's voice in all its triumph.

"She has been found dead on the floor of her bedchamber, somewhere in deepest Africa. An accident apparently . . . she was taking prussic acid for an ailment and drank the entire bottle by mistake. I don't know where Mrs. Thorpe gets these lurid stories."

I put down the coffee cups. Close my eyes. Clutch at the tabletop. Hear a candle fizz and splutter and die. I want Mother to go. I feel her eye upon me. Watching me. I want her to go.

"Good night, Mother," I say, stumbling to the hall, down the corridor, down the stairs to the kitchen. To my sanctum. I can hardly breathe, each inhale labored and tatty. Ann is arranging platters and dishes on the dresser; but when she sees me, she runs and helps me to my chair.

"Miss Landon is dead," I say between gulps of air. "She is gone."

"I'm sorry to hear that, miss. Shall I get the brandy bottle?"

I lean forward and press the heels of my hands against my eyes. "It was she who inspired me to write." I try to find words to explain the presence of Miss Landon in my life, how she has been as guide, as mother, as companion, as teacher. But no words come. Instead I blurt out something else entirely: "She should never have married!"

"Miss Landon is married?"

"Just this year. She went with him to Africa. I can't bear to think of her dying so far away, so alone." I feel a sob creep up my chest. I do not want Ann to see me like this, so I ask her to go to my room and bring down all six volumes of Miss Landon's verse. While she is gone I pour a glass of brandy and toast Miss Landon, even as tears run down my face.

That night my sleep is charged with dreams. Of Miss Landon lying dead upon the marbled floor of her African palace. Of Miss Kelly and her illegitimate daughter dancing upon a London stage while laborers jeer and catcall. Of Louis making love to me in a coal cellar while Mr. Arnott urges him on with wild cries. Each dream floats seamlessly into the next, until I am trapped in a tableau so terrifying I awake sodden with perspiration. I slip from my bed, sink to my knees, and pray for Miss Landon. I pray that Jesus will take her unto him, that she is somewhere more tolerant, charitable, joyful. And through my prayers, her words weave a ragged path: *Oh, what a waste of feeling and of thought have been the imprints on my roll of life! . . . To what use have I turned the golden gifts which are my hope and pride!* All Miss Landon's golden gifts have gone, I think. Just as she foresaw . . . Amen, amen, amen.

Eventually the sun struggles up and I remember it is Lady Montefiore's last breakfast at Bordyke House. I decide not to tell her of Miss Landon's death, for I cannot fall into another unseemly fit of weeping. Instead I involve myself most particularly in her breakfast preparations, making sure a spotless lace-hemmed napkin has been laid at her table, that the cruets have been polished to a shine, that her favorite breakfast of deviled kidneys is garnished with the freshest, greenest parsley.

Later, when she leaves, after much talk of exchanging letters, she calls out from her carriage window, "You won't forget to write to my friend, will you?"

Her words come to me like the call of a bird to its mate, rousing me from my misery. I will do it, I think. I will do it for Miss Landon!

As her carriage bowls away, dust and grit rising in its wake, I raise my hand to wave. Above, the sky sprawls, vast and faintly blue. And it feels to me as if I lift my hand to Heaven, to the spirit of Miss Landon, to my own destiny.

I have no early flowers to fling . . . But I shall write a play for Miss Kelly's theater and I shall dedicate it to the brave and bold spirit of Miss Landon.

CHAPTER FORTY-SIX
ANN

TEA AND BREAD, BREAD AND TEA

After the departure of Lady Montefiore—and the death of *her Miss Landon*—Miss Eliza changes. Or so it seems to me. She still cooks, but with a vengeance now, as if the wind is at her heels. And she is jumpy, even a little snappy, in spite of Bordyke House having no boarders at present.

I tiptoe around her, as meek as a mouse, wondering if it's me that's made her as tart as a codling. Have I disappointed her in some way? Every now and then, as she's writing at the kitchen table, she lifts her head and asks me the oddest of questions. Yesterday, she asked if I thought a recipe could be a work of art, like a poem or a picture. I was on my hands and knees, scrubbing fat stains from the flagstones. I thought about it for a bit and then I said, "Reading a nicely written recipe must be very satisfying for a lady."

She peered down at me, as if she was surprised I'd answered. As if she was surprised there was someone else in the room.

"Do you really think so, Ann?" She rested her chin in her hand and studied me, as if I was a stray cat that had chanced into the kitchen. "I dream of a time when people read recipe books for pleasure, as they read novels or verse. Can you imagine that?"

"You mean ladies sitting in their parlors reading aloud from a book of recipes?" I'll admit I laughed at that. I could not help it. Such a strange notion of hers, for everyone knows that kitchen work is despised by ladies.

"I'm serious," she said. "I like to imagine Mrs. Thorpe and all her good church gentlewomen reading a cookery book for the sheer pleasure of it. And gentlemen too! Why should cookery books be relegated to dark greasy shelves in dark greasy kitchens? I foresee a time when they're stored in libraries or displayed in parlors!"

I snorted with laughter. But then she shot me such a peevish look, I muffled my snorting and scrubbed harder at the floor so that the damp coldness of the stone pushed farther into my bones.

"Our book must be a pleasurable read, Ann. I am quite determined to make it so." And she bowed her head low over her paper and I heard nothing but the scratching of her nib.

Our conversation has given me two thoughts. First, I should like to send Mam a cookery book. Which means I must find the pluck to ask Miss Eliza if I can borrow one. Second, I should like to read Miss Eliza's writings, her recipes that are as beautifully penned as poems. She keeps her recipe writing in a portfolio of marbled card with a leather spine and brown ribbons that she ties in a bow to stop the pages falling from it. It wouldn't be right to open it, but what if she were to leave her papers out?

It's not until a few more days have passed that I get the opportunity to peek at her writings. I'm removing the stones from six ounces of olives with a paring knife, to make an olive sauce that Miss Eliza says is commonly served in France with ducks, stewed fowl, and beefsteaks. My fingers are aching and stained a dull brown when she puts down her quill and stretches her arms wide into the air, as if she is very stiff and must get some blood moving around her.

"Would a cushion make you more comfortable?" I ask as she starts rubbing at the small of her back and twisting her neck from side to side.

She rises, her hand still circling on her tailbone, and says she will go to the parlor herself for one. I notice that she hasn't slipped her papers inside the portfolio, so I wipe my hands on my apron and glance, sly, at her pile of pages. The first thing I notice is that there are no numbers. Which is odd because her recipes usually include lots of numbers, for weights and measures and such like. I go to the table, all the time listening for her steps in the hallway. The next thing I notice is that the page isn't laid out for a recipe. Miss Eliza likes to list her ingredients at the end but this page has no list. Nor is there mention of any foods. Is it a private letter? A secret journal?

I start looking over her longhand—which is not so tidy as it should be and has many underlined words—and I know, quick as a flash, that this isn't a recipe. Nor is it a verse. I feel my brow crinkle up as my eyes strain to read what she's written. Something to do with "a lady of independent means" and "a baker who thrusts violently his closed knuckles into a huge mass of tenacious dough." I am puzzling at the word *tenacious* when I hear, quite sudden, Miss Eliza's determined tread approaching the kitchen door. I spring back to the chopping board and take up my paring knife. In my haste, it slips and slices deep into the side of my finger. The brine from the olives goes straight into the cut, making my eyes smart and silent cusses spring from my mouth.

Miss Eliza arranges her cushion in the seat of her chair and gives a long sigh. Yesterday I would have put it down to her grief for Miss Landon, or maybe to the tragedy of her past that I saw in her poems. But now I've seen her writings I'm not so sure. It seems to me she is grappling with something new, something I know nothing of.

"Are you quite well, Miss Eliza?" I ask, binding my cut finger tight with my handkerchief and being careful to sound solicitous but not prying.

"It's only my back," she says.

"They say winter is coming early this year. Likely your bones are feeling it with today's poor weather."

"And how will your father cope if we have snow?"

"He has blankets and he can build the fire high with furze from the common," I answer. I don't mention how long it takes him to do this, the hundreds of hobbling trips, the hours of twisting and bending to get the furze basket on and off his back. How could she possibly understand? "And I will take him these olive stones if I may? For burning."

"Yes, of course. And what do your people do for food in winter? For bread?"

"Bread?" I echo, thinking of the "tenacious dough" I saw written on her page. Perhaps she is writing a bread recipe and I have misunderstood.

"Yes, what will he eat when frost clings to his beard? When his limbs are numb with cold? When ice presses at his door?"

I love hearing her words when the spirit of poesy is upon her, but today her words make me cross. I want to tell her Pa is not a poem. He is a real man, crippled and poor but still a human being. But that is not my place, so I play along as if I too am a poetess: "And when his stomach growls, savage, with hunger?"

"Quite, Ann. Describe it to me in all its coarseness. I must see and hear and feel and smell every detail."

And so I tell her, as vivid as I can, how it feels to be always hungry so that one can think only of food; how it is to wake up with frost upon the blankets and a sharp wind whistling through the rags at the window; how it is to have fingers so iced they can barely pick up kindling from the ground; how it is to be cheated without mercy because you have nothing.

"Cheated?" she asks. "Why cheated?"

"The very poor can buy only the lowliest of things," I say. "We must buy the dirtiest bread and the rankest ale and tea leaves half full of wood shavings." I stop and hear my voice, which has

changed and is as bitter as a dandelion leaf. But beneath its bitterness I hear another note. I cannot put it into words; I know only
that it is not shame.

Miss Eliza makes an urgent waving motion with her hand,
as if she wants me to continue, as if she hasn't noticed that my
tongue has lost its usual meekness. And so I tell of how Mam
made "tea" by soaking crusts of burned bread in boiling water,
how Pa took the roof from his mouth by eating only raw onions
with his bitter moldy bread, how cheese rinds were bought for
me and Jack so we might grow, how we all got sick from eating meat from diseased animals not fit for market, how Pa's leg
stump made him cry out in pain every night, how Mam lost one
baby after another and four in a single weekend.

When I've told her everything except the worst bits—which
aren't fit for the dainty ears of a lady—I stop talking and go in
search of a skillet, for the olives must be blanched in boiling water and then soaked to remove their saltiness. It's only when I
turn around that I see her eyes are wet, that she is wiping discreetly at a tear. I twist quickly back to the fire for the sake of her
pride. But something inside me soars like a bird. I have made my
mistress cry with the force of my words. In the same way that
her words, her poems, brought me to weeping, so mine have
done the same to her. Strange, that my spirit is soaring even as
I recall the harshness of my past. At least Mam is in her grand
asylum now and Jack is in his shining white kitchen and Pa has
money from his moleskins and the candle ends from Bordyke
House.

A silence falls over the kitchen and in it I seem to hear my own heartbeat and it is steadfast, strong. And then Miss Eliza speaks, her voice loud with feeling and fury.

"If bread is the sole food of so many, it must be good and wholesome. These iniquitous practices must end. They must end!" She slams closed her portfolio, tucks it under her arm, and goes to the larder. I hear her rummaging through the shelves, the tin boxes clanging and the earthenware jars clinking. When she returns, she says, in a most decisive tone, "We shall start a chapter on bread when I'm back from my sister's. I want to experiment with unfermented bread . . . and potato bread . . . and German yeast."

"Yes, Miss Eliza," I say, happy that my words have brought her to this, to a new chapter in *our* book.

"Everyone should know how to bake a loaf of bread."

I nod in agreement. And suddenly I feel assured enough to ask if I can borrow a cookery book. It may not be my place, but I will do it. Tomorrow, when she is calmer, I will ask.

CHAPTER FORTY-SEVEN
ELIZA

BUTTERED CELERY ON TOAST

So. I have overcome my anxiety and started work on a stage play in three acts, about a spinster who befriends a young, impoverished girl. The girl—she has neither name nor age as yet—has a secret. It is only when the spinster discovers that her young friend can read and write that she realizes something has been kept from her. There will be two roles only, for Lady M. informs me that her friend's theater is most intimate with a stage measuring a mere ten square yards.

I'm still working on the cookery book, of course, but the death of Miss Landon and Lady M.'s comments reminded me of the necessity for something more expressive, more imaginative in one's life. And I like the challenge of writing something new— although a play is more demanding than I expected. I must think not only of words and plot, but of motion, of stage props, of music even. I am pondering this, and experimenting with a dish of boiled buttered celery, when Ann returns from market, her basket bursting with thick stems of brussels sprouts, Jerusalem artichokes clod in Kentish clay, and a fine red cabbage so fresh it squeaks.

As she unpacks the basket, she asks if she may borrow a book.

"Of course," I say, lifting bunches of boiled celery from the pan. "Which one in particular?"

"I thought perhaps *The Frugal Housewife*." She points at the small volume in its brown leather bindings, veined with gilt.

"You may read any of my cookery books, Ann. You know that." My mind veers back to my play, which is to make several important points about how Christian ladies could better spend their time and money. I cannot make it too contentious, for it must be well reviewed. But I have to speak out on poverty and education and the fouling of food and—

"It isn't for me."

"Oh?" I say, surprised. "Is it for your brother?"

"Yes," she says very quickly. Too quickly, I think.

"And he would like *The Frugal Housewife*, would he?" I am loath to lose a single volume of my cookery books, for I must constantly check that my dishes are new and original.

"I shall not let him have it for long, Miss Eliza."

"Is he tiring of Monsieur Soyer's collection of books? No doubt they are all French and lily gilded in the French chef way," I say.

"Yes," she says, again too quickly and too full of relief. "That is right, miss."

I examine her face, bent over the red cabbage as she cuts away the outer leaves. Her face and neck are flushed pink, even as her voice is oddly determined.

"I rather rely on that particular book," I say. "Would he like to borrow *The Cook's Oracle* instead? Its author is a constant irritation to me, with his pompous verbosity."

"Jack would be very appreciative, only I was thinking of the size. A smaller volume would be less costly to post."

She keeps her gaze on the cabbage and I notice her knuckles, red and rough, gripping the handle of the blade. I remind her to remove the stalk of the cabbage by splitting it first in quarters. Still she will not meet my gaze.

"It is not for your brother, is it, Ann?" My mind is darting now from the scenes of my play to the scene spilling out in front of me. Secrets and lies, I think. Here—in the kitchen of Bordyke House, my sanctum. "Jack cannot read, can he?"

"No, miss." She bows her head. "How would you like the cabbage cooked?"

"Stewed very slowly in butter," I say. "Then we shall add vinegar and serve with broiled sausages and good gravy. Who do you want to lend my book to?"

There is a long silence, as if Ann is preparing an answer for me. Or deciding whether or not I can be trusted with the truth, whatever that may be.

"Aren't we friends, Ann?" I say gently. "If you tell me your secret, I'll tell you mine."

Her head jerks up and she looks straight into my eyes, quite startled. Her upper lip quivers as she puts down the knife. I cannot tell if she is shocked at my possessing a secret or terrified at the prospect of revealing her own.

"When two people work together as closely as we do, it's difficult to keep secrets," I say. "And not always beneficial."

"How do you mean?"

"Secrets inevitably mean lies and it's not right that friends lie to each other, is it?" I keep my voice soft to hide how much her distrust has affronted me. Indeed, I am rather hurt by it. Haven't I been good to her?

"Oh, miss. I didn't mean to . . ." Tears well in her eyes and she wipes at them with her hands that are stained a deep purple from the cabbage. "It's my mam. She's not dead." Ann starts to weep in copious gulps, her slight shoulders shaking. I turn away, suddenly overcome by disappointment. I have this odd sense of something curdling inside me. As if some inarticulate hope has separated and soured.

"So your mother is alive?"

Ann nods limply. "Yes and no," she says, but is so choked by sobs she can say no more.

"Where is she?"

"A lunatic asylum." She presses her eyes with her cabbage-stained hands and something about them—the red-raw knuckles; the grazed, scabbed fingers; the stem-thin wrists—moves me to tenderness. In spite of her lies. In spite of the sour stream of regret and discontent winding and looping within me.

"And she would like to see a cookery book?"

Ann swallows noisily. "I could not tell you, miss. I am sorry for my lies and deceit."

Words from long ago spill into my head: *I woke to the dark truth . . . rous'd from dreams of bliss to know thee false . . . to feel that there was agony in this . . .* And suddenly I know that this is not her doing, that others have put her up to this. "Did Reverend and Mrs. Thorpe ask you to keep this concealed from me?"

"They said I would not find a situation if anyone knew. What's bred in the bone, they said . . ."

"Bred in the bone indeed!" I feel my loathing and contempt for the Thorpes gather inside me, spreading from my blood to my bones to the backs of my eyes.

Ann blows her nose on her sodden, ragged handkerchief, then returns to slicing the cabbage, which she does very slowly and cautiously as if she thinks the blade could slip at any moment. "She's in an asylum and the nurses don't believe she can read and write. I wanted her to see what I'm helping with. She's not seen a new book of recipes—the one she had was fifty years old."

"Of course you may lend her one of my cookery books. And when ours is published, she must have her own copy." I pause, and as my disgust at the Thorpes ebbs, something in Ann's story piques me. "How did your mother come by her education?"

"I don't rightly know. She lost her mind when I was eleven years old, a little bit at a time, until she no longer knew who we were or what was what."

My mind swerves back to my play. Could I set a scene in a lunatic asylum or would that be too unsavory for the ladies and gentlemen of London? Could I split the tiny stage in two, one half a country hovel and the other a richly decorated drawing room? I prod absently at the bunches of celery simmering on the fire. I can feel Ann's eyes upon me, as if she is waiting for something, but I'm absorbed in my plot, in its twists and turns, and how they are to convey my feelings and rouse the audience from its lethargy.

When Ann speaks, it is in such a quiet voice I barely hear her over the bubbling of the celery and the slicing of cabbage and the clattering of Lizzie's pattens on the scullery floor. "You wanted to share a secret with me, Miss Eliza?"

CHAPTER FORTY-EIGHT
ANN

POTATOES IN THE FRENCH WAY

I don't know how I have the gall to ask, but the question flies from my mouth like a baby bird tumbling from its nest. And once it's out, there's no putting it back.

I'm in such a state, after showing myself to be a liar and talking openly of Mam, that my thoughts are all hither and thither. It was the way she called me her *friend* that most overpowered me, flipping the cheeky question from my gullet. For I'm quite sure that Ma'am would never call Hatty a *friend*. Nor would Mrs. Thorpe call her maid a *friend*.

I concentrate hard on what I'm doing: weighing butter on the scales, melting it in a pan, sliding in the cabbage. Will she answer me? Will she tell me of the lover from her verses? Or something of Mr. Arnott that made her change her mind about marrying him? A shiver of expectation and excitement and fear runs down my spine. For I remember Pa's words—that no lady wants her servant as a *friend*—and I know it was wrong to ask.

"You are right. I promised an exchange of secrets." She lifts the celery from the pan with a gravy spoon and lays it in a colander to drain. Then she slices off a piece and puts it in her mouth. "Too soft," she murmurs. "I should have drawn it from the fire earlier. It has lost its bite entirely."

"I'm sorry, miss," I say, for it was I that distracted her with my weeping and my talk of Mam.

"Make some toast, Ann," she says. "And put some good butter to melt. We shall sample this celery on a slice of crunchy smoky toast."

I busy myself with the toasting fork—and wait for her secret. I hear her nib scratching, then the sound of her shaking over the powdered chalk to dry the ink, which means she's finished her page. My face grows hotter and redder from the flames. The smell of toasting bread, browning and crisping, wafts around my face. Finally she speaks.

"My secret," she says, pausing to blow off the chalk, "is that I am writing a play!"

"Oh." My voice is flat with disappointment. So those were the writings I peeked at the other day. Not love letters or a journal of the heart, but a play for the stage.

"For a new theater run by a lady in London. If I cannot be a poet, perhaps I can be a playwright."

"An author of plays *and* cookery books," I say, to remind her of *our* book, which only yesterday she was speaking of as a *work*

ANNABEL ABBS

of art. I feel disheartened by her secret. As if a fine carriage has rolled over me, with its ironclad wheels, and I have disappeared between earth and sky. I try very hard to remember the writing I saw . . . something about a baker and a lady. A peculiar play, I think. Is that what London ladies like to see upon the stage? Not much of a secret though . . .

"Indeed!" She gives a dainty clap of her hands, and then, most abrupt, asks if I would like to visit Mam while she's away at her sister's. "You may take some of our preserves and a loaf of the bread we shall be baking next week. Take some for your father too, dear Ann."

My heart lifts. *Dear Ann.* She has forgiven me my lies! "Thank you, Miss Eliza," I say, as I pull the hot toast from the fork. "You seem very pleased to be visiting your sister and I'm happy for you."

"I am pleased, Ann." Her voice rises and falls and is full of her smile.

"Will she come to stay with us one day?" I arrange the toast on a platter and my stomach gives a low groan.

"I doubt it," says Miss Eliza. "We are too busy. Now, let us sample celery on toast. Shall we strew it with some herb?"

I frown, but there's no time to dwell on her words, for she wants my opinion on the celery. I've not eaten celery since I was a girl, but I remember its taste—warmish and savory with a hint of lemony bitterness that goes sweet on long cooking. I run through the herbs in the garden that are still fresh and green. "A shame the lovage is long gone," I say. Sage, thyme, rosemary . . .

too strong, I think. They will overpower the celery. "A thin grating of nutmeg?"

"Minced parsley, if we had it fresh," says Miss Eliza. "Let's sample a plain and then a nutmeg-strewn toast, shall we?"

As I cut the toast into four squares, I think about this mysterious sister, Mary, who's never been mentioned—quite unlike Miss Eliza's governess sisters, Catherine and Anna, who are often spoken of. My curiosity gets the better of me and as I pass the celery toast, I boldly ask if Mary has children.

"Yes, she has several."

I wait for her to tell me more of her nieces and nephews, their names and ages, how bonny and lively they are. But she says nothing, just chaws on her toast and stares at the nutmeg grater, as if she is deep in thought about the celery. I'm right, for a minute later, she says, "I prefer it quite plain. It has no need of nutmeg."

Then she gestures at the window, where the dusk is pressing at the glass. "How sudden the dark comes now," she says as I clear away the plates and trim and light the oil lamp.

To cheer her, I say, "Soon you will be with your sister again."

She nods. "Mary's house is most comfortable. Her husband is highly respected and they have the finest carpets and the brightest silver."

It strikes me that she's regretting not marrying Mr. Arnott. But then she leaps up, as if her verve is quite restored. "Supper! Only you, Hatty, and me tonight. Shall we have salted haddock? Gently heated through upon the gridiron . . . and served with . . ." She pauses, her pale hands clasped upon her chest. "Let us fry potatoes in the French way. They must be crisp and light brown, piled into a dish and sprinkled with fine salt. Such a handsome dish!"

And it's as if the thought of food, and supper, and cooking, has rescued her from melancholy, and it cheers me to know that cooking can truly lift her spirits.

CHAPTER FORTY-NINE
ELIZA

BAKED APPLES WITH CLOVES AND CINNAMON

The Colchester-to-Grundisburgh coach jolts along, stopping only once. Here I take a short walk while my fellow passengers—a rough, uncouth couple with faces like pickled eggs—eat in the tavern.

On my walk I look into a beer shop and observe several hovels, taking note of the filth and disease, the animals that appear to live alongside the occupants, the scrawniness and hopelessness of it all. For years I have chosen not to see such things. For years I have turned away and preoccupied myself with poetry, with love, with myself.

I ask for directions to the nearest bake house, but receive only bald, feebleminded stares. Bread—the staff of life—is much on my mind. And yet not one hovel contains an oven. How can bread be baked without an oven? Indignation simmers in me, and only when it calms do I wonder if my mind is purposefully, furiously keeping busy. So that other subjects can be pushed deftly aside.

The coach rolls on, and as the light drains from the sky we reach the outskirts of Grundisburgh. The air is chill here, with a piercing southwesterly wind that carries a faint tang of the sea and makes me pull my cloak tight around my shoulders. My heart beats faster, harder. My hands grow hot and clammy in their gloves. I suddenly wish I'd taken Mother's advice and refused Mary's invitation. But no, I could never have done that. Whatever olive branch Mary wishes to offer me, I am ready to receive it. I think of my portrait—a small pen-and-ink silhouette—rolled up within my shawl of saffron silk and smuggled at the last minute into my traveling trunk. Was I rash to bring it? Certainly I was extravagant to have it made at such short notice. But something about Ann, her confession, awakened in me an obscure need for something I can barely understand, let alone put words to. God knows I have tried. Perhaps Mary will have my portrait framed and hung. Or perhaps she will scathingly return it to me. Or worse. Perhaps she will hide it, burn it even.

Suddenly we are stopped and the coach driver shouts, "This is where Dr. Gwynne lives." Their house is jealously guarded by iron railings and tall black gates. The windows flare with light and are generously wreathed with swathes and swags of chintz and velvet. An oil lamp smokes in a porch of newly whitewashed brick, and upon the front door gleams the hulking brass head of a lion with a brass striker hanging from its brass jaws.

They must have heard the slurring wheels of the carriage or the thwack of my trunk being cast upon the ground, for within seconds a bevy of eager children, their faces as sharp and bright as pinheads, is at the window. They tap on the glass and wave and squash their noses against the panes so that the glass blooms with their breath. So many of them! I search immediately for Susannah, hoping to recognize a familiar feature. But in the breathy commotion I cannot tell one child from another.

And then Mary and Anthony, sleek haired and well nourished, are at the door, kissing me upon the lips and urging me inside. Instantly I smell cloves and cinnamon and baking apples. I want to follow the scent to the kitchen. I want to still my hands by slicing and chopping. I want my mind to shed its nervous clutter and think only of temperatures and cooking times and the pairings of flavors and textures. For a second I wonder if there isn't some way I can spend time in the kitchen. The two of us cooking together, conferring, tasting, while the kitchen hums gently in the background. And it seems to me that the kitchen, with its natural intimacy, is more conducive to friendship and love than any other room in the house. The steady, indeterminate pattern of days spent there; the heady unforgettable smells; the warmth and succor of its confined space.

"But don't you look well," gushes Mary, whose cushioned cheeks glow like coals. "Do you not agree, Anthony, my dear?"

Anthony takes my cloak from my shoulders and nods. "Indeed you do, Eliza."

And then the children—hundreds of them, or so it seems—tumble into the hall, all laughing and talking and pushing to be near me. Again I seek blindly for Susannah, but the children are all dressed alike, white smocked, blue stockinged. The bustle,

the noise, the shrill clamor of it all overwhelms me, even as
Mary calls on them to be quiet and remember their manners.
How does she live with this cacophony? I think.

I am introduced to the children one by one: Anthony Junior,
Tatham, Minna, Anna, Emily, Helen, Hammond. And finally
Susannah. She stretches up and kisses me with her pink, pursed
lips. I smell soap on her newly scrubbed skin and wait for some
sort of emotion to sweep over me. I feel only the dimmest sense
of affection. I wait a moment, stroking abstractedly at her hair.
But there is no sudden spurt of maternal love, no visceral desire
to grip her to me, no rush of raw longing. What I feel, above all,
is curiosity. As she steps away I scrutinize her, searching for myself in her features. She has my dark hair, my pale skin, my long
slender neck. But her eyes are not mine . . . Her eyes are deep
set, brown with tiny flecks of gold, long thick lashes that curl
as if they have been scraped through a butter curler. They are
his eyes, unshuttered, unsparing. And I am reminded, instantly,
of *him*.

The younger children pull on my hands and skirts, and the
older ones look me over from the corners of their eyes. Anthony
puts his hand on the small of my back, guiding me into the parlor where a fire flickers, red and violet, and where endless shelves
display endless lines of books bound in calfskin.

Anthony sees me eyeing the books with a prying, envious expression. "Excessively dull medical books," he explains, batting
at the air.

"They remind me of our old home, before we sold our library,"
I say. "I'm glad you have such a collection. It is right that children

grow up with books around them." I wonder if my volume of verse is in among the medical tomes, if Susannah has seen it or read it. But no, Mary was always shamed by my *unfettered sentiment*, as she once put it. If there is a copy of my poems here, it will be under lock and key.

The smaller children tumble upon the Turkey rug, where they push and shove and make hideous faces, sticking out their pink tongues and waggling their fingers in their ears. They seem unable to sit still, even for a second. They poke at each other's rib cages and fall upon one another and call each other vile names. The older children egg them on with much mirth, as if my presence is of no consequence. Surprised, I look to Anthony for discipline, but he is busy settling himself into an armchair and Mary has gone to give orders to the servants.

I snatch constant looks at Susannah, observing how she tilts her head when listening, how she bats her thick lashes in irritation, how she slaps at her brothers with a peculiar flapping motion of her hands, how she wrinkles her nose and scratches at her head. And then she sees me looking at her and flashes me a smile, so blithe, so lopsided, I am reminded again of *him* and of his smile that seemed to curve in two.

"Susannah, won't you sit beside me?" I pat encouragingly at the sofa. She catches Anthony's eye and he nods his assent. The little girl, my very own daughter, creeps to the sofa and springs upon it like a cat. She snuggles beside me and I feel the warm damp weight of her leaning into me. My arm lifts, as if of its own accord, and reaches around her shoulders.

And that is how we are when Mary returns.

CHAPTER FIFTY
ANN

BAVARIAN BROWN BREAD

I get two rides to Barming Heath. The second is with a tanner who huffs stale breath all over me and blows pipe smoke in my ear. After a mile of this, he puts his brawny hand upon my knee and asks how I shall repay his kindness. I answer, very stoutly, that being a good Christian girl I want no more of his ungodly talk. My words, so full of assurance, take me quite by surprise. They come from my mouth of their own accord. Only after I have jumped from his cart, do I hear Miss Eliza in my words. The neat force of her, the determined politeness. I have learned all that from her, I think, and a warm feeling comes over me.

This warm light feeling stays with me all the way to the lunatic asylum, in spite of the weight of my basket that grows heavier with each step. In it are two jars of preserves, a pat of fresh butter, and a pot of thick cream, as well as a loaf that Miss Eliza calls our *Bavarian brown bread*—from a Professor Liebig whose books and pamphlets have been arriving by mail coach all week. Underneath all this lies a cookery book, for I am determined to show the nurses that Mam can read. It will be a small miracle, of course, for she has read nothing for years. But Miss Eliza assured me that *no one forgets how to read. Ever.*

There's a sharpness on the back edge of the wind today. And when it gets into my mouth and nose I sense an ice-and-pepper tang. It blows up as I reach the asylum, whipping my hair from its cap, nipping at my chapped lips, gusting up my skirts. When the lodge keeper draws back his hatch, the wind blows straight through, making the papers on his table fly into the air so that he growls, irritated.

"I am here to see Mrs. Jane Kirby, my mam," I say, pushing him a sixpenny bit.

He looks at the coin and frowns, as if he's not sure whether to take it. I push it a little farther, wondering why he doesn't snatch it up in his usual swift way.

He screws up his little hogish eyes, then looks at the paper on his desk, holding it down with a bony fist, for the wind is still blowing through the open hatch. I pull my shawl tight around my shivering shoulders and hope they will bring Mam to me somewhere warm. Perhaps I can see her bedchamber today, feel the softness of her feather mattress and the thickness of her quilt. She is all bones, so a skinny mattress and skinny blankets will be no good at all.

The lodge keeper coughs, his eyes circling over the sheet of paper. Around and around.

"I can read," I say, tentative, for I do not want to hurt his pride.

"Likely you can, missy," he says, with another cough. "A gentleman came for Mrs. Kirby yesterday."

"Oh," I answer, surprised. No one has called Pa a gentleman for as long as I can remember. I wonder why he didn't mention anything when I delivered the candle stubs and rabbit ears last week. "That must be my father. He has only one leg," I say, wondering if he rode with the miller, and hoping he wasn't turned away like I was on my first visit.

The lodge keeper's mouth drags up and down as he peers at the paper. Then he looks up but does not catch my eye. "The gentleman what came yesterday had two legs."

I stare at him, confused. "A gentleman with two legs for Mrs. Kirby? For my mam?"

The lodge keeper nods slowly, licking at his dry lips. "He took her away."

"No, you are muddling my mam with someone else," I say, impatient now. "Show me that paper." I push the sixpenny bit so it's touching his knuckles and make a grab for the paper. Perhaps there is another Mrs. Kirby, or a Mrs. Kirkby, or a Mrs. Kribby, someone else who has been cured by the doctor and collected by her husband.

He pulls the paper back, his face coloring. "I know what my eyes have seen and my ears have heard, missy. I have no need of reading."

"Well then, tell me where she has gone," I say. "Or who has collected her."

He grabs at the sixpenny bit and puts it in his pocket, as if he no longer feels compelled to leave it. And in that moment I know he's telling me the truth, that he's about to reveal something he shouldn't.

"'Twas a clergyman. He saw the superintendent for a private meeting."

The wind falls away and for a minute everything goes very still. Even the old, dry leaves stop scurrying along the ground. Is it possible Reverend Thorpe—for who else could it be?—has taken her home? That she has been cured and made ready for the parish again? But as soon as these thoughts strike, I see the folly of them.

My voice falls to a whisper. "Where did he take her?"

The lodge keeper closes his lips tight and stares hard at his sheet of paper. Only this time his eyes aren't going around and around. I take a shilling from my purse and shove it toward him.

He looks at the coin and I see his mouth working, as if he's fighting with his own soul. "Please have the money," I say. "For your troubles."

"She was in the Dead House. Likely for some time," he says after a long pause. "It's full to bursting right now."

I frown, not understanding his words, not understanding what a Dead House is. "Is she still there?"

"He took her to St. Margaret's Church in East Barming." He pushes the coin back to me. "It's where the lucky ones go, those that aren't sold."

"Sold?" I echo, baffled.

"That's right—their skull caps is cut off and their lunatic brains are cut open. You're lucky she had a Christian burial with a proper man o' the cloth."

Black spots start rushing and swarming before my eyes. All at once I see nothing but the endless black spots. Behind them, the lodge keeper is blurred, his nodding head disappearing in a spin of blackness. I hear his voice, muffled: "Are you all right, missy?"

As my mind gropes through the storm of black spots, words from somewhere rush at me. I catch them, hold them fast, say them, silent, over and over: *Life's silver cord torn apart, the golden bowl broken. Life's silver cord torn apart, the golden bowl broken* . . .

"You can walk to East Barming; 'tis just over a mile as the crow flies. Look for the spire. Hers'll be the only fresh grave; all the rest is sold to the surgeons."

Through the swirling speckled spots, I see the lodge keeper gesturing through the hatch, back to the road, down to the left.

"But she had somewhere to go," I say, numb. *Life's silver cord torn apart, the golden bowl broken. Life's silver cord torn apart, the golden bowl broken.* "I was her silver cord and she was my golden bowl." Through the fading black spots I see the lodge keeper give me an odd look, his hand reaching for the hatch, reaching to shut me out.

Somehow I find my stumbling way to St. Margaret's Church, tears blurring my eyes as I beg directions. All the time I am haunted by the thought that Mam's death is my fault—for if I had stayed home with her, she would surely be alive. And if I had been stronger, more like Miss Eliza and less like my feeble wavering self, I would have demanded to see Mam after she tripped over a shovel, which I now know was a lie to keep me away. My tears stop when I reach the graveyard. At the back is a small mound of newly turned earth. Not a single bloom lies upon it.

Not a single piece of fresh foliage. Dead, curling leaves blow over it and gust away. I scour the ground for footprints and find only one. The imprint of a hobnailed boot. No sign of anyone else. Only the fresh-turned earth, black and crumbling. Only the crows screeching from the leafless trees.

I take the preserves from my basket, along with Miss Eliza's copy of *The Cook's Oracle*. I cannot leave without commemorating Mam. Without remembering that it was she who taught me to read. It was she who taught me to write. I place the book so it sits squarely in the midst of the broken earth. A tombstone of sorts. Its leather cover, stained where buttery fingers have gripped it, shines faintly from the black soil. I kneel in the cold mud and put the jar of damson jam on top of the quince marmalade and place them on the book. I have made her a sepulchre, I think. A gravestone as respectable as any. I arrange the loaf of Bavarian brown bread and the pat of butter and the jar of cream to make a crucifix. Then I kiss each one—the book, the jars, the bread, the cold black earth.

When I'm done and have wiped the crumbs of dank soil from my lips, I notice the wind has dropped to a sullen breeze. I take up my basket, pull down my cap, hug my shawl to my ribs, and begin the long walk back to Tonbridge.

CHAPTER FIFTY-ONE
ELIZA

CURRANT CAKE

Mary presides efficiently over the children's tea, chastising the nurse, dispatching the sulky maid to and from the kitchen, issuing a steady stream of commands. Do not talk with your mouth full. Do not eat with your fingers. Do not open your mouth when you chew. Do not pick at your nose. Do not take God's name in vain. Do not put your napkin on your head. Do not tease your sister. Do not poke the baby. Do not drop crusts on the floor.

Within a few minutes, I am stupefied with boredom, while my head throbs from the relentless cacophony. I try to watch Susannah from the tail of my eye, but she is interested only in gobbling scones or elbowing her brother. I feel a curious detachment, not only from her, but from the entire rabble of nephews and nieces. It occurs to me, most uncharitably, that I would not mind if I were never to see them again. The thought shocks me with its bluntness, with its lack of feeling. Perhaps love comes with time, I think. Perhaps if I had seen more of them, I would feel a modicum of affection. Perhaps if Susannah had grown up with me, I would feel a mother's love.

Minna shrieks so shrilly I put my hands to my ears in an involuntary movement that Mary, with her omniscient eye, spots. "Ah, Eliza, my dear. They are in high spirits because of you. They are not always so unruly."

I lower my hands into my lap, where they twist at a napkin. I want to excuse myself and slip to the kitchen or to my bed-chamber, but I know Mary wishes me to observe the children at tea, although I have no idea why. No sane woman would make an old maid sit through such bedlam. I wonder what I would do if this was a play. How might I end it? How might I hold the audience's attention? Could I pull the cloth from the table so the crockery and cutlery crashes to the floor? Could Mary grab the bread knife and plunge it desperately into her heart? I need something to bring an instant ghoulish hush to the stage . . . For a few minutes I am completely lost in my thoughts, in my stage directions and props and when to bring the curtain down. Until Mary's voice cuts reproachfully into my head.

"Eliza? Eliza? Susannah is talking to you . . ."

I look up and see Susannah's eyes upon me. And *he* flashes before me. A memory so vivid, so acute, my nails dig into my palms.

"I'm sorry." I shake my head. "I was thinking of something else altogether."

"Mama says I may read to you tonight."

I give a thin awkward smile. Mary, who is cutting a vast currant cake, halts and beams at Susannah. "Why not show your aunt how you can read in French?" She plows the knife into the cake then turns to me. "A French master comes to the house every week, more for the benefit of Hammond and Tatham, but Anthony thought Susannah should join the lessons. She has such an ear for French, my dear."

"My French is much better than Hammond's and Tatham's," adds Susannah, picking out the currants from her cake and pushing them to the edge of her plate. The currants have not had their stalks removed, I note testily.

"Do not brag, Susannah." Mary turns to me again. "Her French is very good, my dear. Uncannily so."

I flinch, wishing she would cease her innuendo. Her constant references to the long-gone past—which I have worked so hard to delete—give it a weight and substance that drags on me, fatigues me. The baby starts to cry, and I see Susannah flick a currant at Hammond. Suddenly I long for the composure of Bordyke House, the quiet presence of Ann, my books of recipes and poetry, my quill pen and its brass inkpot, food that has been carefully prepared, properly prepared. Food that is eaten slowly, voluptuously, morsel by morsel and mouthful by mouthful. Not like this table where it is all gobbling and devouring, or mangling to a pulp, or little sticky fingers slipping crusts and currants to the floor.

"If I am to hear you read, I must ready myself." I make my voice amiable, jolly. The voice of a fond maiden aunt. "So I shall rest for an hour, if you will excuse me."

"You must be rested for dinner." Mary saws at the bread, which is not properly risen. Then she looks up and fixes her eye on me. "We have important things to discuss."

I feel a moment of confusion. As if some mystery has drifted into view but hovers just out of reach. And then it races toward me and suddenly I understand her letter. She does not want to renew sisterly relations with me. She wants something—*from* me.

Dinner is a dull affair, each course less appetizing than the one that precedes it. I gnaw my way through leathery overcooked mutton; boiled potatoes that have not been peeled with sufficient attention and are still hard at the core; shredded cabbage that has been overcooked and not correctly drained; and finally a rice pudding that has been cooked with neither raisins, almonds, lemon peel, nor flavoring of any sort. The awfulness of the food distracts me from the conversation to come, the *important things to discuss*. I have now worked out what these important things are: Mary and Anthony Gwynne are in need of money.

All through dinner I am braced and ready with my answer. Namely, that I have received no advance from Mr. Longman and there will be no money for several years to come. I am also braced for questions about my refusal of Mr. Arnott, for recriminations and accusations of failing Mother and Father and my sisters, *slaving as governesses*. But none come. Instead, Anthony proves to be a font of knowledge on Professor Liebig and his nutritional theories. For an hour we discuss the importance of nutrition, even as we chew on food that has been cooked dry of all goodness. The irony of it goes unnoticed by Mary, who is constantly distracted by the children's scampering feet overhead or by something she has forgotten—a hem that remains undone, a sock heel not yet darned, a misplaced boot that must be collected from a neighbor.

Finally, the port arrives with a tiny crystal glass for Anthony. And with it, the *important things*.

Anthony pours himself a glass and then clears his throat. Mary clears her throat too, so I do not know who is to make the request for money. I see them catch each other's eye and so, to spare them embarrassment, I hold my hand up and say, "Please don't worry. I know you need money for Susannah, and you shall have it. But I have no advance from Mr. Longman, so it will take some time. I have given myself ten years to prepare my cookery book."

Mary's face flames but before she can speak Anthony has both palms in the air, stroking at it, as if to stop me speaking.

"You have quite misunderstood our invitation," he says. "We have asked you here to offer Susannah back to you."

The blood drains out of my face, then rushes back in a sweep of mortification and confusion and shock.

"Given your refusal of Mr. Arnott, it seems unlikely you will have your own family now," says Mary. "We love Susannah as if she were our own, but it is not right we should keep her. Mother says you have a young girl helping with your book and we thought, now that Susannah is twelve, perhaps you could use Susannah instead. Mother has agreed."

My own daughter, I think. I can take Susannah home with me. I shall be a mother. A mother!

"You can explain it very easily," says Anthony, pouring himself another glass of port. "You can say she is a niece from Suffolk come to help you. Her costs will be covered by the wages of your kitchen maid."

I close my eyes and instantly scenes swim before me: Susannah and I at market together; me teaching French and literature to Susannah; the pair of us cooking, tasting, conversing, discussing books and baking, poetry and puddings. I shall introduce her to the verse of Mrs. Hemans and Miss Landon. And when I visit the bold Miss Kelly to discuss my play, Susannah shall accompany me and I will tell the truth of her.

"Well, what do you say?" There is a crack in Mary's voice and when I open my eyes I see that hers are glazed with tears.

"Let Eliza sleep on it," says Anthony gently.

I nod, determined not to make a hasty decision. But I am tingling all over with the promise and possibility of *my daughter*. "I will hear her read now, as I promised," I say pushing away my chair and almost running from the room.

Susannah is propped upon a mound of knitted cushions in a little painted bed. I touch the bedstead and its metallic chill gives me an instant sense of relief: bedbugs do not take so well to metal. It strikes me this may be my first truly maternal thought, and I feel slightly startled at how it came upon me, as if by instinct. Is this motherhood? Will other motherly feelings follow in the wake of a single fear of bedbugs in my daughter's bed?

"I will recite you a poem," says Susannah, her scrubbed pink cheeks shining in the candlelight. She starts reciting, fast and in a single breath so that the words spill into one another: "'Will you walk into my parlor?' said the Spider to the Fly. ''Tis the prettiest little parlor that ever you did spy; the way into my parlor is up a winding stair, and I've many a curious thing to show you when you're there.'"

I sit beside her and put a clumsy arm around her shoulders, waiting for—for what? For a deluge of motherly feelings, I think. She is still rattling away, so I try and concentrate on the words . . . "'I'm sure you must be weary, dear, with soaring up so high; will you rest upon my little bed?' said the Spider to the Fly. 'There are pretty curtains drawn around; the sheets are fine and thin, and if you'd like to rest awhile I'll snugly tuck you in!' 'Oh no, no,' said the little Fly, 'for I've often heard it said, they never, never wake again, who sleep upon your bed!'"

"You've remembered the words splendidly," I say, although something about them unsettles me. Images of spiders and unsuspecting flies shuffle through my mind. Which of us is Spider and which of us is Fly? If I were to pluck her from this rowdy boisterous home—where she has a respected doctor as a father—would she one day thank me or would she one day hate me? And what if I cannot cultivate feelings of fondness for her? What if it starts and ends only with the fret of bedbugs?

"Do you know the rest, Susannah?" She doesn't answer and I see she has fallen asleep. I stoop to kiss her cheek, hot and faintly sticky with the residue of cake soap. A thrill runs over me . . . my own daughter! How will it be to have her at my side, in my home, the two of us cooking, reading, reciting poetry together? I kiss her cheek again, letting my lips linger, wondering if this is how Mary feels when she kisses her children good night. It is such a contented feeling, I cannot help but kiss Susannah a third time before blowing out the candle. I am just tiptoeing from her room, when a ball hits me on the side of my face. I turn, my cheek fizzing with pain, and glimpse Hammond and Tatham scampering down the hall.

My earlier contentment turns instantly to irritation. Why is Mary not here to scold them? I think, stroking my throbbing cheek. And where is the nursemaid? I try to remain calm because Anthony's words are repeating in my head . . . that I must sleep on my decision, that I must not rush into anything. It is only as I creep past Mary's bedchamber that I realize why she is not chiding Hammond and Tatham. She is in her room. Weeping.

CHAPTER FIFTY-TWO
ANN

PLAIN POUND CAKE

I don't stop at Bordyke House. Miss Eliza's not due home for another day and I have questions. For Pa. For Reverend Thorpe. For Mrs. Thorpe. My feet are sore and stinging. Blisters burst and ooze at my heels and on the tops of my toes. An east wind full of spite and frost has risen from nowhere, whipping my face raw. My fingers are threads of ice. But the pain is nothing next to the din in my head. So many questions, all tripping over each other, a heaving, squirming sprawl of questions. How did Mam die? Why did no one tell me? Why did Reverend Thorpe bury her in an unmarked grave miles from her home? And beneath these, other questions maunder. Less keen, less sharp. Like a grumbling ache that will not pass. Questions I should have asked long ago: Did something make her a lunatic? Did something happen I know nothing of? Did *I* drive her to lunacy? Is her lunacy to be my fate too?

I know I should go home first and ask Pa. But I don't trust him to tell me the truth. And the rectory is on my way. I shall stop at the rectory, I think. I shall put on my *Miss Eliza voice* and insist on a proper burial for Mam in her own churchyard.

I go to the back door, squeezing past a dog cart and a pony at its hay bag. When I ask for the reverend, a housemaid looks me up and down, says he is out, and tries to close the door.

"Mrs. Thorpe, then?" I ask. The wind blusters past me, lifts the housemaid's apron, tugs at her cap.

She nods and shuts the door. And when it next opens, there is Mrs. Thorpe, dressed in stout black silk, her face dragging in different directions. As if she doesn't know which expression to muster. Finally she settles on a look of resignation.

"Come in, Ann Kirby," she says. "My husband is not here but you can wait."

"Maybe you can help me, Mrs. Thorpe." My hands shake beneath my shawl as I follow her to the parlor. I would rather be elsewhere. I don't feel comfortable among her china knick-knacks and velvet cushions. I wish I had gone home to Pa, but it's too late. Mrs. Thorpe points at a plain wooden chair as she lowers her thick rustling skirts into a velveteen armchair. She looks at me with her eyebrows raised, as if she wants to know the nature of my business.

"I've come about my mam." My voice is very quiet, and a gold clock in a glass case chimes as I speak. "I believe Reverend Thorpe has buried her, all the way over by Maidstone." Tears prickle in my eyes.

Mrs. Thorpe nods, brisk. "That is correct. He has been very

good to your family, Ann Kirby. I am sure you will want to thank him when he arrives."

I blink, baffled at her words. "But how did she die and why was I not told?"

Mrs. Thorpe picks up some embroidery from a basket on the floor and, very casual, begins to stitch. "She fell down the stairs and broke her neck in the asylum. Mr. Thorpe was informed and took it upon himself to make the necessary arrangements. He is with your father at this very moment although I expect him back imminently."

"Yes, that is very kind of him." My lips wobble as images crowd into my head. Mam tumbling down hundreds of stairs in that huge, gray building. Why wasn't she tied to a nurse? She would never have fallen if I had been caring for her. Guilt presses down on me.

"Indeed it is. He is a busy man. And an exceptionally generous man—he paid seven shillings for her coffin. The reverend is a saintly man, Ann Kirby."

"But why is she buried so far away?" I grind my nails into my palms to stop the tears from bursting forth.

"We cannot have the dregs of lunacy in our graveyard, Ann Kirby. Our bedchamber overlooks the graveyard and we hope to have our own children, God willing." She stabs at her embroidery, not looking at me once. "Besides, I like to open the window for fresh air."

I stare at her pale, tight face. Is she saying that Mam's madness might rise from a coffin, from the earth, and infect her through an open window?

"Yes, the reverend and I cannot take any risks." Then she looks up, straight into my eyes. "The truth, Ann Kirby, is that she has not been your mother for a very long time. My husband saved you—and her—from a life bereft of dignity and propriety. The time for mourning was when she first lost her mind. After that she was no longer a mother, merely a lunatic."

I look away, at the china ornaments on the mantelpiece, at the little framed embroideries and watercolor pictures that crowd the wall, at the yellow roses that twist and writhe upon the rug. I try to summon pictures of Mam before her madness, but they do not come. Not until I turn my foggy head and catch sight of a Bible on a little table by the window. And in that moment, she comes to me. And I am ten and crouched beside her, turning pages of a book. The air is thick and steamy and smells of apples and honey. A wasp buzzes and its drone mingles with her words. She's speaking in her low, calm voice, her fingertips stroking my cheek. She's telling me books must be treasured, that books will always be my friend.

I grip the picture to me, but it fades away. Later, Pa threw all the books upon the fire, ripping them page by page and shouting that we must have warmth or we would die. Mother was mad by then, but still she wailed and sobbed. Father bound her to the window so she could not hurl herself upon the flames.

"She is still my mother and I want her buried in Tonbridge," I say, surprised at the boldness of my voice.

Mrs. Thorpe bends and pulls a padded footstool from beneath her plump chair. She rests her feet upon it, as if she has had a hard day laboring, and resumes her needlepoint. "How did it begin,

Ann Kirby?" she asks, very slow with her eyes narrowing. "What were the first indications of her mental decay?"

I pause, unsure what to say, whereupon she rings the brass bell at her belt and tells the parlormaid to bring tea and two slices of plain pound cake no thicker than her little finger—which she jabs at the air so there can be no mistaking how thin to cut the cake.

"Think back, Ann," she says, her features quite soft now, almost smiling. "What did you notice first?"

I don't want to talk about Mam to Mrs. Thorpe, but I'm suddenly very hungry and thirsty, and it strikes me that if I'm polite, perhaps Mam can be buried proper, in Tonbridge. Where Pa and I can place wildflowers upon her grave every week.

I answer her question uncertainly, for it was many years ago and I was but a child.

"She could not remember what seeds she had planted," I say. I don't say that nasturtiums burst from every inch of soil, that we had no potatoes or leeks that year, that we ate nasturtium seeds until our mouths burned. Did she stop being my Mother then? I wonder. Was that the moment I became *her* mother? Mrs. Thorpe's words have left a sour taste in my throat, but I know there is some truth in her words. At some point, my mother ceased to be the mother I had known. And yet, to me, she was still Mam . . . my mam.

"She became forgetful?" Mrs. Thorpe is smiling at me, a peculiar smile that looks as if it has been stuck upon her face with clay. "What next?"

"Her words were mixed up and she could not find them," I reply. I don't tell her how one day, when Mam couldn't seem to find any words at all, she took the iron kettle from the fire and threw it at Pa. Or how, after that, she spent hours and hours lying on the mattress. Just lying there. Doing nothing. Saying nothing.

"When did she start . . . wandering and . . . removing her clothing?" Mrs. Thorpe coughs and inspects her embroidery.

"That was more recent." All at once I don't want to say any more. I don't want to think of how Mam behaved in the last year. Toppling over as if she were drunk, crying, shouting, lying like dead for hours and hours, pissing on the cottage floor, running half naked up and down the streambed. I don't want to remember her like that. "She could not reason," I say simply.

Mrs. Thorpe's face sets hard again. "And how about you and your brother? Are you becoming forgetful?"

"I must get back to Bordyke House." I stand abruptly, no longer caring about my manners or the promised pound cake or seeing Reverend Thorpe. Suddenly I loathe Mrs. Thorpe and her nasty nosy questions, and I want to be in Miss Eliza's kitchen with her poems of despair in front of me. A line of her verse floats toward me. I pluck it from the air and hang on to it, tight . . . *Come to my grave when I am gone, and bend a moment there alone* . . . I will find a way of getting Mam buried in Tonbridge, I think, even if I have to dig her up with my own bare hands.

CHAPTER FIFTY-THREE
ELIZA

POTATO BREAD ROLLS

Of course I cannot *sleep* on Mary and Anthony's offer to return my daughter. After an hour of inner turmoil I rise and dress myself. I creep down to the drawing room, but the fire is almost out and the air is stiffening with cold. I make my way uncertainly to the kitchen quarters. Past the scullery, where a housemaid sleeps upon the floor. Past the washhouse, where someone snores loudly from behind the door. In the kitchen, the stove still radiates a little stale heat, the copper pans glimmer in the moonlight, and a beetle trap clicks and clacks as insects fall between its jaws. I close the door behind me and let the serenity, the quietude of the room soothe me. I have an inexplicable urge to do something with my hands—to write or slice or knead. Anything but this endless clenching and unclenching of my fists. I light a candle and look for a quill pen, an inkstand, paper, but see none. Unless I can still my hands, I cannot think, I cannot put my mind in order.

I had not expected Susannah to be returned to me. I had never dared hope for such a thing, although I have often dreamed of how a life with my daughter might be. But now the moment has been sprung upon me and I am plagued with doubts. For me and for her. It pains me to confess it, but I do not have Mary's sanguine motherly nature. And in the anxious hours of night I am beginning to wonder if there is perhaps something wrong with me . . . for even when I kissed Susannah I felt only contentment. Not the true, deep love I suspect Mary feels. Of course, my hand reached involuntarily to check whether Susannah's bed frame might harbor bedbugs. But what if that was only from concern for my own welfare? Above all, my mind keeps returning to our introduction in the drawing room, when I felt merely curiosity. None of the warmth and affection I imagined would pour into me at our first meeting. Am I unnatural in some way?

I look about the kitchen, and my eye falls upon a flour tin and a basket of potatoes. I find a paring knife hanging from the dresser shelf and begin scraping the potatoes, dropping long spirals of mud-crusted peel into a bowl. I give each twisting length of peel a thought as I dispose of it: Would my daughter be more contented alone with me, or with a full family replete with siblings and father? Do I have the attributes of a good mother? Does Susannah belong to me because I bore her or to Mary who raised her? What makes a mother?

As I drop the final peeling into the bowl, I have an overwhelming sense of *wanting*. Of wanting Susannah for myself. Of wanting to possess what is rightfully mine. A memory of her birth comes to me: she is in my arms, her head streaked with blood, her face crumpled like a blanched walnut. Madame le Duc, in her long white apron, bends over me, giving me brandy from a china feeding cup. Susannah gnaws on my nipple. I feel again the pain, the relief, the sheer exhaustion of it all. Pierre never visited, never saw her.

One day, as I was waiting to return to England, I received a letter from him. I didn't keep it but its words are impressed upon my mind. And the scene of its arrival is set, as if in aspic. I can remember all those vivid little details: the air pulsing with the warm scent of lilac; the Normandy light falling, like gold, across the floor; the creaking of the rocking chair with its cane upholstery; Father reading and pulling at his mustache; Madame le Duc humming to Susannah. I was looking out of the long narrow window, wishing I was well enough to walk along the beach again. The beach where Pierre and I had spent such joyful times, walking and talking, our hands fluttering, grazing, unable to keep apart.

Of course the beach had also been my downfall. The softly sloping dunes where I had taken him in my arms, where we had kissed as we had never kissed before. He had asked me to marry him, of course. He said the French way was to make love before marriage, that there was no shame, that as his wife I would be half French. I don't regret it. For many years, I feasted from that one night of passionate love ever since, recalling his sumptuous skin, the touch of him, the sand sinking softly beneath me.

When I realized I was with child, it was too late. By then I'd heard the talk of his philandering. With servant girls and seamstresses, with ladies and with lace makers. It seemed that no one was immune to his desires and yet all this had passed me by. I saw then my future . . . a wife, far from home and cast aside, unable to trust a single maid, a single friend. Not for all the silver in Spain would I be that forlorn little wife.

At first the jealousy was unbearable. I could think of nothing but how he touched them, how he kissed them, the words he slipped into their ears. The jealousy bore into me, green and sour, until I could think of nothing else. Until I was no longer myself. Then one night I decided to express my feelings on paper. I wonder now if it wasn't God's obscure guidance—for the writing of verse was my savior. A week later, I returned Pierre's ring. He fell upon his knees, begged me to think again, said all the talk of other women was lies and slander. I wavered. He was so very handsome, so dashing, so charming. So famed for his courage and bravery upon the battlefield. I felt my body melt and cry out for him, but my mind was stronger. And I was fortified by poetry.

That evening I returned to my lodgings and wrote poem after poem. A month later I knew for sure I was with child. I was bursting from my corset, my monthly bleeding had ceased, I could take no food before midday. Still my mind was resolute: I would not be Pierre's submissive prowling wife. I wrote to Mary, who had married Anthony and become stepmother to his three children and was also with child herself. I wrote only for advice: my sleep was broken every night by fierce cramps in both legs and the morning nausea was unbearable. But she informed Mother, who refused to correspond with me. Father, however, hurried to Normandy. He tried to persuade me to take back Pierre, to make a marriage of form. But I would not. I could not. I had found a voice in my writing, a voice that kept me steady. A voice that seemed to offer me a means of escape. Already I was imagining a little booklet of verse, an audience. I knew there was truth in my words and that, if they had helped me, they could help others. Even as I grew big with Pierre's child, I was nurturing this other secret child—my verse. By the time of my confinement Pierre had found himself a new fiancée and Father had halted all attempts to *return me* to him. But my secret love child—my poetry—was well and truly bonded to me, warm and alive with a beating heart all of its own.

There was only one matter on which Father was intractable: I was not to raise the child myself. Already Mother and Mary had agreed the Acton family must not have its good name stained by a bastard child. Such a stain would have made marriage for my sisters unattainable, business for my father and brother difficult, a social life for Mother impossible. And as for me, the education in which Father had invested would have been worthless.

"How will you find a husband?" he asked. "How can you be a governess or a school mistress or a lady's companion, if you have a child?"

Pierre's letter arrived that afternoon, as the shadows lengthened, as the running swell of the sea grew louder in that long-windowed room. He wrote with a proposition: that he and his wife-to-be adopt Susannah and raise her, in France, as their own. It was a generous offer and Father urged me to consider it. I knew then that I could lose my child forever. I wrote to Mary and Anthony and begged them to take Susannah. Mary's letter came swiftly—she would take Susannah, but only on one condition. Only if she could raise Susannah entirely as her own. Only if I forfeited all maternal rights. Forever.

Susannah was mine for a mere month. Did I love her for that month? Can that month compare with her many years as Mary's daughter? I remember the wrench of handing Susannah to my sister. For a week I suffered. For a week the emptiness at my elbow and my breast was an aching throbbing pain. My leaking milk was like a wound until Madame le Duc bound my chest in cold cabbage leaves and strips of linen. I wrote poetry day and night. But then, one bright morning, I walked out through woods of pine and birch. Foxgloves and wild clematis and briar roses were bursting from the earth. Birdsong shook the air. Swifts snipped at the sky. I knew then that I must publish a collection of my poems. Not only the tragic ones but new verse, about the glory of life, the joys of solitude, the majesty of nature. I hurried back to England and set to work, finding printers and subscribers, writing new poems, editing the old ones. Pierre was quite forgotten. Even Susannah had faded to a dim memory. After a while I struggled to recall her features, to hear the pitch of her cry, to remember the milky softness of her skin.

All this floods back to me as I chop potatoes, as I pump water into a pan, as I place the pan upon the stove and pray for sufficient heat to bring it to the boil. While the potatoes simmer I weigh out flour by rushlight and hunt for yeast in the pantry, being very careful not to wake the supine creature—a parlormaid?—sleeping upon the floor. My thoughts turn to Susannah. What is right for her? To rip her from her family? Her home?

As I tip the flour into a bowl, I hear the beetle trap click-clicking. Not once, but several times, as if a train of insects has been gobbled up. I measure out the yeast and prod at the potatoes. I can tell they are properly mealy from how quickly they crumble. Perfect for potato bread rolls, I think. Only then do I remember Ann. It was she who told me of a bread her mother made using potatoes rubbed, quite hot, through a coarse sieve.

If Susannah comes to me, what will happen to Ann? If Susannah comes to me, how will I make the money I need to be truly independent? To secure *her* independence? If Susannah comes to me, how will I complete my cookery book, my play?

As I drain the water from the potatoes, my conundrum clears into a simple question: What do I most want for my daughter? And through the smoking, spitting rushlight, an answer comes. Clear and concise.

CHAPTER FIFTY-FOUR
ANN

SMOKED HAUNCH OF BADGER

I leave the rectory and return to Bordyke House. Hatty takes one look at my long face and hugs me to her, very hard.

"Go to your Pa first thing in the morning. I can do your work and I'll tell Ma'am. Miss Eliza ain't due back just yet," she says. Later that night, after she blows out the candle, I tell her everything.

"You're lucky Reverend Thorpe has dealt with it," she says, in her matter-of-fact way. "At least your mam's in consecrated ground. I've heard tell of pauper lunatics being thrown into lime pits. No grave, not even a coffin. They just put 'em in a shroud and throw 'em in a hole."

Her words startle me out of my grief. Mrs. Thorpe's comment about the cost of Mam's grave flies into my head. Seven shillings for a coffin. Why would Reverend Thorpe do that? I fling back the cover and sit bolt upright. All the hairs on my arms are on end. My mouth feels as dry as sawdust. So dry that when I speak my voice is hoarse and croaky. "Are you sure, Hatty?"

"Oh yes. Paupers from the workhouse are treated likewise, only their hearts are chopped open. With idiots, it's the skull. Cracked open like a nut, they say. They can't very well bury them after that, can they? So they tip 'em in a lime pit."

I don't answer her, for the darkness is seething all around me, muffling her gabble so that everything blurs. All I can think of is Reverend Thorpe, hurrying to the asylum, getting Mam's body to the nearest church, paying for the coffin, not breathing a word.

"And you ain't had to pay a penny. So Reverend Thorpe has done you a service. Anyway, it's not so far, is it? I'll come with you and we can plant it up with spring violets, make it the prettiest burial plot in the place. And you can save for a headstone."

"But why would he do this for us? He hates us."

"Because he's a man of the cloth and God told him, I suppose."

I put my head beneath the cold sheet and close my eyes. Something seems odd to me, very odd. I think of the times I visited the asylum, how eerily silent it was. No other visitors, no parish officers, no hearses or carriages. I glimpsed tradesmen of course, but they had always disappeared around the back, like the miller. And yet Reverend Thorpe had been there. A few days before me.

The following morning I rise early, leaving Hatty to black the stove and pump the water and fill the coal scuttles and lay the fires. I find Pa at the cottage, pegging out fresh moleskins for the puny December sun to dry. He leans for his crutches, but I put up my hand and tell him not to move. Then I squat beside him and start crying, huge scraping sobs that judder through me.

"She's in Heaven," he says. "'Tis better for her. And Reverend Thorpe got there in time to have her properly buried. She's in God's own hands now."

"Why can't she be buried here?" I sob. "Near enough for us to visit . . ."

He shakes his head. "Mrs. Thorpe didn't want her too close. And then there was the extra expense of getting her body here. I couldn't ask that of him. What matters is that she's had a Christian burial, Ann."

I nod, my sobs dying in my throat.

"Her funeral would have been a sparse and dismal affair. Best left to the reverend." Pa takes my hand in his and jerks his head at the neat line of moleskins beside him. "Will you come home, Ann? I'm making a few coins from the moles and the reverend has offered us the bones and eel skins from his kitchen. Seems he's partial to eel, but he don't use the skins which dry very nice and make a lovely garter for gentlemen with aching knees. We could scratch a living, the two of us."

I stare at the little gray moleskins with their long pale claws, pegged firmly into the ground with small wooden stakes. I should come home and look after Pa, I know that. But as I think this, something tugs at my insides, sucking out all the air in my lungs. I wipe my eyes and think of Mam, of all the hours she spent helping me with my letters. Did she teach me to read and write so that I can *scratch a living*? I think of Jack in his shiny white kitchen, of Miss Eliza bowed over her quill pen. I imagine myself at market, selling Pa's greasy candles and scrawny mole-skins from a barrow. I cannot believe that is what Mam intended for me.

He nods toward the kitchen. "Can you smell that?"

I sniff at the air, catching something meaty, woody, smoky at the back of my nose. "Are you cooking in there?"

"I've a haunch of badger smoking in the chimney. The rever-end has agreed I can lay traps in his garden. You won't go hungry here, Ann."

All this talk of the reverend is confounding me, unsettling me. I have a feeling that Pa is not telling me everything.

"Why did the reverend have Mam buried? Why didn't he leave it to us? Or to the asylum?"

Pa sucks at his cheeks and says nothing for a long time. I feel the cold and wet of the soil seeping through my skirt and petti-coat, spreading over my skin and into my bones. "Does he do that for all his parishioners?" I feel confused, for everyone keeps telling me how good the reverend is and yet I cannot forget all his little acts of meanness.

Eventually, Pa speaks. "No," he says. "No, he does not."

"So why for us?"

He strokes absently at a pegged moleskin, still sucking in his cheeks. "You must not breathe a word, Ann. Do you promise?"

I nod, more flummoxed than ever. I feel very hot inside my cold damp clothes, a flushing heat that comes from nowhere and makes my skin scald, my face burn, so that I must throw off my shawl and loosen my bodice.

"Reverend Thorpe and your mother were cousins. We were sworn to say nothing, to no one."

My eyes grow big and disbelieving.

"And so he feels an obligation. Not much, but a little. His wife believes madness to be in the blood. She makes it hard for him, but she has the money. Not him."

"So he is a relative of mine?"

"If we do not shame them—with drinking or madness or crime—they will help us. But we must say nothing of the family connection. They were shamed by your mam marrying so far beneath her, but now they are shamed by other things, by my crippled leg, by us being paupers. But mostly they do not want the taint of madness upon them. Do you understand, Ann?"

I nod and stand up. The smell of smoking meat gusts from the cottage, making me feel hollow and hungry. And in that second, my future is suddenly, blindingly, as clear as glass. I think of Miss Eliza, the way she speaks always with purpose. I try and copy her voice, strong and clear.

"I cannot scratch out a living here, Pa. Mam would not have wanted it. And I don't want it. I want more—I want to be a cook. I want to help Miss Eliza finish her book of recipes." And only God knows how long is left to me, I think. Only God can spare me from the lunacy.

I help Pa up, adjust his crutches for him, motion to the cottage. "I shall insist that Mr. Thorpe takes you back. It is the very least he can do for us." As I walk beside Pa, it seems to me that I am a fraction taller, a little straighter. As if something inside of me has grown.

"You'll take a slice of my badger ham, won't you, Ann?"

"I will," I say. "But then I'm going straight to Mr. Thorpe." And I have never heard my tongue so determined, so decisive.

CHAPTER FIFTY-FIVE

ELIZA

CHOCOLATE ALMONDS, GINGER CANDY, AND PALACE BONBONS ON OSIER TWIGS

I am pulling an iron tray of potato rolls from the oven, straining to see if the crusts are sufficiently browned and crisp, when the kitchen maid appears, her hands scrabbling at the ribbons of her apron. She cries out in surprise, for the mantel clock shows it is barely six and the rushlight throws only the slenderest beam upon my person.

"It's only me, Miss Acton," I tell her. "I have made a fire, so that is one less task for you."

She peers, bemused and still half-asleep, at the rolls.

"Potato rolls," I explain. "They stay moist longer than any other bread and the flavor is excellent. Do you have a rack?"

The girl gawps at me as if I am speaking in a foreign tongue. After a few seconds she comes to her senses and pulls a rack from a cupboard on the wall. "I'm sorry, ma'am," she says, blinking.

"Only Mistress Mary rarely comes to the kitchen. I thought you was an intruder."

"Indeed not," I say briskly. I leave instructions for the rolls to be served warm with very fresh salted butter, and return to my room to find the portrait of myself I brought for Susannah. As I'd rubbed the boiled potatoes through a colander, stirred in the flour, kneaded the dough, and cut it into squares, my mind had cleared and sharpened. And now I have a plan and must put it into action.

I take the portrait from my trunk and a letter wallet from my bag. From the wallet I take a poem I wrote to Susannah after Mary took her from me . . . I read it again, and think how poignantly it reads, but also how distant it sounds, as if it has been penned by someone else, someone I barely know. All that repetition of the word *forget-me-not*. How lacking in originality it seems. How obvious.

I roll the poem into a tight cylinder and slip it inside the rolled portrait, pausing briefly to unroll it and inspect my silhouetted pen-and-ink self. She too seems another person. Even though she is so newly inked. She is no longer me, I think. In the same way that Susannah is not mine. Too much has passed. How can we be mother and daughter without that bond of time and nurture to sustain us?

I think of the expression on Mary's face when Anthony offered Susannah back to me. The way her lips trembled, the light draining almost imperceptibly from her eyes. I recall the weeping I heard from her room. I remember how she watched over the tea table—correcting the children's manners and grammar, straightening their collars and cuffs—and how she can talk of little else. Could I be like that? Do I want to be like that? I look again at the portrait, searching the eyes for signs of who I was. Could I have been like Mary? Could I have been as happy a mother as she is? I try to picture myself with a boisterous brood of children, but the picture in my mind's eye is a watercolor and will not hold, the colors bleeding and fading. Perhaps if I picture it in oils, I think. Still it tears and frays and will not hold. I look at the rolled-up portrait with its inner rolled-up poem—reassuringly firm and tidy—and speak to my old self: *Perhaps you were never intended for motherhood, perhaps you were made differently, made for something else.*

While I wait for Mary to wake up, I take ink and quill, and note down my observations on potato rolls . . . More salt is needed than with regular wheaten bread. And less liquid. And the fire must be gentle, if they are to succeed. My nib scratches over the paper as I add my final observation: the potatoes must be of the best quality, the very best. Only when my notes are complete do I take a clean sheet of paper and start writing instructions for my will. Susannah may not have her blood mother but I am determined she has her independence, that she has choices. For without choices, we are nothing.

Later, when I've completed the notes for my testament, I go in search of Mary. I find her in the nursery, instructing the nursemaid on which outfits the children are to wear. Already the room is pandemonium: the boys are fighting, the girls are bickering over hair ribbons, the baby is wailing, three musical boxes are clamoring, and Mary's sartorial instructions are being delivered most emphatically. I retreat and wait impatiently in the corridor. Now my mind is made up I want to return to Bordyke House as swiftly as possible. Ann will be there, I think. And the kitchen will be quiet, industrious, purposeful. I shall be able to proceed, unfettered, with my work.

As Ann comes to mind, I have a sudden longing to take her a gift. Something dainty and delicious. Chocolate almonds, ginger candy, barley sugar . . . in a pretty bag tied with satin ribbon . . . I make a mental note to ask Mary if there is a confectionery shop nearby, but already the mental note is lost, for my mind is crackling with ideas of confectionery. Our book must have a confectionery chapter, I think. Nougat, as I ate it in France, crammed with pistachios, almonds, filberts. Palace bonbons of candied citron on osier twigs. Orange-flower candy made with the freshest blossom. How odd—no sooner does Ann come to mind than I am running over with ideas and inspiration. It strikes me then that Ann is more daughter to me than Susannah.

Mary appears, breathless and bustling, from the nursery. "They are always full of spirit in the morning!" She laughs and fans at her face with her fingers, as if the exuberance of the nursery has warmed her. Then her face falls. "We shall miss Susannah terribly. She is so loved by us all." She turns away and fumbles for a handkerchief. When she speaks again, her voice is low and muffled, as if she has the handkerchief pressed against her mouth. "But Anthony is right and we cannot keep her forever. Not now that you have chosen to be husbandless, not now that she can live with you under the guise of a niece or a kitchen maid."

"Mary." I put my hand upon her arm. "I have decided it is better for Susannah to stay with you. As soon as I am able, I shall send an allowance." I pause and a strangled gasp splutters from my sister's throat. I continue, rapidly, efficiently, and to the point. "I shall leave her everything in my will, so there will be no financial burden on Anthony. And no difficulty for you finding her a husband. There is just one thing . . ."

Tears are streaming, in gullies, down Mary's pink disbelieving cheeks. "B-But she is yours . . ." Her stammer is mingled relief and shock and bewilderment. As if she cannot understand my decision, even as it fills her with joy.

"There is just one thing," I repeat. "I have a small portrait of myself that I would like to give to Susannah. I shall leave it at your discretion how best to explain it."

"She must not be tainted by scandal." Mary sniffs into her handkerchief.

"No," I agree. "'I may have sinn'd . . . but be the curse upon my head—O, let it not descend to her.'"

Mary looks up, her eyes pink and wet. "That is so beautifully spoken, Eliza."

"I quote the verse of Miss Landon," I explain, my voice wavering. "I was once told that husbands wouldn't allow their wives to invite Miss Landon into their homes. I do not want a similar fate for Susannah."

"Nor for you," says Mary, suddenly sounding cheerful and resolved. "Scandal and shame are to the detriment of all of us."

I nod absentmindedly. It strikes me that, as Susannah's "aunt,"
I can do more for her than I ever could as her hapless, ill-starred
mother. And yet . . .

"I shall go and inform Anthony—he will be delighted." Mary
gives a little satisfied clap of her hands. "And then I must deal
with Cook who is very upset and about to give warning. She
is under the delusion that I have forgotten my place and used
her kitchen before she was up." She laughs as if such an idea is
quite preposterous. But before I can confess to my kitchen *crime*,
she hurries to the stairs, her voice issuing commands to the
air: "Hammond, are you dressed yet? Anthony, where are you?
Bessy—tell Cook I am coming . . . And can someone put the dog
outside?"

It pleases me to see Mary so full of cheer, to know that Susannah is so deeply loved. But thoughts of *scandal and shame*
pluck at me. There is a finality in those words, I think. An un-
ambiguous instruction that makes my dream of dedicating my
cookery book to Susannah a misguided folly. It will need a new
dedication, I think, as I return to my chamber to pack up my belongings. Words and phrases spin through my head: a line from
Mrs. Hemans? A dedication to the memory of Miss Landon? No
doubt Mother will wish it dedicated to her . . . Should I dedicate
it to Mary in gratitude? Or to Father who had me educated and
is still in exile?

I shake my head, trying to rid myself of all these swilling
thoughts, for I would much prefer to think of candied fruits and
caramel. But as the coach rolls back to Colchester, and then an-

other jolting coach to Tonbridge, Susannah will not leave my mind. I am determined she inherits something sizable from me, be it money, or . . . or . . . Only when my journey is finished do I realize that I have come home empty-handed, my intended gift of chocolate almonds or ginger candy for Ann quite forgotten.

CHAPTER FIFTY-SIX
ELIZA

HER MAJESTY'S PUDDING

I cannot shake the idea of dedicating my cookery book to Susannah. Back at Bordyke House I pull down my volume of *Domestic Cookery*, which states most clearly in its introduction that it was written for *the authoress's own daughters*. I read those words again and feel a prick of envy. But then my eye is caught by the frontispiece and its accompanying line: *By a Lady*. And another possibility comes to me. If I published anonymously—another unknown, nameless *lady*—perhaps I could safely dedicate my book to Susannah. It would be my gift to her, along with the future proceeds of the book.

As I ponder this I notice a line at the bottom of the page, a line I have never previously noticed:

Sixtieth Edition

Suddenly I no longer want to be anonymous. Not even for Susannah. In my mind's eye I see my book—sixty editions of it—with my name emblazoned across the opening page and stalking down the spine. There is something about this image that makes me tremble, even as it makes me feel taller, less flimsy. I have lived at the whim of chance, but if my book ran to sixty editions, Susannah would inherit a substantial estate. She could live freely, like a gentleman or a wealthy widow. I balance *Domestic Cookery* in my palm and imagine my own book being passed from hand to hand, from mother to daughter, from neighbor to sister, from friend to friend. Of one thing I am sure: recipes speak. They carry within them their own language. And to remain anonymous is an act of cowardice. For when we strip away our name, we remove the certainty so necessary for a new housekeeper. I look at my shelf of recipe books: Carême's *Patissier Royal*, Raffald's *Cookery*, Glasse's *Art of Cookery*, Clermont's *Cookery*. Each name in proud, gleaming gilt. And it seems to me that these recipe writers have been my companions, not only guiding me with their instruction but offering friendship—even as they infuriated me with their ill-measured ingredients and inelegant prose. They have softened the edges of my seclusion, filling my kitchen with accomplices. I turn over Mrs. Rundell's book and inspect the nameless spine. I shake my head, for company is never nameless. What sort of woman ekes out her friendship in anonymity?

The door rattles open and Ann appears, her gait so unusually brisk and bright that I forget all thoughts of *sixty editions*.

She asks about my journey and my sister's family, then says, "Are we to be very busy today, Miss Eliza?" There is a glitter to her voice, as if she has swallowed a saucer of golden ingots. And for a second I am envious of how uncomplicated her life is. She has felt hunger and cold, of course. But she has never battled her own ambition, or felt the sting of spinsterhood with all its untold duties, or experienced the lashing tongue of disapproval. She simply *lives*.

Ann looks at me, as if she can see my envy in the green glare of my eyes, then says, "Or are you working on your play today?"

"I'm thinking of visiting Lady Montefiore," I say quite unexpectedly, the words bolting from my mouth as if of their own accord. "She wishes to read my play and I wish to meet her theatrical friend, Miss Kelly." I feel a sudden urgency to complete my play, to see it performed in London, to hear lines—that I have written—bounce from the walls of a theater. At the same time I hear the call of my cookery book. And my head hums with hundreds of recipes impatient to be cooked in kitchens everywhere. "So little time," I murmur, too quietly for Ann to hear.

"I worked on a new dish while you were away. A pudding." She ties her apron tight around her waist. "Milk, cream, vanilla, eggs, and sugar."

"Oh," I say, slightly unsettled at the jauntiness of her tone, at its *certainty*. "A custard. Did it curdle?"

She ignores my question and tells me that she garnished her pudding with branches of preserved barberries. She asks if I would like to see it. But before I can answer she scuttles to the pantry, returning with a clean pudding cloth over one arm, and my best platter—on which wobbles a custard as large and pale as a harvest moon. Atop are woven branches of barberries that wink like garnets. For a second I am speechless. Her creation—for it is nothing less—is picture-perfect.

She offers me an egg spoon and jabs at the platter. "Go on, Miss Eliza. I saved it for you to taste first."

I dip the spoon into the custard's wrinkled rind and lift it swiftly, curiously, to my lips. As I do so, I'm aware of a sense of serenity washing through me. My anguish over dedications, the lurking accusatory voice that lives inside my head, all of it slips away. And there is only cream and vanilla. It occurs to me that although this glorious pudding is her creation, Ann is partly my creation, and I am partly her creation. Cooking and tasting have provided their own stage and we are performing on it at this very moment.

"Have you a name?" I nod at the quivering pudding, marveling again at Ann's use of barberry branches for decoration. "What about barberry custard?"

Ann smiles, more to herself than to me. "I've called it Her Majesty's Pudding."

"For Queen Victoria." I nod approvingly.

"Oh no," she says. "For my mam who died and was buried without my knowledge."

The egg spoon clatters from my hand. Why has Ann not mentioned her mother passing away? I feel perplexed and hurt, but Ann merely wipes at her eye with the pudding cloth, then turns back to the custard and pokes at the barberry branches. "I don't want to talk about my mam," she says. "Besides, the custard is named for you too, Miss Eliza. You are now my queen."

Something clots briefly in my throat. But then Ann is speaking again, and her words leave me dumbstruck. "I have a new rich relative, but I can't say nothing because he is a secret!"

I stare at Ann, and wonder if the girl is touched with fever, if the death of her mother has sparked a fire in her brain. But another glance at her barberry custard tells me this cannot be the case. I feel panic at the edges of me, moving through my veins, blotting out my surprise and confusion and hurt. Blotting out the joy of hearing her call me *her queen*.

"A rich relative?" I repeat foolishly. But my mind is frothing. Is she about to leave Bordyke House to live with her *rich relative*? To look after her widowed father? Or to join her brother in Monsieur Soyer's famous kitchen? No wonder her tone is jaunty! No wonder there is a fresh spring in her step!

"Yes," she says, her gaze swiveling to the window. "I can't say any more, but it has made me feel . . . bolder. And so did getting Pa's job back, and making and naming my own pudding." Her eyes turn back to me and they have lost their customary shyness. "I have you to thank, Miss Eliza. You have . . ." She pauses and I see her lips working, searching for the right phrase.

"Emboldened you?"

"More than that . . . Nourished me." She tips her chin, as if pleased at her choice of word. Then she falls silent, and I wait for her to say that she wishes to give notice. Instead she turns on her heel, hurrying Her Majesty's Pudding back to the pantry. Leaving me to mull her newfound audacity: Will it take her from me? Is my kitchen sufficiently spacious to accommodate two bold cooks?

My head feels too small for so much confusion and doubt. So I return to Mrs. Rundell's recipe book, my thoughts scrambling back to my own cookery book and the problem of its dedication. I wipe at a buttery fingerprint on the spine, then dust off a smudge of flour. And as I do so a name flashes before me. Ann! I would like to dedicate my book—*our* book—to Ann . . . But no, that would never do. No writer ever dedicated a book to a servant, and Mother would be incandescent with rage. I must find a dedication that encompasses Ann *and* Susannah, that speaks to anyone in need of a kitchen companion, that includes all those exiled from their kitchens . . . rich and poor, married and unmarried, Jewish and gentile . . . Words begin to cut and fold in my head. I need words that are clear, simple, to the point. Like my recipes. Like me . . .

I close my eyes. I can hear the fire hissing with a thousand breaths, Ann humming in the pantry, the clink and clank as she arranges bottles and jars. And from this music, a line drifts into my head. A line that is clear, simple, complete. The perfect dedication:

To the Young Housekeepers of England

I write it down and slip it inside the pages of my play. And then I repeat it under my breath. "To the Young Housekeepers of England . . . To the Young Housekeepers of England."

And I like it. Yes, I like it very much.

EPILOGUE
1861
Greenwich, London

ANN

I find her cookery book at the bottom of a chest where I keep
spare blankets for Mr. Whitmarsh's motherless girls: *Modern Cookery*. How sturdy and handsome it looks, in its wine-red
leather bindings, embossed on the spine, stitched at the edges—
and her name in gold so bright it glitters. I open the book and
turn to the title page. I can't help but smile: *Modern Cookery, in All
Its Branches: Reduced to a System of Easy Practice, for the Use of Private
Families . . . in a Series of Receipts which Have Been Strictly Tested,
and Are Given with the Most Minute Exactness . . .* Oh, Lord, how we
tested! I turn to the contents page, laying the book side by side
with my so-called gift from Mr. Whitmarsh: *Mrs. Beeton's Book
of Household Management.* And then I go through both, recipe by
recipe. By 5 P.M. I have barely covered a quarter. But already I can
see which way the wind blows. Mrs. Beeton has filched at least
a third of our recipes. The very same dishes, but made flat and

dull, and with new titles of her own making. Granted, her placing of ingredients at the beginning rather than the end is clever.
But there's nothing more than that.

Reading our recipes all over again has made my tongue hum.
Like it used to. Before I came to Mr. Whitmarsh's house and he
told me he would dine only at his club for *career reasons*. Before
his daughters refused to eat anything but burned-to-a-crisp mutton cutlets with plain boiled potatoes and plain rice pudding. I
lost heart when I came here. Mr. Whitmarsh wanted me laun-
dering his shirts and his daughters' frocks, and scrubbing the
floors, and boiling up the rags he needs as chief dispenser at the
Royal Greenwich Hospital. He gave me enough money for cutlets, potatoes, rice, and milk. And not a penny more. Meanwhile
his belly grew plump and soft on green turtle soup and suet pudding. Gobbled at his club for *career reasons* . . .

I put the books to one side, take a sheet of paper, and write
myself a shopping list. Tomorrow I will cook real food. Miss
Eliza's food. Why else has the man given me a cookery book? As
I write out the ingredients from my favorite dishes, the flavors
and tastes return to me, reaching beneath my tongue, collecting
sweetly in a pool at the base of my throat: a brace of young well-
kept partridges, fresh button mushrooms, port wine, fine salt, a
firm flavorsome cucumber, very fresh green spinach. And pudding? Why, of course! It must be the pudding we tested over and
over: the elegant economist's pudding. How she liked that name!
And how apt it was—for she was both elegant and thrifty. To my
list I add: a pint of stoned raisins, fresh milk, and newly laid eggs,
lemon grate, bitter almonds, a few drops of ratafia.

I say not a word to anyone, but two days later I tell Mr. Whitmarsh he is to eat at home tonight. He looks at me, baffled. I slip a hand inside my neckline, flirty, and say, "For *career reasons*, sir." And then I wink, as bold as brass.

When he gets home, his girls are already fed their overcooked mutton cutlets and tired rice pudding, and I have dressed the table like an altar. Best damask tablecloth. Best Wedgwood china. Best crystal. The three-pronged silver-plated forks. A fresh bunch of sage at the ceiling to keep the flies away. He sniffs at the air, confused and wary. As if he thinks I'm about to poison him. Then he looks at the table, laid for two, and frowns. "Am I not dining alone?"

"I shall join you, if I may, sir." I blush, for it's not a servant's place to suggest such things, even when she shares her master's bed. "It's all cooked and keeping warm. But I can eat below if you prefer?" Oh, the barefaced cheek! I never heard myself so brash and saucy. Mr. Whitmarsh raises one sprouty eyebrow, then shrugs. And so I eat beside him, in a high-backed chair with a napkin shook out upon my knee. Like a married woman dining with her husband.

Over supper—spit-roast partridges stuffed with field mushrooms and served with a mushroom and port wine sauce, and stewed cucumbers, and spinach turned from a mold and richly buttered—I tell him of my life before I came to him. Of how Miss Eliza Acton and I worked ten years on a cookery book. Of how she wanted it to bear my name too, beneath hers. But I refused. I felt it weren't my place. We fell out over that, for she could not understand it and was mortally offended. And then I found out she had a child, a girl she'd kept hidden from me all those years. It was my turn to be mortally offended. For by then I thought we were firm friends.

Mr. Whitmarsh eats, drinks, nods. No doubt thinking of the medicines he must dispense tomorrow. So I continue rambling on about my past . . . For reasons that were stupid and regrettable, I left Bordyke House. Miss Eliza asked me to stay and help with her next book, which was to be on nothing but bread. But we had been too long together—cooking side by side fifteen hours a day for ten years—and she had become quite the preacher. Always angry about poverty and the injustices of life although she'd never had a hungry day! Later, when she was living in Hampstead and working on her book of bread recipes, she sent me a signed copy of *our* book. In her letter she said her "niece" was helping out. Even then she refused to say it was her *daughter*. She wrote that her play had been a great success but that she was too tired to write plays or poetry now and that her mind was going. She could not remember simple things, she said. She forgot to put her full address, writing only Miss Eliza Acton, Hampstead, London. So how was I to write back to her?

Mr. Whitmarsh is barely listening to me, for when I put this question he nods and chaws and says my food is the finest he has ever eaten and why didn't I tell him I was a mistress of the kitchen?

"And now she's dead," I say, ignoring his question as he has ignored mine. "And I think it was the madness that came upon her because that was how my mam started her slow descent . . . forgetting little things. And knowing this frightened me so that

I didn't want to think about Miss Eliza, or look at our book, or cook. But now . . ." My voice trails off as I wonder how best to explain that Mrs. Beeton's plundering of our recipes has reminded me that life is short, that it comes only once, that it must be grabbed and gulped at. And not left out to spoil and rot.

He cocks an eyebrow, then lifts a partridge bone to his mouth and sucks noisily upon it. "Better than my club, far better, and all the time you've been scrubbing floors, my Ann . . ."

"I am tired of scrubbing floors and charring mutton cutlets for your girls, sir." I put my knife and fork down. "I want to be your cook. You can entertain your gentlemen friends here. Mrs. Beeton says home dining is very fashionable in polite society." I almost spit when I say *Mrs. Beeton*—the cheek of her!

"Only in households where there is a wife who acts as hostess," Mr. Whitmarsh says, curt. No mention of *my Ann* . . . "I cannot invite the doctors' wives if I do not have one myself."

I take a deep breath. "I am tired of being your servant. I wish to be Mrs. Whitmarsh and to cook your supper every night and converse with your gentlemen friends and their wives. And to sleep always in your bed." My face blushes hot but I look right at him, straight in his eye. If he says no, I'm decided: I'll go elsewhere and find a position as cook. Monsieur Soyer is dead these past two years, as is my brother Jack, but there are other places I can go. I have heard talk that Lady Montefiore has opened a Jewish soup kitchen in the East End of London. Likely she would take me . . .

He looks down at his plate and slurps at his mushroom and port wine sauce, very slow as if he's thinking. Then he looks up and grins. "Why else do you think I bought you a book of household management, my Ann?"

My addled brain dances. "So you will accept my hand in marriage, my Benjamin?"

He laughs. "Only if your pudding is as good as your partridge."

"Oh, it's better," I say. "The elegant economist's pudding is the best sweet dish ever baked."

Acknowledgments

I'd like to thank the following for their continued support and inspiration: my mother, Barbara, who introduced me to the twin delights of cooking and reading recipe books when I was a mere toddler; my mother-in-law, June, for her superlative collection of English cookery books and for teaching my husband to cook when *he* was a mere toddler; my first readers—my mother; my husband, Matthew; Sharon Galant and Thomasin Chinnery at Zeitgeist Literary Agency; and my friend Rachel Aris—all of whom provided invaluable feedback; Gladstone's Library, where I spoke on the subject of Eliza to an audience that listened (and kindly ate my Eliza cakes and biscuits) with such enthusiasm I was inspired to stop researching and start writing; the antiquarian cookery collections at the British Library, the London Library, the Guildhall Library, and the Wellcome Library; Beverley Matthews, archivist at Tonbridge School; Emeritus Professor Maggie Humm; and, of course, my family—Matthew, Imogen, Bryony, Saskia, and Hugo—who have dutifully eaten my Eliza-inspired cooking for longer than they can remember. Thank you!

A final and special acknowledgment to the many teams across the world who have played a part in publishing *Miss Eliza's English Kitchen*: my US agent, Claire Anderson-Wheeler, whose title-creating skills are unsurpassed; Lucia Macro and her splendid team (Asanté Simons, Danielle Finnegan, and Holly Rice) at William Morrow, who kicked off publication with exceptional edit and design skills; in the UK, my agent, Sharon Galant, has worked diligently and tirelessly, while Sara-Jade Virtue and Alice Rodgers at Simon & Schuster brought their considerable enthusiasm and talent to the process. And lastly, thank you to all the publishers and translators who are currently working out how to translate the many obscure culinary terms used by Eliza Acton and Ann Kirby: I wish you luck.

Special recognition must go to Eliza Acton herself, and to all the women of history who were brave and audacious enough to write under their own names. I hope this novel goes some way to acknowledging how difficult, complicated, and courageous this decision was.

About the author

About the book

Insights,
Interviews
& More...

Meet Annabel Abbs

About the author

Aaron Hargreaves

ANNABEL ABBS is a writer. Her first novel, *The Joyce Girl*, was published in 2016 to great acclaim and has sold across the world. It tells the fictionalized story of Lucia Joyce, forgotten daughter of James Joyce, and is currently being adapted for the stage. Her second novel, *Frieda*, was published in 2018 and immediately became a London *Times* Book of the Month and then a London *Times* Book of the Year, as well as being featured on BBC *Woman's Hour* and in *Tatler*, *Good Housekeeping*, *Red*, and all UK national newspapers. The novel—which has been translated into eight languages—tells the dramatic story of Frieda von Richthofen, the woman who inspired D. H. Lawrence's *Lady Chatterley* and later became his wife. Abbs's coauthored work of nonfiction, *The Age-Well Project,* was published in 2019 under the name Annabel Streets. Her latest nonfiction book, *Windswept: Walking the Paths of Trailblazing Women,* was published in 2021 and recounts the walking adventures of eight extraordinary women who found solace in wild landscapes. ❧

Note from the Author

In 1996, I was lucky enough to acquire the cookery book collection of my mother-in-law, June. After leaving school in 1946, June studied home economics. She started her career at *Good Housekeeping* magazine, but later retrained as a cookery teacher. During this time—and long before it was fashionable—June began collecting old cookery books, eventually amassing a library of more than two hundred. It was here that I came across Eliza Acton, as well as Maria Rundell, Alexis Soyer, William Kitchiner, Hannah Glasse, Hannah Woolley, Agnes Marshall, Mrs. Beeton, and many, many other cooks and cookery writers. It was only on closer examination that I realized Eliza Acton's recipe writing was head and shoulders above that of her peers, rooted in her personal history as a thwarted poet. Although Eliza was writing nearly two hundred years ago, the message to her readership of "young housekeepers" is more relevant today than ever before. Thrift and the avoidance of waste, nutritious food for good health, the need to master plain cookery, cooking with care and fresh ingredients, learning from "other nations," and the importance of making good food available to everyone . . . these resonate as much now as (if not more than) they did in 1845. And so I leave the last word to Eliza: "It is not, in fact, cookery-books that we need half so much as cooks really trained to a knowledge of their duties."

Indeed, Eliza, indeed. ∾

Historical Note

Eliza Acton's 576-page cookery book took a decade to complete. Published in 1845 as *Modern Cookery, in All Its Branches: Reduced to a System of Easy Practice, for the Use of Private Families*, it was an immediate success and became a bestseller within weeks of publication, staying in print for more than seventy years. It's now widely regarded as the first cookery book written for general use and its author as the first modern cookery writer. The book—which sold more than 125,000 copies within thirty years—returned to print in 1966 and has been reprinted several times since.

Eliza's biggest innovation was listing the ingredients for each *receipt*, as recipes were called at the time. *Modern Cookery* was the first book to include accurate measured lists of ingredients, a concept extended by Mrs. Beeton and now followed by cookery writers everywhere. Not only did *Modern Cookery* include ingredient lists with each recipe but it also gave precise notes on timings and other factors likely to affect the outcome, often under the heading of *Obs.* (a thoroughly contemporary abbreviation of *Observations*). It was also the first cookbook, according to food historian William Sitwell, to include a recipe for brussels sprouts.

Eliza Acton remained in great respect (perhaps more than any other historical cookery writer) by later generations of chefs and writers. She has been described by Delia Smith as "the best cookery writer in the English language" and by food writer Bee Wilson as "great," while *Modern Cookery* was described by Elizabeth David as "unquestionably the greatest cookery book in our language"; by Soyer's biographer, Ruth Cowen, as the cookbook that "took the genre to new heights"; and by Penelope Farmer as "the parent of the modern cookery book."

Eliza was the first known poet/playwright to become a cookery writer, a trend of combining fiction and food writing that continued with May Byron, Mary Virginia Terhune, Harriet Beecher Stowe, Crescent Dragonwagon, Hanna Winsnes, Helena Patursson, Janet Laurence, Alison Uttley, Sophie Dahl, Marian Keyes, James Salter, and many others.

At some point during the writing of *Modern Cookery*, Eliza's bankrupt father returned from exile to England and Eliza's mother left Bordyke House to live with him in Hastings. This left Eliza and ▶

Ann at Bordyke House, where they meticulously cooked and tested recipes. After the publication of *Modern Cookery*, Ann Kirby appears to have parted company with Eliza. According to Eliza's biographer, Ann is not heard of until the 1851 census when she is recorded as living in London as personal servant to the widowed dispenser at the Royal Greenwich Hospital.

While my portrait of Ann is entirely fictitious, my portrait of Eliza is based on several facts. Her poems were published in 1826 and she sold 530 copies, with 352 going to early subscribers. When she took her second volume to Longman Publishers, a decade later, she was indeed told to go home and return with a cookery book. We know she continued writing poetry because a poem of hers was published by Richard & John E. Taylor in 1842, suggesting she wrote poetry for at least twenty years.

Eliza never married, but her first biographers (Mary Aylett and Olive Ordish, *First Catch Your Hare*) were lucky enough to be in communication with her great-niece. It was here that I encountered the story of Eliza's illegitimate daughter who was raised (allegedly) by her sister. This short biography also referred to Eliza's play produced at Miss Kelly's Soho theater. No record of the play remains (most of Miss Kelly's plays were produced anonymously) and no one has been able to track down Eliza's illegitimate daughter, although this is hardly surprising given there was no requirement to register births during this period and illegitimate children (who were very common) were frequently hidden away or absorbed into respectable families. According to Aylett and Ordish, Eliza's daughter was known to have inherited an allowance, and to own a portrait of her biological mother, which she kissed every night, a story that traveled through the generations of the Acton family.

Several mysteries hover over the story of Eliza Acton, many of which have been explored in her more recent biography, *The Real Mrs. Beeton: The Story of Eliza Acton*, by Sheila Hardy. Hardy, despite trawling all the archives, never found any record of Eliza Acton's will. Eliza would have died a wealthy woman and yet neither a will nor her letters have been discovered, leading to speculation that these were destroyed on her death, perhaps to preserve her reputation and the family name by preventing disclosure of an illegitimate daughter. Several of her poems (which struck me with their frankness and intensity) also include missing lines and dedications using asterisks only (a technique employed by Victorian newspapers to avoid libel).

After the success of *Modern Cookery*, Eliza produced a second cookery book: *The English Bread Book*. It never sold as well as *Modern Cookery*. However, during this time, Eliza became a champion of home cooking and nutritious food, persuading the public to eat healthier food and fighting to have harmful additives removed from bread. While Mrs. Beeton later plagiarized almost a third of her recipes, others did so during Eliza's life, prompting her to denounce them, in an 1855 preface to *Modern Cookery*, as "strangers coolly taking the credit and profit of my toil."

She died on February 13, 1859, at the age of fifty-nine. Oddly, her death certificate describes her—in the Occupation column—neither as poet nor writer but as "Daughter of John Acton, Ipswich. Brewer. Deceased." The cause of death is given as "Premature Old Age," now thought to be a euphemism for dementia. Meanwhile her grave was inscribed only with the words "Eliza Acton, formerly of Ipswich who died in Hampstead."

It was in Eliza's poetry and cookery writing that I sought (and partially found) clues as to what happened to Eliza in her youth. It's known she spent time in France (probably on two extended occasions) and that she had a debilitating love affair. At this time illegitimate children were rife in France, with historians estimating that between 30 and 40 percent of all babies born in Paris were illegitimate. Her poems speak plainly of betrayal, envy, and emotional pain. I have plundered them accordingly, adding flesh to a rumor that has doggedly pursued her—that of an illegitimate daughter.

Within two years of Eliza's death, Mrs. Isabella Beeton produced her first cookery book. For several decades, Eliza languished, lost in the long shadow of Mrs. Beeton. It's now known that Mrs. Beeton plagiarized Eliza shamelessly, cutting and pasting hundreds of her recipes and claiming them as her own, going "out of her way to alter the formulations so that no one—and especially not the hawk-eyed Miss Acton, had she lived—could point an accusing finger" (Kathryn Hughes, *The Short Life and Long Times of Mrs. Beeton*). Mrs. Beeton, however, cleverly moved the ingredients list from the bottom of a recipe to the top—where it has remained to this day. ▶

Blank page

Historical Note *(continued)*

Eliza's story took place at a time of unprecedented social upheaval. The early Victorian period saw Britain change irrevocably: the Industrial Revolution; a rising middle class; vast wealth but also unimaginable poverty, particularly among the rural poor; rapid change prompted by new technologies—from gas to electricity to railways. But this was also the era when the first fast and convenience foods appeared, from powdered custard to imported frozen meat. The processed food we consume today had its beginnings when Eliza was writing, and her dislike of it (in particular it's lack of nutritional content) informs both her cookery books.

To provide a richer and more intense flavor of the period and for the sake of narrative flow, I have collasped events that took place over the ten years Eliza spent writing her cookery book into a shortened timescale. ◠

A Note on the Characters

For added authenticity I have based most of the characters in *Miss Eliza's English Kitchen* on real people. However, the Thorpes and Ann's family are entirely fictitious. Mr. Arnott is also fictitious but was inspired by a man of the same name, mentioned twice in Eliza's cookery book. The Curries, Potted Meats, Etc. chapter includes recipes for Mr. Arnott's Currie Powder and Mr. Arnott's Currie, the latter taken directly from Mr. Arnott's written instructions, with the ultimate paragraph as follows: "Next put in a fowl that has been roasted and nicely cut up; or a rabbit; or some lean chops of pork or mutton; or a lobster, or the remains of yesterday's calf's head; or anything else you may fancy." How could I resist making him a character? Incidentally, in her Observations Eliza makes it clear that although Mr. Arnott's currie powder is worth making, his currie is not!

Maria Rundell

Mrs. Maria Rundell's book is frequently referred to by Eliza. Rundell was the anonymous author of *A New System of Domestic Cookery*, published by Longman's archrival, John Murray, in 1806. It became a publishing sensation, running to sixty-seven editions, and is thought to be the reason Longman asked Eliza for a cookery book.

Lady Judith Montefiore

Lady Judith Montefiore was the author of the first Jewish cookbook in English, *The Jewish Manual; or, Practical Information in Jewish and Modern Cookery*, published anonymously a year after Eliza's book. Some of its dishes are very similar to those in Eliza's book (Eliza refers several times to a "certain Jewish lady" to whom she's indebted for her Jewish recipes) and we know that Eliza ate Jewish smoked beef, which she considered "excellent" in the home of a "Jewish lady." It has been speculated that the "Jewish lady" was, in fact, Lady Judith Montefiore of London and of Ramsgate in Kent. ▸

Judith was an extraordinary woman: she spoke six languages, played an active role in the development of Palestine, and was a dedicated philanthropist, involved in numerous charities including the establishment of soup kitchens in the East End of London.

Fanny Kelly

Fanny Kelly was a well-known actress believed to have been part of Eliza's circle of acquaintances. In 1840 she opened a theater and dramatic school in London's Soho so that young women could be trained in drama. She lived with her "niece," who was widely believed to her illegitimate daughter.

Mrs. Hemans and L. E. L.

Mrs. Felicia Hemans and L. E. L. (Miss Letitia Elizabeth Landon) were prominent and hugely popular female poets, writing at the same time as Eliza. Like many female poets of this time, they remain largely unknown. Hemans published more than fourteen volumes of verse between 1818 and 1835, becoming one of the best-loved poets of her time. L. E. L. published her first poem when she was sixteen; and her many novels and poems sold so well she was able to maintain her mother and help fund her brother's Oxford education. However, her reputation as an independent, unmarried writer meant most men forbade their wives from inviting Miss Landon to their homes. She eventually married (after allegedly giving birth to three illegitimate children) the governor of Cape Coast Castle on the African coast, dying four months later in a possible suicide.

Alexis Soyer

Alexis Soyer was a French chef who became Victorian England's most celebrated cook, presiding over the kitchens of London's Reform Club for thirteen years (1837–1850). A born innovator, he was one of the first to cook with gas and famously invented a portable stove. He set up soup kitchens in Dublin during the Irish Famine and helped organize the feeding of militia during the Crimean War. He also wrote several cookery books.

About the book

Kent County Lunatic Asylum

The locations of this novel are also as historically accurate as I could make them, in particular the Kent County Lunatic Asylum, accounts of which make horrific reading. One of the earliest purpose-built asylums, it opened in January 1833. The site was modeled on a prison (the same architect designed Maidstone jail) and described by an inspector visiting in 1840 thus: "massive stone walls, small iron-framed windows, absence of ornament . . . narrow stone stairs, low vaulted ceilings, rows of dark dungeon-like cells . . . tables screwed to the floor, heavy wooden chairs in which patients were strapped, primitive wooden beds with straw for bedding . . . lunatics in coarse scanty clothing, some in strait waistcoats, some in manacles or other form of restraint." The inspector went on to describe finding two men who had been chained to their beds for four and a half years and another twenty to thirty men and women in manacles or "fastened in a coercive chair by a large cuirass of thick leather."[*] In these early asylums it was common for dead patients to be dissected by surgeons who had a particular interest in the brains of the insane.

The Kent County Lunatic Asylum later became Barming Heath Asylum, then Barming Mental Hospital, and finally Oakwood Hospital. It closed in 1994, but its legacy endures in the term *barmy*.

Bordyke House

Bordyke House in Tonbridge, Kent, where Eliza and Ann are thought to have tested thousands of recipes as they wrote *Modern Cookery*, is still a family home, although Tonbridge is—of course—a very different town! ～

---

[*] Geraldine Procter, *A History of Oakwood Hospital from 1828–1982* (Maidstone: Kent County Library, 1982).

Poem Sources

"*The painful beatings of a breaking heart / Are hush'd to stillness . . .*" (Eliza Acton, "The Grave")

"*My first affections, and my last, / Were thine—thine only—fare thee well!*" (Eliza Acton, "L'Abandonnée")

"*Darkly, darkly, Misfortune's wing / Is o'er thee rolling its heavy cloud; / Slowly, slowly, 'tis gathering . . .*" (Eliza Acton , "Cards of Fortune")

"*With what still hours of calm delight / Thy songs and image blend; / I cannot choose but think thou wert / An old familiar friend.*" (L. E. L., "Stanzas on the Death of Mrs. Hemans")

"*affection's chain / Was all too rudely wrench'd in twain . . .*" (Eliza Acton, "L'Abandonnée")

"*blighted hopes, and friendship fled . . .*" (Eliza Acton, "I Know How Vain It Is to Mourn")

"*I am flung neglectedly / Abroad, where fostering love is not . . .*" (Eliza Acton, "Nay Twine the Heath-Flow'r Wild for Me")

"*Few save the poor feel for the poor. / The rich know not how hard / It is to be of needful food . . .*" (L. E. L., "The Widow's Mite")

"*My heart's in the kitchen, my heart is not here, / My heart's in the kitchen, though following the dear, / Thinking on the roast meat, and musing on the fry, / My heart's in the kitchen whatever I spy.*" (Maria Jane Jewsbury, from "A Rural Excursion," in *Phantasmagoria*, vol. II)

"*Sound on, thou dark unslumbering sea! . . . Thou sea-bird on the billow's crest . . .*" (Felicia Hemans, "The Last Song of Sappho")

"*It is a dreadful thing for woman's lip / To swear the heart away . . .*" (L. E. L., "The Marriage Vow")

"*Pause!—'ere thy choice hath clasp'd the chain / Which may not be unloos'd again; / For though of gold the links may be / They will not press less painfully . . .*" (Eliza Acton, "Cards of Fortune")

"*Let not the cares which round me cling, / Obscure one moment's bliss for thee . . .*" (Eliza Acton, "Le Trist Adieu")

"Thy heart, thy heart is cold as stone, / And feels but for itself alone . . ." (Eliza Acton, "Cards of Fortune")

"giant-clouds of shame, / In dark'ning masses, clust'ring came . . ." (Eliza Acton, "Cards of Fortune")

"There is no joy on earth to me / Where thou art not . . ." (Eliza Acton, "Le Trist Adieu")

"Oh, what a waste of feeling and of thought / Have been the imprints on my roll of life! . . . to what use have I turned / The golden gifts which are my hope and pride!" (L. E. L., "Gifts Misused," from *Fragments*)

"I have no early flowers to fling . . ." (L. E. L., "The Forgotten One")

"I woke / To the dark truth . . . rous'd from dreams of bliss / To know thee false . . . to fell / That there was agony in this . . ." (Eliza Acton, "L'Abandonnée")

"Come to my grave when I am gone, and bend a moment there alone . . ." (Eliza Acton, "Come to My Grave")

"I may have sinn'd . . . / But be the curse upon my head,— / O, let it not descend to her!" (L. E. L., "The Dying Child") ∽

Recommended Reading

As ever I am indebted to the work of others, in particular:

First Catch Your Hare: A History of Recipe-Makers, Mary Aylett and Olive Ordish

The Real Mrs. Beeton: The Story of Eliza Acton, Sheila Hardy

Cooking People: The Writers Who Taught the English How to Eat, Sophia Waugh

The Short Life and Long Times of Mrs. Beeton, Kathryn Hughes

A Woman's Work Is Never Done: A History of Housework in the British Isles, 1650–1950, Caroline Davidson

The Victorian Kitchen, Jennifer Davies

The Kitchen in History, Molly Harrison

Taste: The Story of Britain Through Its Cooking, Kate Colquhoun

The Last Food of England: English Food: Its Past, Present, and Future, Marwood Yeatman

The Victorian House: Domestic Life from Childbirth to Deathbed, Judith Flanders

Alexis Soyer: Cook Extraordinary, Elizabeth Ray

Relish: The Extraordinary Life of Alexis Soyer, Victorian Celebrity Chef, Ruth Cowen

Feast: A History of Grand Eating, Roy Strong

A History of English Food, Clarissa Dickson Wright

Food: A Cultural Culinary History, Ken Albala

Scoff: A History of Food and Class in Britain, Pen Vogler

The Art of Eating in France: Manners and Menus in the Nineteenth Century, Jean-Paul Aron

Victorian Women Poets: An Anthology, ed. Angela Leighton and Margaret Reynolds

L.E.L.: The Lost life and Mysterious Death of the "Female Byron," Lucasta Miller

Rural Life in Victorian England, C. E. Mingay

Early Victorian Tonbridge, C. W. Chalklin

The Victorian Asylum, Sarah Rutherford

Life in the Victorian Asylum: The World of Nineteenth Century Mental Health Care, Mark Stevens

A History of Oakwood Hospital from 1828–1982, Geraldine Procter (Oakwood Hospital was formerly Kent County Lunatic Asylum)

Victorious Century: The United Kingdom, 1800–1906, David Cannadine

And most important of all, Eliza's own works:

Poems, 1826

Modern Cookery, 1845 and 1855 (revised edition; note: I have included receipts from both editions in this novel)

The English Bread Book, 1857

Recipes*

Eliza Acton's Pickled Peaches

Take, at their full growth, just before they begin to ripen, six large or eight moderate-sized peaches; wipe the down from them, and put them into brine that will float an egg. In three days let them be taken out, and drained on a sieve reversed for several hours. Boil in a quart of vinegar for ten minutes two ounces of whole white pepper, two of ginger slightly bruised, a teaspoonful of salt, two blades of mace, half a pound of mustard-seed, and a half teaspoonful of cayenne tied in a bit of muslin. Lay the peaches into a jar, and pour the boiling pickle on them; in two months they will be fit for use.

Peaches 6 or 8: in brine three days. Vinegar, 1 quart; whole white pepper, 2 oz.; bruised ginger, 2 oz.; salt, 1 teaspoonful; mace, 2 blades; mustard-seed, ½ lb.: 10 minutes.

Eliza Acton's Broiled Eels with Sage

Kill, skin, open, and cleanse one fine eel. Cut it into finger lengths, and rub it with a mixed seasoning of salt and white pepper, and leave it for half an hour. Wipe it dry, wrap each length in sage leaves, fasten them around it with coarse thread, roll the eel in good salad oil or clarified butter, lay it on the gridiron, squeeze lemon juice over, and broil it gently until it is browned in every part. Send it to table with a sauce made of two or three ounces of butter, a tablespoonful of chili, tarragon, or common vinegar, and one of water with a little salt.

Eliza Acton's Chocolate Custards

Dissolve gently by the side of the fire an ounce and a half of the best chocolate in rather more than a wineglassful of water, and then boil it until it is perfectly smooth; mix with it a pint of milk well flavored with lemon peel or vanilla, add two ounces of fine sugar, and when the whole boils, stir in five well-beaten eggs which have been strained.

---

* Recipes taken from both the original (1845) and the revised (1855) editions of *Modern Cookery*.

Put the custard into a jar or jug, set it into a pan of boiling water, and stir it without ceasing until it is thick. Do not put it into glasses or a dish until it is nearly or quite cold. These, as well as all other custards, are infinitely finer when made with the yolks only of the eggs, of which the number must then be increased.

Rasped chocolate, 1½ ounces; water, 1 *large* wineglassful: 5 to 8 minutes. New milk, 1 pint; eggs, 5; sugar, 2 oz. Or: chocolate, 2 oz.; water, ¼ pint; new milk, 1 pint; sugar, 2½ to 3 oz.; cream, ½ pint; yolks of eggs, 8.

Eliza Acton's Boiled Swan's Egg

Swan's eggs are much more delicate than from their size, and from the tendency of the birds to feed on fish might be supposed; and when boiled hard and shelled, their appearance is *beautiful*, the white being of remarkable purity and transparency. Take as much water as will cover the egg well in every part, let it boil quickly, then take it from the fire, and as soon as the water ceases to move put in the egg, and leave it by the side of the fire—without allowing it to boil—for twenty minutes, and turn it gently once or twice in the time; then put on the cover of the stewpan and boil it gently for a quarter of an hour; take it quite from the fire, and in five minutes put it into a basin and throw a cloth, once or twice folded, over it, and let it cool slowly. It will retain the heat for a very long time, and as it should be *quite cold* before it is cut, it should be boiled early if wanted to serve the same day.

NB: Eliza serves these in a green salad, first removing the yolks and mashing them with herbs, spices, butter, minced onion, and lemon juice, then returning the mixture to the whites and arranging the whole lot on a bed of dressed lettuce.

Eliza Acton's Tonbridge Brawn (Pig's Head)

Split open the head of a pig of middling size, remove the brain and all the bones, strew the inside thickly with fine salt, and let it drain until the following day. Cleanse the ears and feet in the same manner; wipe them all from the brine, lay them into a large pan, and rub them well with an ounce and a half of saltpeter mixed with six ▶

Recipes *(continued)*

ounces of sugar; in twelve hours, add six ounces of salt; the next day pour a quarter of a pint of good vinegar over them, and keep them turned in the pickle every twenty-four hours for a week; then wash it off the ears and feet, and boil them for about an hour and a half; bone the feet while they are warm, and trim the gristle from the large ends of the ears. When these are ready, mix a large grated nutmeg with a teaspoonful and a half of mace, half a teaspoonful of cayenne, and as much of cloves. Wash, but do not soak the head; wipe and flatten it on a board; cut some of the flesh from the thickest parts, and lay it on the thinnest; intermix it with that of the ears and feet, roll it up very tight, and bind it firmly with broad tape; fold a thin pudding-cloth quite closely around it and tie it securely at both ends. Place the head in a braising pan, with the bones and trimmings of the feet and ears, a large bunch of savory herbs, two onions, a small head of celery, three or four carrots, a teaspoonful of peppercorns, and sufficient cold water to cover it well; boil it very gently for four hours, and leave it until two parts cold in the liquor in which it was boiled. Take off the cloth and put the brawn between two trenchers, with a heavy weight on the upper one. The next day take off the fillets of tape, and serve the head whole.

Eliza Acton's Soup in Haste

Chop tolerably fine a pound of lean beef, mutton, or veal, and when it is partly done, add to it a small carrot and one small turnip cut in slices, half an ounce of celery, the white part of a moderate-sized leek, or a quarter of an ounce of onion. Mince all these together, and put the whole into a deep saucepan with three pints of cold water. When the soup boils take off the scum, and add a little salt and pepper. In half an hour it will be ready to serve, with or without straining; it may be flavored at will, with cayenne, catsup, or aught else that is preferred, or it may be converted into French spring broth, by passing it through a sieve, and boiling it again for five or six minutes, with a handful of young and well-washed sorrel.

Meat, 1 lb.; carrot, 2 oz.; turnip, 1½ oz.; celery, ½ oz.; onion, ¼ oz.; water, 3 pints: half an hour. Little pepper and salt.

18

Obs.—Three pounds of beef or mutton, with two or three slices of ham, and vegetables in proportion to the above receipt, all chopped fine, and boiled in three quarts of water for an hour and a half, will make an excellent family soup on an emergency: additional boiling will of course improve it, and a little spice should be added after it has been skimmed and salted. ∾

Reading Group Guide

1. What do you think this book is about?

2. In what ways—if any—are Miss Eliza and Ann Kirby similar?

3. Ann is changed by her job in Miss Eliza's kitchen. But how does Ann's presence change Miss Eliza, if at all?

4. The themes of female duty and obligation ring through this novel. To what extent did Miss Eliza and Ann overcome the social and personal expectations placed upon them?

5. The novel is, in part, a coming-of-age novel. In your view, which events played the most pivotal role in Ann's shift from girlhood to womanhood? Could the coming-of-age theme also apply to Miss Eliza?

6. What role did food, and its preparation, play in the development of the two women?

7. The novel explores the mother-daughter relationship, ultimately posing the question: What constitutes a mother? How did you respond to the decision Miss Eliza made in the penultimate chapter?

8. The novel contains many acutely observed moments of domesticity. Which of these scenes stood out most for you, and why?

9. As they cook together, Ann and Eliza are able to navigate borders and boundaries, and to have conversations that might not have happened elsewhere in the house. How does cooking help facilitate this?

10. The novel, set almost two hundred years ago, is rich with historical detail. Since that time, what has been gained and what has been lost?

11. What additional value, if any, did the Historical Note add? What did it bring to your experience of the novel?

12. Can a recipe be plagiarized? ∽